SPEAKING CULTURALLY

SUNY Series in Human Communication Processes
Donald P. Cushman and Ted J. Smith, III, Editors

SPEAKING CULTURALLY

Explorations in Social Communication

Gerry Philipsen

STATE UNIVERSITY OF NEW YORK PRESS

Published by
State University of New York Press, Albany

Printed in the United States of America

Production by E. Moore.
Marketing by Dana E. Yanulavich

For information, address State University of New York
Press, State University Plaza, Albany, N.Y., 12246

Library of Congress Cataloging-in-Publication Data

Philipsen, Gerry, 1944–
Speaking culturally : explorations in social communication / Gerry
Philipsen.
p. cm.—(SUNY series in human communication processes)
Includes bibliographical references and index.
ISBN 0-7914-1164-8 (PB : alk. paper).—ISBN 0-7914-1163-X (HC :
alk. paper)
1. Language and culture—United States. 2. Sociolinguistics—
United States. I. Title. II. Series.
P35.5.U6P47 1992
306.4′4′0973—dc20 91-33107
CIP

10 9 8 7 6 5

Contents

Preface

Speaking Culturally is written to introduce students to the ethnography of communication by presenting a series of cases and commentaries pertaining to speaking, one of the principle media in which communication is accomplished. The ethnography of communication is a complex method, perspective, and body of writings, and the studies presented here can necessarily only suggest some of the many insights into human communication that it offers. Nonetheless, the reader of this book will, I believe, be introduced here to some fundamentals of the ethnographic spirit in the study of communicative conduct. It is hoped that that spirit will lead the interested reader to further study the methods and materials of the ethnography of communication.

The book brings together several previously published papers (chapters 2 through 4) and 4 chapters written expressly for it (chapters 1, 5, 6, and 7). It consists of a series of studies of communication in particular social worlds and of chapters that introduce and retrospectively comment on the particular studies. Thus, the book presents a series of reports as well as a series of interpretations that place the separate reports in some kind of perspective.

Chapter 2 is based on two previously published articles: my "Speaking 'Like a Man' in Teamsterville: Culture Patterns of Role Enactment in an Urban Neighborhood," *Quarterly Journal of Speech* 61(1975), 13–22, and my "Places for Speaking in Teamsterville," *Quarterly Journal of Speech* 62(1976), 15–25. Chapter 3 is based on my "Mayor Daley's Council Speech: A Cultural Analysis," *Quarterly Journal of Speech* 72(1986), 247–60. Chapter 4 is based on Tamar Katriel's and my "'What We Need Is Communication': 'Communication' as a Cultural Category in Some American Speech," *Communication Monographs* 48(1981), 301–17. Grateful acknowledgment is made to the Speech Communication Association for permission to reproduce these articles here and to Tamar Katriel for her permission to reproduce our jointly authored paper.

The reports that I have presented here are drawn from studies of communicative conduct in two cultures. Here I have labeled those cultures, respectively, Teamsterville culture and Nacirema culture. These labels require some prefatory explanation. The people who produced the communicative conduct from which I have drawn my reports of Teamsterville culture do not use the word Teamsterville to refer to themselves or their speech community. It is a name I have supplied, after the modal occupation—truck driver—of the people who live in the neighborhood I call Teamsterville. I do not mean to suggest that the people there are members of the Teamsters' union, nor do I mean to suggest that Teamsterville and its ways are to be associated with Teamsters in general. I am concerned here with a particular speech community, which I have named in such a way to suggest something about the work activities of those who live there. Nacirema (American spelled backward) is a term the anthropologist Horace Miner (1956) coined to refer to some Americans and some of their culturally distinctive habits. Nacirema does not refer here to a particular group of people or to a particular locale, but refers rather generally to a particular culture, a particular way of thinking and acting—a way that does not necessarily include all North Americans or all citizens of the United States of America, but which is prominently associated with some of the history and some of the contemporary texture of life that can be observed there.

Of course, I am fundamentally indebted to those people whose speech I have examined here and whose speech I have treated as expressions of, respectively, Teamsterville and Nacirema cultures. Whenever I consulted with someone in either of the two ethnographic projects, anonymity was promised and thus I cannot acknowledge persons by name. I have tried here, and in other reports I have made about these two cultures, to honor those who provided me with culturally revealing expressions, by reporting, as faithfully and as carefully as I was able to, what they said and did, and by trying as best as I can to appreciate their expressions as worthy of my respect rather than as objects of criticism. Readers will have to judge, as best as they can, the degree to which I have succeeded in this regard.

As to friends and colleagues who have helped with this project, no anonymity was promised and, I hope, none is desired. There are so many people who helped with various aspects of this book that I cannot name all of them. But there are a few people whose contribution should be acknowledged and this I am most pleased to do. Mary Jo Rudd helped me with the early Nacirema fieldwork in Santa Barbara, California, particularly with the analyses of dinner time conversations. Tamar Katriel deserves special mention in connection with the Nacirema project. She joined me once the project was initiated and was a coauthor with me on chapter 4. The opportunity for this intercultural collaboration was, for me, invaluable. That her work on the Nacirema project was her introduction to the ethnography of communication, to which she has since become a distinguished contributor, is a source of special pleasure to me. Cheryl Marty-White provided the fieldwork materials for the study of "K," presented in chapter 3. I am very grateful for her generosity in allowing me to use these materials. Mary Toepel typed the final manuscript skillfully and efficiently, and this material assistance was invaluable to me. Sandra Cross and Lisa Coutu provided valuable bibliographic help.

Three people have been especially helpful to me in the writing of this book, not so much for their specific contributions as for their inspiration and encouragement. In my view, there would not be an "ethnography of communication" without the scholarship and presence of Dell Hymes. If this book has in some small way contributed to the program of inquiry that he first commissioned in 1962 (Hymes 1962), I will feel satisfied. Whatever contribution it might make, the present work would not have been possible without the program Hymes has made possible. In this regard, too, I would like to express my appreciation to Professor Hymes for his encouragement and advice to me as I have tried to work within the ethnography of communication. It is a special pleasure when one discovers that a great scholar whom one admires for his work turns out to be as kind and as helpful to a younger scholar as Professor Hymes has been to me.

Don Cushman, of SUNY Albany and its Press, has been a fast friend and critic for many years. It was only through his encouragement that the present book has been completed. Donal Carbaugh provided an unusually helpful review of the manuscript. His work in the ethnography of communication, his collegiality over many years now, and his perceptive comments on this book's contents have been a source of great help and inspiration to me.

I hope that when readers have finished with the book, they will understand what I mean when I say that it would be hopelessly Nacirema of me to absolve others of any blame for whatever shortcomings it may have. Nonetheless, I can only thank the many critics, colleagues, and students who have helped me think through the themes of this book. Many have helped in ways which I cannot fully appreciate and acknowledge, but I am mindful that much is owed to many.

PART I

Introduction

Chapter 1

SPEAKING IN ITS CULTURAL CONTEXT

"We don't want no yahoos around here." These were the first words I heard as I stepped across the threshold of one of the many taverns in Teamsterville, a working-class, multiethnic neighborhood in Chicago. As I approached, I heard the sounds of convivial neighborhood speech, men talking and laughing as they drank together. But when I, a stranger, crossed the doorway, the warning to "yahoos" punctuated the talk, and then voices hushed, and all ears and eyes followed my every step to the bar. Eventually, talk resumed, but not the lively roar it had been before I appeared; for like other Teamsterville taverns, this was not merely a public place open to anyone, but an enclave in which some but not other personae were welcome, and I was an intruder. There was no sign outside the tavern, because "everybody" knew who belonged there and those who needed a sign to welcome them were not among that circle of insiders. I entered this back region of Teamsterville life because I was studying the community's places for speaking, prominent among which were corner taverns.

That this particular scene was the chief place where these men talked; that they talked boisterously when I was not there and stopped talking when I entered; that eventually one man came to my bar stool and asked me "where are you from and what's your nationality?"; that upon hearing my answer, he told me that he was Sicilian and that Sicilians cut the throats of men who invaded their territory and "messed with their women"; that throughout Teamsterville there were corners, corner bars, porches, and streets where socially segregated groups talked about ethnicity and locality, and what it meant to be a man or a woman. All of these and many other things eventually became known to me as elements in a pattern of spoken life in Teamsterville. To know these patterns, and to know the life they constituted for those who lived it, was the goal of my inquiry. And to learn about speaking in Teamsterville, in its cultural particularity, was a tactic, a means among other means, to reach the larger end of learning firsthand whether and how it is that speaking is a radically cultural mode of communicative activity.

When I first entered Teamsterville, the community appeared to me as merely a series of unconnected streets, buildings, people, and activities. By the time I left it over three years later, it was, for me, not just a setting, but a scene, a place suffused with activity, with meaning, with significance, not only for me, but more importantly for those who had grown up there and those who lived there permanently. As a student of communication, what eventually struck me most about Teamsterville and my experiences in it was that one way to think about this community was as a speech community, a universe of discourse with a finely organized, distinctive pattern of meaning and action.

After spending several months in Teamsterville, I began to notice there a practice, a habitual way of speaking, reinforced by the expressions of Teamstervillers. It was difficult to detect and not much easier to describe, but it was salient enough that it was hard to ignore, both practically and theoretically. That practice consists of infusing a concern with place into every conversation. In Teamsterville, to my surprise, if one's interlocutor did not know one's "nationality" it would be asked at the beginning of the conversation, and it seemed that every reference to a person included a reference to that person's ethnicity. The same is true for residence: references to where the person lived, or was from, permeated everyday speech. In addition, where persons stand in relation to each other according to a social code of power and position—a person's place in the social hierarchy—was mentioned directly or indirectly in virtually every conversation in which I participated.

Teamsterville concerns for social and physical placement were, in their pervasiveness and importance, alien to my way of thinking and speaking. It took some time for me to notice that there was something there to notice—a pattern of emphasis and salience of the cultural category place, expressed in many symbols of social and physical space. To the extent that I was learning what potentially significant aspects of the world the Teamstervillers thought and spoke about, and that I was learning the local vocabulary and expressions for symbolizing those aspects of experience, to that extent I was learning about a culturally distinctive system of symbols and meanings.

Much of my learning about the importance of place in Teamsterville culture was, one might say, academic. It was an interesting subject for mental exploration, a phenomenon of some curiosity to one who was interested in cultural differences across peoples. But another kind of learning was more personal.

In my work in Teamsterville I was responsible for supervising the after-school activities of several groups of neighborhood young people who participated in the program of a neighborhood youth center. By training and preference it was my practice to discipline young people who had violated the center's rules by talking with them, trying to understand their feelings, to discuss the cause of the problem, and to talk out ways of improving conduct in the future. Soon, word of my methods was broadcast around the neighborhood and my reputation as a man who used words to influence youths was secured. Much to my surprise, and eventually frustration, this practice of mine led to the conclusion, by the neighborhood boys, that I was a homosexual (in their eyes a man who uses speech to influence boys is not really a proper "man" and must be a "queer," in that a "queer" is not a proper "man").

Here I faced a neighborhood belief about speech behavior, that a man who uses speech to discipline boys is not a real man and therefore must be a homosexual. The application of this belief to my conduct led to a situation in which it was, for some time, nearly impossible for me to perform effectively my duties in the youth center. Only after some months of reflection, and the use of a revised strategy of self-presentation, was I able to work effectively (as a man) among these boys.

When I left Teamsterville, after nearly three years of field research, it was with a new sensibility that I heard the speaking of "mainstream" Americans. That new hearing led me to do fieldwork among middle-class, college educated Americans living in southern California and the Pacific northwest regions of the U.S.A. These people, whom I call by Horace Miner's term "the Nacirema" (Miner 1956; read Nacirema backwards), speak the English language, as do the Teamstervillers, but their ways of speaking it, and of living, differ. Among the features of Nacirema communicative conduct contrasting with that of the Teamstervillers' is the great effort the former make to facilitate the expression of unique feelings and thoughts. The Nacirema emphasize that each person is unique and Nacirema speech practices not only reflect that belief but indeed serve to make it true.

In California, my student Mary Jo Rudd and I observed, and listened intently to tape recordings of, Nacirema conversations at family "dinner time." This is a speech event in which participants insisted relentlessly that all family members be allowed a turn at talk, indeed be encouraged to talk—because each person "has something to contribute." We found that the people we observed believed strongly that one's place in the family, defined by a role such as "father," should not be a basis for interrupting or curtailing the speech of others, because each person's contribution is believed to be uniquely valuable. For these Nacirema, speech is a way to express one's psychological uniqueness, to acknowledge the uniqueness of others, and to bridge the gap between one's own and another's uniqueness. It is a means by which family members, for example, can manifest their equality and demonstrate that they pay little heed to differences in status—practices and beliefs that would puzzle and offend a proper Teamsterviller.

In Seattle, my student Tamar Katriel and I listened to many Nacirema tell their life stories—stories in which great moral weight was placed upon interpersonal "relationships" in which each party was not only free, but also felt a sense of pressure, to express and celebrate their uniqueness, and to explore and understand the other's distinctive individuality. The sense of boundary sharply dividing occasions and personae, so prominent among Teamstervillers, was either not expressed or, where it threatened to be present, was aggressively opposed.

Although it might appear that the Nacirema, with their penchant for individualism, do not have a common culture, we learned that among these individualistic, seemingly relativistic, people, there is a discernible, common culture, one that underpins its communicative conduct. For the Nacirema, such folk concepts as "self," "relationship," "work," "openness," "growth," and "communication" provide a systematic vocabulary of perception and motive. To understand Nacirema speech, as its speakers and hearers understand it, to understand the motives they use in organizing and interpreting their social experiences, to know what it means to be a Nacirema—these all require that one have knowledge of the culture-specific meanings of these Nacirema symbols. The phrase "what we need is communication," expresses a key theme for the Nacirema. It is a saying whose explication articulates one foundation of a way of talking about, and living, one's life, a way that has produced culturally distinctive rituals and myths in which "communication" is a central concept.

It is hard to immerse oneself in an alien cultural world, as Teamsterville was to me, and be unchanged by it. For me the contact with Teamsterville life brought into sharp relief several aspects of Nacirema culture which, at one time, I had taken for granted. That such terms as "communication," "self," and "relationship," and the ideas to which they refer, are cultural constructions and not universally given experiences, was easier to grasp after struggling to learn a culture such as Teamsterville's. To hear a Nacirema's statement that "each of us is an individual," as a deeply cultured, even quaint, statement, is made easier after having spent three years listening to Teamstervillers talk about persons as "Italians," "Poles," "Lithuanians," and so forth—as persons whose being is defined more by their social than by their psychological characteristics. To hear, as a deeply cultured statement, the Nacirema's insistence that each child should express themself because of the child's potentially "unique contribution" to a family conversation is facilitated by listening for three years to Teamstervillers insisting that a child should be seen and not heard.

THE ETHNOGRAPHY OF SPEAKING

The written reports of Teamsterville and of Nacirema spoken life, placed side by side and compared and contrasted, reveal a picture, or a hearing, of speaking as a deeply cultured process. The implication of this view is that to understand speaking in a particular speech community, one must come to understand how it is culturally shaped and constituted. Ethnography is the process of coming to the understanding of such shapings and is the reporting of such understandings. An ethnographer of speaking is a naturalist, who watches, listens, and records communicative conduct in its natural setting. The ethnographer describes what is to be found in a given speech community as well as what regular patterns can be observed there. For example, the ethnographer might document all observable instances of speech behavior in a community, noting not only that speech occurred or not, but also where, by, and with whom, in what language(s) and dialect(s), in which verbal forms, about which topics, as part of what interaction sequences, and with what observable consequences.

From many observations of the speech behavior of a people, the ethnographer generates two classes of statements. One is a statement of what is there to be observed in the speech community—for instance, that there is a recurrent event in which a particular kind of speech activity occurs, that two languages are spoken, that there is a repertoire of riddles, and so forth, and, of course, what the event, activity, languages, and riddles are. A second statement is a statement about patterns of amount, of frequency, or of qualitative association and significance. A qualitative pattern specifies the conditions under which something occurs and what its meanings are to those who produce it. These statements of existence and pattern are initially derived from field observations and then are tested by further observations. The discovery of patterns is preliminary to interpretation and explanation, and for these tasks the ethnographer formulates a theory of a people's ways of speaking. Such a theory consists of statements about the culture, the local system of symbols and meanings, perceptual and value premises, and ground rules.

Culture, as it is used here, refers to a *socially constructed and historically transmitted pattern of symbols, meanings, premises, and rules* (the definition is adapted from Geertz 1973, p. 89). That a culture is socially constructed and historically transmitted implies that it could have existed before any given set of interlocutors and, potentially, endures beyond them in time. It implies furthermore that it is neither biologically endowed nor the invention of any particular individual, but is something socially constructed. Like all socially constructed inheritances, individuals can, to some degree at least, do what they will with them, but individuals do not choose the cultures to which they are initially exposed and they cannot easily change them in one generation. Although individuals can alienate themselves from a culture's terms and two interlocutors can, between themselves, negotiate the force a culture's meanings and rules have for them, and although individuals and interlocutors can construct meanings not given in any known culture, these meanings and rules are not cultural. A culture transcends any individual or any individual's social network, such that two people who meet for the first time can partake of a common culture and use it in making sense with each other. Likewise two people might never meet and yet partake of a common culture, a culture that is available to all who hear its terms spoken in public life.

Every common culture of which interlocutors might partake, and which they might use in speaking together, includes, among its parts, a part devoted to the symbols and meanings, premises, and rules pertaining to speech and, more broadly, to social communication. A symbol is defined as a "vehicle for a conception" and symbols are "tangible formulations of notions, abstractions from experience fixed in perceptible forms, concrete embodiments of ideas, attitudes, judgments, longings, or beliefs." The "conceptions" are the "meanings, notions, definitions, and so forth, which symbols express" (Geertz 1973, p. 91). Premises express beliefs of existence (what is) and of value (what is good and bad). A rule is a prescription, for how to act, under specified circumstances, which has (some degree of) force in a particular social group. A cultural code of speaking, then, consists of a socially constructed and historically transmitted system of symbols and meanings pertaining to communication—for instance, the symbols "Lithuanian" or "communication" and their attendant definitions; beliefs about spoken actions (that a man who uses speech to discipline boys is not a real man); and rules for using speech (that a father should not interrupt his daughter at the dinner table).

The ethnographer of speaking observes (audits?) the flow of social life in order to discover there, and to represent, in writing, the portion of a culture that is devoted to communicative practices. What a culture symbolizes (that subset of experience it marks off for conceptualization and naming), what it symbolizes with (the symbolic forms with which meanings can be expressed), what beliefs and values it posits, and the array of prescribed and proscribed actions it specifies, constitute a system sui generis. Because they are distinctive, the ethnographer must discover such particularities in each speech community. But this does not mean that the ethnographer has no heuristic tools to use in the study of particular speech communities. The hearing and representing that constitute ethnography are guided by the use of a descriptive framework, such as that proposed by Dell Hymes (1962, 1964, 1972), a system of categories for observation developed through systematic inquiry and analysis, and which is a general outline of the contexts and components of ways of speaking. Furthermore, the accumulation of many such studies, many different ethnographies of speaking, provides comparative knowledge that the ethnographer uses to help inquire into the distinctiveness of any particular case. The descriptive framework and the accumulated representations provide the materials that ethnographers, when they take the role of theorists, use to think about, to generalize about, the enduring, general characteristics of speaking as a universal feature of society.

The ethnography of speaking, then, consists of hearing and representing distinctive ways of speaking in particular speech communities. An ethnography of speaking is a report of a culture, as that culture thematizes communication and of the ways that culture is expressed in some historical situation. This conception of speaking, of culture, and of ethnography rests upon an assumptive foundation, to which I now turn. An exposition of this foundation should reveal why it is that ethnography, and the kind of comparative analysis that ethnography makes possible, is such an important methodology for the study of speaking as a mode of communicative conduct.

AN ASSUMPTIVE FOUNDATION

Speaking is Structured

Albert Einstein is reported to have written that "God may be subtle, but he isn't plain mean" (Wiener 1954, p. 183). With these words he expressed eloquently a basic tenet of scientific dogma, that although the world might appear to be random, there is, after all, order in it, and humans can discern that order, if with some difficulty. Ethnographers of speaking have produced a research literature that confirms and illustrates what was at one time only assumed: that everywhere speech is heard, there is structure in who speaks, to whom, in what language(s), through which channels, on what occasions, in what settings, for what purposes, in what sequences of action, and with what instrumentalities.

Whenever people speak, they organize their speech in ways not governed only by rules of grammar or by physical laws. That is, even though, in any communicative situation, it might be grammatically acceptable and physically possible to make any of two or more linguistic choices, such choices are not randomly produced. Recent sociolinguistic studies provide massive evidence that such choices as which language to use in a particular situation (for bi- or multi-lingual speakers), how to address an interlocutor, whether to delete or add sounds to words, whether to talk or remain silent, are strongly patterned (Hudson 1980). Conversation analysis studies demonstrate that speaking turns in conversation are precisely coordinated, hesitations and pauses are delicately organized, and interaction is finely synchronized (Moerman 1988). Studies of nonverbal signaling behavior in humans have recently afforded a picture of interaction as organized not only within but across modes of sign behavior (Wiemann and Harrison 1983). As Dell Hymes wrote, anticipating some of the many discoveries made about the structure of spoken life, "speaking, like language, is patterned, functions as a system, is describable by rules" (Hymes 1962, p. 131).

To say that speaking is structured is not to say it is absolutely determined. It is patterned, but in ways that its creators can circumvent, challenge, and revise. Its rules are violated, new rules and meanings are created, and therein play is brought into structure just as structure is brought into play. Furthermore, any given speech community is, to use Hymes's phrase, an "organization of diversity." The patterns of speaking in any community are fashioned from diverse, even discrepant, motives, practices, and preferences, but nonetheless there is, in any particular community, a knowable system in its language use. To acknowledge that the patterns are mutable and that they subsume diverse strands does not negate the fact that, nonetheless, there is a pattern.

One of the surest ways to experience the structure in speaking is to step from one society to another, to situate oneself amid the sounds and stratagems of an alien speech community, because such new hearings bring the essential structure of both communities into sharp relief. Such a stepping, such a situating of oneself, not only provides a way to hear one community's sounds as structured, it is also a first step in discovering that wherever there is a distinctive social community there is also a distinctive way of speaking.

Speaking is Distinctive

"Speech," Edward Sapir wrote, "varies without assignable limit as we pass from social group to social group" (1921, p. 4). The sounds of any particular communal conversation may be drawn from a universal repertoire of noises, but what the noises will be, mean, and accomplish, are matters of local provenance. The conditions and contingencies of spoken life give rise to particular vocabularies, moral rules for using speech, and habitual ways of speaking as an instrument of social action. Wherever there is a spoken life, there is a distinctive system of predicables, preferences, and practices for spoken conduct.

Until quite recently, "speaking" as a department of culture had been neglected in studies of speech and in studies of culture. It had been considered a given, something that is what it is, wherever it is found. Of course, it has long been known that languages differ and that ways of life differ; and cultural differences in speech behavior have long been noted in passing. But until the last twenty five years, Sapir's statement notwithstanding, speaking—the use in social interaction of language and other symbolic resources—was taken for granted as something that does not vary across cultures.

A striking way in which speaking was taken for granted was in the implicit assumption that speaking is, primarily or even exclusively, a means for transmitting information. That is not always or everywhere its primary or exclusive function. In Teamsterville, for example, much of speech behavior functions, not primarily to report or to describe, but to link—that is, to link interlocutors in a social relationship, to affirm and signify the interlocutors' sameness and unity. At the Nacirema dinner table, statements about one's experiences serve not only to inform listeners about those experiences but to give speakers an opportunity to express their uniqueness, to differentiate the speaker from the others. This suggests not only that something more than information transmission is being done with speech, but also a difference, across groups, in *what* gets done.

In Teamsterville a parent is expected to use physical punishment to discipline an errant child; among the Nacirema a parent is expected to use supportive speech as the first tactic in discipline—a difference in rules. The Nacirema concept of "communication" is, if not unknown, at least not prominent in Teamsterville speaking—a difference in meaning. What these peoples and others are doing, and what their speaking activities mean to them—these are culturally shaped and defined.

An implication of assuming that spoken life is distinctive is that communicative conduct can never be fully understood, predicted, or explained without knowing the distinctive culture in whose terms, and the distinctive social context in which, it is spoken. Speaking is always speaking somewhere, with some group of people, in some language, and it is always shaped by and a part of some social life. To understand speaking in any particular instance is, in part, to understand a distinctive way of life. Making sense of a particular communal conversation, then, requires local knowledge, knowledge not only of speech sounds but of a local system of symbols and their meanings, of community mores, and of indigenous patterns of message-making and interpretation.

Based on recent research, it has become a truism to say that the communication technologies available to and used in a society have a profound effect on the character of its social life. Language and speech are universally present in all societies, but the availability of literacy, print, and telecommunications varies across time and place. The presence or absence of these different technologies of communication, it has been argued, is a fundamental factor in the character of any society. As Ruth Finnegan, who has reviewed much of this literature, has written recently:

> Because communication is so fundamental we tend to take it for granted and not to reflect overmuch on the various forms it takes. But a closer analysis of communication patterns—and particularly the various technological channels through which communication can flow—suggests that it may have far greater influence over our social and economic life, even perhaps our mental make-up, than one might at first suppose (Finnegan 1988, p. 16).

One need not disagree with the claims that societies differ in their communication technologies and that these differences have important consequences, to make the complementary claim that how any one of these media is shaped and functions in lives and societies varies as well. The claim I am advancing is that *speech* is "so fundamental that we tend to take it for granted and not to reflect overmuch" on the various ways it is thematized and enacted in speech communities. Finnegan has written, "the universality and fundamental importance of language for human society may be overlooked. In fact verbal communication through humanly developed language is common to all societies and can be seen as the universal background against which all other forms of communication take place" (1988, p. 167). I would add that this "universal background" is itself highly particularized in terms of what any particular people has to say about it and in terms of what they do with it.

The idea that speaking varies across cultures, in the ways suggested above, was first put forth in an explicit way by Dell Hymes in his article "The Ethnography of Speaking" (1962). He made two assumptions. The first, which has been discussed above, is that speaking varies cross-culturally; that is, as a domain of human activity it is thematized distinctively across cultures, and in different societies there are different ways of speaking. This distinctive treatment includes whether speaking is included in the cultural system and, if so, what symbols, meanings, premises, and rules there are pertaining to speaking in the culture. The second is that speaking is a key to, or a metaphor of, social life. And thus, given that speaking, as a socially and culturally structured practice, varies across speech communities, its analysis as a cultural system reveals, in particular cases, something about the distinctive society and culture of a people. For example, that the Teamstervillers believe speech, one of the media of communication, to be efficacious in signaling and ratifying solidarity, where there is some basis for a solidary bond, as well as for revealing and reinforcing perceptions of social difference, where there is some basis for recognizing such differences and that the Nacirema have an extensive vocabulary for, and system of beliefs pertaining to, "communication," suggest something about meaning and action in the contexts in which a code is used.

In every speech community there is a social pattern of language use—that is, some ordering in what is actually done in the speech activity of a community. And there is a cultural ideology—that is, a system of beliefs and prejudices about communication. These, taken together, reveal a culturally distinctive way of acting and a culturally distinctive way of experiencing social life. These articulating with each other, in the life of a person or group, constitute—that is, make up, bring about, or enact—a distinctive social reality.

Speaking is Social

It is in moments of sociation that people speak: when they huddle together in intimate pairs or families, organize their labor for mutual gain, govern and submit to each other as citizens of a state, or unite as a tribe. Not every social moment is a speaking moment, but every speaking moment not only occurs in, but also contributes to, a particular moment of sociality. Speech is not merely a medium of or an accompaniment to social interaction but also shapes and constitutes social life. "Oral communication," wrote Father Walter Ong, "unites people in groups" (1982, p. 69). As, he continues, "the spoken word proceeds from the human interior and manifests human beings to one another as conscious interiors, as persons, the spoken word forms human beings into close-knit groups" (p. 74). But oral communication unites people not merely into *a* group but into a particular humanity manifested in particular words and practices, and that particularity has an ideational and experiential substance that is distinctive and thus is a powerful resource for constructing personal and social meaning. It is a resource by which a *particular* humanity is established; a *particular* sense of sociality is a consequence of a *particular* social life.

To know, and to use appropriately, the meanings, rules, and speech habits of a local group signals and affirms that one is a member of it. To know the local parlance, but be unwilling to use it, or feel not permitted to use it, or to feel that using it would insinuate oneself somewhere that one does not belong, reveals a relationship, perceived or real, that places one at some distance from the group. To have once used the local parlance and then to eschew it because one is "beyond all that" places one in relation to the group, as a former member or as one temporarily distanced from the group. These patterns of use and nonuse have expressive import for the individual and the audiences to which they are revealed and addressed, because they are intricately woven into the texture of lives and societies. Knowledge of, and ability to participate in, a particular community's spoken life are not only resources for information transmission but are resources for communal identification, and communal being, as well. Speech is both an act of and a resource for "membering."

A culture and a social community are not exactly one and the same but it is hard to imagine either existing except in some integral relation to each other. A culture, as defined here, is a system of meanings, an organized complex of symbols, definitions, premises, and rules. To speak of Teamsterville culture is not to speak of a geographical or political unit but of a code. A community consists of a group of people who are bound together in some relation of shared sentiment and mutual responsibility. A neighborhood is not a code and a code is not a social group, but a neighborhood *as community* is bound together, in part, by its local code of meanings and mores, and a code has its intelligibility and its force in some particular communal association, be it neighborhood, network, or nation.

It is when code and community jointly meet that the full power of culture is most strongly experienced. It is in an actual social community that the full sense can be felt of a culture as set forms that precede utterance and action, that constrain and enable what can be said and done in speech. A culture devoid of a context has no practical force, a context devoid of a culture has nothing to transform it from a mere physical setting to a scene imbued with significance for those who play out their lives against it.

THE DISCURSIVE FORCE OF COMMON CULTURE

Not all of life is spoken life, to be sure. Juxtaposed with the forces of nature, tradition, class, and economics, and with the consequences of individual differences in beauty, intelligence, strength, and virtue, speech might appear to be of relatively little importance in the total scheme of life. Certainly it has its limits as a department of the human experience. Once at a dinner party I listened to a man tell about how several professors of economics at the university at which I taught were notorious for their extreme political views, views systematically woven into their research and teaching, to the degree that the university's essentially conservative establishment found these professors to be quite troublesome. "Of course," he said, and then laughed, "that would never be a problem in your field." I never queried him as to the meaning of his remark. But I think he believed speech is of such little social, political, or economic significance that, of course, there is little about it that could be controversial—the stakes are too low to take the subject very seriously.

There are no simple answers to the question of whether speech is a trivial or a powerful thread in the social and biographical fabric. One claim is that there is a world of hard substance—the material facts of economics, power, biology, and the nearly as brutish facts of tradition and fashion—against which speech is mere accompaniment, vessel, or mirror of the important aspects of life. A contrasting claim is that personal identity, social reality, and social action are constituted in—created, negotiated, and transformed, as well as reflected in—the communicative conduct of which speaking is a part.

The ethnographic views, or hearings, represented in this book reveal that speech shapes and constitutes lives and societies in powerful ways. But the ethnographer is quick to add that although talk plays an important role in every life and society, how it does this varies considerably. The ethnographer is always concerned to inquire into how speech enters into a particular life and society, what its situated distinctiveness is. Thus, the ethnographer can affirm the importance of speech and of studying it, but will also insist that because its importance is expressed in distinctive ways across societies, much of what is important to know about speaking is situated, cultural knowledge.

One way to show how speech shapes life differently in different societies is to think of different ways of speaking as expressing culturally distinctive codes, or ideologies, of personhood, society, and communicative action. That is, every cultural way of speaking is a distinctive answer to the questions (1) What is a person? (2) What is society? and (3) How are persons and societies linked through communication? Teamsterville and Nacirema cultures are instructive illustrations. In Teamsterville, the person is fundamentally a persona, a bundle of social identities, such as "man," "Italian," "young," and a resident of 33rd Street. Society is existentially and morally prior to the person—it existed prior to the individuals who are part of it and it is more important than any individual. Communication is a process in which psychological similarities and social differences are manifested so as to link individuals in relations of solidarity and hierarchy. This is an ideology of honor, in that persons are accorded value to the degree that they embody and promote societal values of hierarchy and community.

For the Nacirema, on the other hand, the person is a psychologically unique individual; society is built up from the acts of autonomous individuals and itself is of value only in the degree to which it enhances the individual. Unique persons link themselves to others by communicating their uniqueness to each other while simultaneously paying homage to their social equality. This is an ideology of dignity, in that in this code the individual is an object of ultimate value.

A code of speaking provides a system of rules and premises that is a rhetorical resource—that is, a resource that can be used in appealing to others to act. It also marks off a universe of meaning and supplies a system of interpretive resources with which interlocutors can make sense with each other. And in terms of answering questions of ultimate meaning, in terms of providing individuals and societies with ways to answer questions about why they exist and where they fit in a scheme of sense and meaning, a code of speaking provides the resources for creating a sense of coherence and form. Codes of speaking are, from this vantage point, rhetorical, interpretive, and identificative resources.

THE PLAN OF THE BOOK

The various points of view presented in chapter 1 have not been proposed as uncontestable assertions so much as considerations that legitimate what is to follow. What follows is a series of case studies, two based on Teamsterville culture and two based on Nacirema culture, which explore how these cultures thematize speaking as a medium of human communication. The considerations—or assumptive basis—of chapter 1 suggest that by inquiring into distinctive cultures one might find there distinctive treatments—distinctive systems of symbols and meanings, premises, and rules—of this medium, and it is this possibility that is the object of exploration.

Before proceeding, a word should be said about the presentation of two cultures within one volume. A piece of advice given to authors of books is to fix in the mind a single image pertaining to the subject of the book and to allow that image to shape and inspire one's research and writing throughout the project. In writing this book I have tried to keep in mind an abstract image—that of interlocutors speaking with each other—and to keep foremost in mind the question of what happens when people talk. This has been difficult because as soon as I have imagined a hypothetical image of persons speaking, particular images, drawn from memory and field records rather than from imagination, replace the constructed image in my mind's eyes and ears. The hypothetical image is much like a photographic negative or an outline drawing, but the particular images are colored with the sounds and tones of particular lives, occasions, and communities. Thus the image of speaking invariably gave way to images of "speaking," the quotation marks implicating an activity given a particular meaning in particular worlds of discourse.

The chapters that follow are about the cultural coloration given to speaking, rendering it in particular instances of its realization a fundamentally cultural activity. What happens when people speak, what their speaking consists of and what it means to them, are constructions made, I argue, in the terms and tropes—the colors—of particular cultures. I have begun in this chapter by introducing the research theme and the perspective that has produced, and informs, its development. There follows a series of four chapters in which case studies of "speaking" are presented. Chapters 2 and 3 present case studies of Teamsterville culture, 4 and 5 of Nacirema culture. These case studies are further interpreted in chapter 6, a chapter that comparatively analyzes the two cultures examined in the case studies, revealing two underlying codes—or social rhetorics—of personhood, society, and strategic action. Finally, drawing from the materials and interpretations presented in the previous chapters, a theoretical synthesis is made in chapter 7—a synthesis in which several ways in which speaking is "speaking" are formulated and illustrated. The integrating theme of the book is, then, that whenever people speak, they participate in an activity that is thoroughly cultural. And the implications of this are presented through a detailing of ways this fact impinges upon the process of social communication.

PART II

Speaking in Teamsterville Culture

Chapter 2

PLACE AND PERSONAE IN TEAMSTERVILLE SPEAKING

Talk is not everywhere valued equally, nor is it valued equally in all social contexts. Speaking is an object of a high degree of interest, elaboration, and positive evaluation in some cultures, such as those of the Barundi (Albert 1972) and St. Vincentians (Abrahams and Bauman 1971), but is relatively deemphasized in other cultures, such as those of the Paliyans (Gardner 1966) and the La Have islanders (Bauman 1972) (see also Braithwaite 1982, Philipsen 1986, and Carbaugh 1989 for systematic reviews). Cultures are not only varied but are also internally diverse in the emphasis they place on the value of talk. In all communities there are some situations where "silence is golden" and some where talk is the most valued mode of social behavior (Basso 1970, Philips 1970). Each community has its own cultural values about speaking and these are linked to judgments of situational appropriateness.

Teamsterville, which is located on the near south side of Chicago, is a neighborhood of blue-collar, low-income whites who share a cultural outlook on communication. Teamsterville's cultural (shared, tacit) understandings about the value of speaking are sharply defined and susceptible of discovery, although they are not written down in native treatises on effective communication, nor can native informants necessarily verbalize them.

One manifestation of cultural outlook is the local view of the appropriateness of speaking versus other actional strategies (such as silence, violence, or nonverbal threats) in male role enactment or self-presentation. Whether and how well a man performs in a manly way is a principal criterion in Teamsterville for judging whether his behavior is appropriate and proper to the social identity, "male." Manliness is a theme of much neighborhood talk about self and others, and a Teamsterville man is aware that his social performances will be judged frequently as to their manliness. To know how to perform, or present oneself, "like a man" in Teamsterville as elsewhere is to be privy to implicit understandings shared by members of the speech community—that is, to have access to the culture. It is because the male role is highly important in the culture that description of the place of speaking in male role enactment reveals much in general about the community's valuation of talk.

A Teamsterville outlook on settings or locales also informs native understandings about speaking as a situated mode of social activity. In addition to the personae, which the culture marks for speaking "parts," the culture also marks particular scenes for occasions of talk. There are no labeled conversation areas or orators' arenas in the community, but its worldview includes social boundaries, scenes, and scenes within scenes referring to everyday stages upon which a particular kind of dramatic action may unfold. The native view of settings, and of the activities they most appropriately realize, specifies, among other things, places for speaking, and in turn that specification permits an inference about the place of speaking in Teamsterville.

"Place" is used here in several senses but each contains various ideas of location, such as a position in a social hierarchy, a physical setting, or the niche properly occupied by a thing, person, or idea. In this sense one speaks not only of things but also of people and ideas as having a place "in the scheme of things." A place can also be regarded as a perspective from which one discovers or explores a subject by the use of mental images. "Place," then, may simultaneously suggest notions of social, physical, perceptual, and heuristic location.

The phrase, "places for speaking in Teamsterville," uses each of these senses of the word "place." Although this paper locates speaking in social and physical space, primarily it locates speech in the community's culture. Teamsterville's outlook on the occasioned uses of speaking suggests that a sense of place—at once both hierarchical and physical—is a "major unifying perception" in its cultural worldview, a perception that creates shades of meaning and interpretation regarding speech as an instrument of communication and social life. Two features of place—personae and scene—are perspectives that have special relevance for exploring Teamsterville's images of the world, and for thereby discovering where its people locate speech in their cultural scheme of things.

Four Teamsterville place concepts form a simple taxonomy of culturally defined places for speaking. Each is labeled by a native place term, and is defined in terms of the kind of setting to which it refers, the personae whose presence in it create a scene, and how the scene-personae configuration creates an occasion for talk. Scene, personae, and talk thus are interwoven aspects of the design I use in reporting Teamsterville places for speaking.

COLLECTION AND ANALYSIS OF DATA

I had two periods of contact with Teamsterville. The first was a twenty-one month period during 1969 and 1970 spent as a social group worker in the neighborhood. The second, which began after a twelve month absence from the neighborhood, was for nine months in 1971 and 1972 devoted exclusively to fieldwork research.

Participant observation and interviewing were used as techniques of data collection, and data were analyzed using an ethnography of communication model (Hymes 1962, 1972). All available data, including field records of speech behavior, informants' statements (spontaneous and elicited), and tape-recorded verbal interaction provided the evidence from which the culture pattern was inferred, and against which it was tested. Thus, multiple sources of data were used in constructing descriptions and verifying hypotheses relevant to the inferred culture pattern (Webb, Campbell, Schwartz, and Sechrest 1966).

One research technique was particularly useful in constructing the culture pattern. The two episodes analyzed in this paper draw attention to the role enactments judged ineffective by Teamsterville residents. Native reactions to out-of-role behavior are instructive because they bring into sharp focus role expectations which have been violated (Goffman 1959; chapter 5). While exclusive use of this technique could produce a distorted view of the culture pattern (Naroll 1970), it is useful as one source of clues to discovery of a pattern. The episodes reported below are clues to discovery. They provide concrete instances of a pattern verified systematically through ethnographic research (Keesing, 1970).

SPEAKING "LIKE A MAN"

A Teamsterville native shares tacit understandings about the situational appropriateness of speech behavior—specifically, that in some situations speech is appropriate in male role enactment, but that in others it is not and its use casts doubt on the speaker's manliness. Three classes of situation can be discerned: those marked in the culture for a relatively great amount of talk by men, those marked for minimal talk by men, and those in which an emphasis of the verbal channel is proscribed for effective male self-presentation and for which other means of expression are required.

Following are brief analyses of the first two of these classes of situation and a more extensive analysis of the third.

When the social identity relationship of the participants in a situation is symmetrical, the situation can appropriately realize a great amount of talking by a Teamsterville man. Specifically, the participants in a speaking situation should be matched on such identity attributes as age, sex, ethnicity, occupational status, and location of residence. The participants should be longtime friends. Speaking is a dominant focus of all-male social interaction in corner groups and corner bars. For boys the street corner, and for men the corner bar, is the principal setting for sociability. Speaking is a dominant activity in these settings. Typically, small groups of boys "hang" on their own corner, and groups of men have their own corner bar, a public drinking establishment claimed by them as their "turf," a territory to which outsiders are not invited or welcomed. Teamsterville men seek out other men of like identity, in well-established locations. These are the situations in which it is most appropriate and proper for a man to produce a great quantity of talk.

A high quantity of speaking is considered inappropriate in situations in which the participants' identity relationship is asymmetrical. Such relationships are, for the adult man in Teamsterville, those with a wife, child, boss, outsider to the neighborhood, or a man of different ethnicity. Certainly, Teamsterville men do speak to their wives, girlfriends, children, and employers, but these are not contexts of relationship that call for a high quantity of speaking nor are these the "natural" situations in which to engage others in a state of talk. Thus one criterion in Teamsterville for marking a speech situation for men is the variable, the social identity relationship of the interlocutors. In speech situations the relationship is symmetrical on relevant identity attributes; in nonspeech situations the relationship is asymmetrical.

For some situations the question is not so much whether there should be a great quantity or frequency of talk but rather what mode of action is to be emphasized in male self-presentation, and it is this kind of situation I have selected for more detailed analysis. Specifically, an analysis of the Teamsterville data produces the generalization that when a man must assert power over or influence another person, speaking is disapproved as a dominant means of self-presentation and in such situations other means of expression are preferred, sometimes required, if the actor's male role enactment is to be credible to those who witness it. Three instances of this class of situation have particular relevance for a Teamsterville man: when he responds to insult, an insult directed either at him or at his female relative or girlfriend, when he seeks to influence the behavior of a status inferior, such as a child; and when he asserts himself in politics or economics. These instances of the class of situation are analyzed and illustrated below.

It is not uncommon that a Teamsterville man must respond to insults directed at him or at the reputation of a woman relative or girlfriend. An episode illustrates the Teamsterville view that an emphasis of the verbal channel is not appropriate for men in such situations. A settlement house group worker took a group of Teamsterville boys (thirteen and fourteen years of age) on a trip to Old Town, an entertainment area in Chicago. On the drive from Teamsterville to Old Town, conversation turned to the topic of defending the honor of women. The question was put to the group worker, who was not a native of Teamsterville: "What would you do if a guy insulted your wife?" The group worker responded that he did not know, that it would depend on the situation. The answer did not satisfy the boys, who pressed the question by asking, "But you'd hit him, wouldn't you?" The worker answered that he did not know, that he probably would not hit him, or fight, but would instead probably try to talk to him or persuade him to leave. The boys, however, pressed the point, and became increasingly nervous and upset, to the point that their moving vehicle was shaking from the activity. They were, as I recorded it at the time, visibly agitated. As the group drove off Lake Shore Drive, a main highway in Chicago, into the Old Town area, all of the boys, who were usually enthusiastic about Old Town visits, clamored to go home, saying they did not want to go to Old Town after all.

How can the Teamsterville boys' apparently sudden decision to go home be explained? In spite of their fondness for Old Town, the boys were—on this and previous occasions—uneasy about many of the people they expected to meet there, and they freely verbalized their apprehensions of blacks, "hippies," and "pot-smokers." On a typical walk with the boys on Wells Street—Old Town's main street—some of the boys would always be close to the side of their adult group worker. At the start of the trip in question, the boys apparently assumed they would be in the company of a normal man who protects those in his care in their culturally prescribed way, for example, by fighting for them as he would for the honor of female relatives. When the boys learned, through the discussion in the car, that their adult companion of the evening was not the kind of man who protects those dependent upon him in what is for Teamsterville the culturally prescribed way, they became frightened. The boys' definition of the situation had been radically altered by the conversation in the car. The closer they got to Old Town (where, they could reason, they might need an adult for security), the uneasier they became. To the boys, given their assumptions, the situation was threatening. The boys faced a problem of trying to deal with an alien situation, created by the man who said he would choose silence or talk when fighting is, to the boys, the proper and appropriate response.

A second episode is about the Teamsterville reaction to a man who did not know—or who for some other reason did not act in conformity to—a local conception of appropriate role enactment. Again, the outsider's out-of-role behavior was the choice of speech over fighting as the preferred mode of self-presentation in an exigent situation, one that required a man to influence the behavior of his status inferiors. The episode, which took place over a period of days, was prompted by the trouble a Teamsterville settlement house had with teenage boys in its youth program—the boys were undisciplined, rude, and defiant of authority. The director of the program approached the problem in what he thought was a constructive and sympathetic way, by trying to reason with the boys, to involve them in decision-making, to understand their feelings, and so forth. These were techniques that had, in other settings, proved effective for the director. The strategy was not effective in Teamsterville; the boys became more rebellious and more verbally abusive and disrespectful of adult staff members.

John, a longtime resident of the neighborhood, embodied the local norms of the strong, physically aggressive male. John, who witnessed much of what went on during teen program hours, had to face, as I now interpret it, a dilemma. On the one hand, the director of the program had a position of high status in the community, and he was a married, adult man. On the other hand, the director did not physically subdue the boys, as John thought he should. John's dilemma can be phrased as the resolution of conflicting information: either the director was not a normal male or the role expectation of corporal punishment and the speech proscription for men in such situations was not applicable.

John dealt with the dilemma in three stages. He apparently ruled out the possibility that the director belonged in the nonnormal category. One reason why it would be hard for John to assign the director to the nonnormal category is that the director was married, and in Teamsterville marriage is automatically accepted as proof that a man is not a homosexual. An illustration of this is that in a group discussion at the Teamsterville settlement house someone interpreted my wearing of colored socks as a sign that I was a homosexual; the assertion was quickly disputed when someone else said, "He can't be queer, he's married." At first John hinted, and eventually stated outright, that the director ought to "beat the hell out of these kids." He even expressed his willingness to help and reassured the adult that he could obtain the boys' parents' permission for such action. John's suggestion was reinforced by his explanation to the nonnative that Teamsterville boys interpreted the verbal strategies as a sign of homosexuality, a point I verified repeatedly in other observations and through elicitation of role expectations from informants.

Having failed to change his interlocutor's behavior to conform to Teamsterville expectations, John adopted a second strategy, shifting from persuasion to an attempt at rationalizing the behavior. Since the director failed to live up to the social-moral code, John sought to interpret the behavior in light of another code. It was illegal, he reasoned, for someone in the position of director to hit minors: "I know you'd like to hit these kids, but someone in your job can't do it, it's against the law, but I know that you'd like to hit them." It appears that John was beginning actively to reevaluate the alien behavior. However, recourse to "higher authority" as an explanation apparently did not satisfy him for long.

John's third and final strategy can also be described from a moral perspective. The director was not immoral (homosexual), or guided by an extralocal morality (legally bound not to hit minors), but was now, in John's eyes, so proper that he was able to transcend the expectations that apply to mere mortals. John said to the director: "You know what you are, all the trouble you get from these kids, I don't know how you can keep from belting 'em one; you're a saint, that's what you are." The director's speaking strategy had been interpreted and rationalized. John applied several levels of the Teamsterville moral code to account for the alien behavior, to preserve the director's role enactment as appropriate, proper, and convincing. The preference of a verbal to a physical role enactment was itself a message in the community, but John had to search for a meaning to that message with which he could comfortably live, a meaning that was at each stage of his interpretation a moral one.

In both of the above situations—an insult by a stranger and rude behavior by the boys—the Teamsterville man discerns a threat to the credibility of his role enactment as male. The challenge requires a response, a self-presentation that answers the challenge. What resources for self-presentation are appropriately available to him? Speech is the currency of social interaction when participants have similar social identities, including membership in a close-knit friendship group; speech purchases an expression of solidarity or assertion of status symmetry. Therefore a response in which speaking is the dominant mode of self-presentation has little value as a counter to the threat—indeed, the threat itself might be an inappropriate assertion of status symmetry. A speech surrogate as the dominant means of self-presentation purchases an assertion of distance, difference, or status asymmetry, and may therefore appropriately be used to counter the threat. The man must respond in such situations and the sanctioned resource for responding is something other than talk.

In Teamsterville speech is judged appropriate for male self-presentation in assertions of solidarity but not in assertions of power over another person. "Responding to insults" provides a neat illustration of this two-point theme. First, when an outsider to his group insults a boy's girlfriend or mother, to take a speaking "part" is to run the risk of having one's performance judged to be ineffective. By not defending his girlfriend physically the boy invites further attacks on himself, inferiority feelings for himself, and possible future attacks on the girl. After all, the Teamsterville boy would reason, who will protect her if her boyfriend is not "man enough" to defend her? I am here describing, as a construction from relevant data, the Teamsterville boys' own conceptualization.

As in any study of norms, so in this, rules do not necessarily predict behavior. Speech, at least as a dominant mode of response, is *judged* ineffective as role enactment when dealing with an insult to a woman under a man's protection when the offender is an outsider. However, if a boy insults a peer's mother or girlfriend (the mother or girlfriend of a member of his own corner group), speech is judged an effective, appropriate means for neutralizing the attack. Preferred is a verbal put-down, which in effect humiliates or defeats the attacker, but a simple appeal to stop is also appropriate. Speech is, in the situation defined, a sanctioned resource for acting to respond to the exigence of the situation. It should be emphasized that speech is efficacious for an expression of power only in the context of a previously established, continuing relationship based primarily on a solidarity tie. The strength of the tie supports the verbal appeal, and a verbal strategy but serves to activate the solidarity ties, which are themselves persuasive resources.

Teamsterville residents not only believe that speech is inappropriate and improper in dealing with a threat from an outsider, but that its use will bring negative consequences to the boy, such as future attacks on himself and his friends. So too, when a Teamsterville adult man wants to affirm or assert power over or influence the behavior of a child, the use of speech is not only ineffective but may also entail damaging consequences for the man's reputation. The principle is seen in action in the failure of a man to respond to verbal abuse from a child by a show of physical power. For the child to challenge the man with speech, particularly brash speech, is an initiation of status symmetry, a challenge that, if met only with talk by the adult, is not met at all. The use of speech by the child signals to the other a comment about the relationship, an implicit announcement that the speaker is in a solidary relationship to the hearer. And in Teamsterville, as elsewhere, assertions of solidarity are judged to be the prerogative of the more powerful member of a pair (Brown and Gilman, 1960). For the man to restore the relationship to its properly asymmetrical state requires the use of an effective cultural resource for that situation, and such an effective resource is physical fighting or nonverbal threat, not talk. One informant summarized the Teamsterville view when he responded to my question of how a man would be judged if he talked to an erring child before spanking him: "I don't know of that ever happening. That just wouldn't be natural for a man to do."

In Teamsterville, speech is proper and functional in asserting male solidarity, but not in asserting power and influence in interpersonal situations. In critical symbolic ways, as protector and master of a house, the Teamsterville man disvalues speech as a resource for male role enactment. In another critical way, as breadwinner, speech is not an integral part of earning a living or of other aspects of economic life. A list of Teamsterville occupations, prepared from my survey data and corroborated by government census figures, suggests that the Teamsterville man requires relatively little verbal interaction in connection with his employment. And yet, when the Teamsterville man needs a job, or must deal with the civil authorities, or must plead a case, what means of persuasion are properly available to him? I would coin the phrase a "rhetoric of connections" as the answer to the question, meaning that connections with a political leader, a prospective employer, or other kinds of officials, are personal resources that may be morally and effectively marshaled in times of personal need. Whereas speech is not a resource critical to male role enactment in exigent situations, connections have a very real value. When I raised the subject of connections with my male informants, each of them smiled broadly. Apparently they were pleased by mention of the subject and enjoyed discussing it. Each emphasized the personal importance of connections and told how he himself had used connections successfully in some situations requiring effective action. "The more connections a man has, the more he is a man," is how one informant explained it.

For the Teamsterville man, minimal emphasis of talk in work settings is one part of a pattern of minimal talk with outsiders to the neighborhood, with persons in positions of authority who are not longtime associates, and with white-collar persons, with whom there is a perceived status difference. Most of the Teamsterville man's necessary contacts with "outsiders" are mediated through a local precinct captain, Catholic parish priest, or union steward. The politician—a precinct captain or his block assistant—serves as an intermediary in matters of employment, law, politics, social welfare, and various other matters, thus minimizing the resident's direct dealings with the outside world. This is an extension of a widespread European pattern that extends from minor secular situations to religion. In the European countries of origin of Teamsterville residents, not only in politics are dealings with authority normally conducted by means of an intermediary, but also in the sacred realm, where the resident does not directly address the deity but relies upon such intermediaries as ministers, priests, or holy figures to whom he prays. It should be noted that the intermediary principal redefines situations requiring assertion of influence from the use of speech by the suppliant to the use of solidarity or locality ties with the intermediary, who is eventually to state the case for the resident. Speaking is easy and appropriate for the intermediary in virtue of his higher social status and his demands for convincing role enactment as an intermediary.

The concept of the intermediary was confirmed in conversations with informants, who verified the "rule" of access to outsiders through an intermediary. In addition, the concept proved useful in explicating what I had, previous to formulation of the principle, viewed as inexplicable behavior. Throughout my years as employee-participant and as ethnographer-participant observer at a Teamsterville settlement house, I had occasion to observe on numerous occasions the following illustration of the intermediary principle in action. The settlement house required that any teenage boy wishing to join the group work program in the middle of the school year come to the office to register and speak to the director. Whenever a teenage boy came to register, however, he always brought a friend, someone who was already a member of the program, who stated the newcomer's case, while the applicant stood by as if mute, although he might later prove to be capable of loud and frequent talk. My uninformed response, born of being socialized to a very different culture, was skepticism about a teenage boy who could not come on his own and speak "as a man." In Teamsterville, however, I discovered that many of these applicants were speechless only in situations of their choosing. To speak "like a man" in Teamsterville required knowing when and under what circumstances to speak at all.

Teamsterville residents do not think in terms of organized action for community improvement, nor do they think in terms of using a verbal strategy for self-assertion. I asked one block politician, who praised the connections system for satisfying the needs of individuals and families, whether a community group would be able to secure some needed improvement through a persuasive campaign. I tried phrasing the question in several different ways, but my interlocutor would or could answer my question only by pointing to the ways in which individuals secured personal favors through the effectiveness of an intermediary in the social or political system. The connections system—and the local conceptualization of its efficacy—is based on personal ties to intermediaries. My interviews of longtime residents and my own experience produced only two instances of a community group that organized a persuasive campaign for community improvement. Both instances were described by respondents as following this pattern: first, the groups tried to promote a cause through a group-organized persuasive campaign, including appeals through news media, but the groups did not have connections and the campaigns failed; then someone in the neighborhood who had connections noticed the campaign and acted to secure the needed action. The importance is not the actual, but the reported, result of using personal connections in attaining the desired end. In Teamsterville, speech and group action are not regarded as effective methods for attaining difficult goals, and sometimes speech is thought to be counterproductive.

In summary, speech in Teamsterville is not an effective means for the display of a manly role before one who is not a peer. If an assertion of power is necessary, custom sanctions other means of expression. Naturally, the means vary with the nature of the situation. If one's addressee is of lower status—a child, a woman, a member of another Teamsterville ethnic group—the power assertion may rely on nonverbal threat or physical combat. When one's addressee is of higher status—a boss, an outsider from a more prosperous neighborhood, a government official—male power assertion may properly employ personal connections with an intermediary who states the resident's case for him. When speech is used in asserting influence among peers or in securing the services of an intermediary, the role enactment is effective because of the strength provided by the established solidarity tie rather than the style or content of the verbal message. Just as the woman who has learned her roles in the speech community knows her place is in the home, so a man who has learned his roles in Teamsterville knows his "place" when it comes to speech behavior. He asserts himself in civil or economic affairs through an intermediary, and is neither so bold as to engage in talk with those far above him on the social scale nor so lacking in self-esteem that he must use speech to deal with those below him. To be able systematically to render a convincing performance of the male role in Teamsterville requires control of the culture, particularly the part of the culture that specifies the efficacy of speaking in appropriate, proper, and convincing role enactment.

PLACES FOR SPEAKING

A sense of neighborhood has a deep and compelling significance to the dwellers of Teamsterville. The socio-spatial boundaries that residents perceive as "the neighborhood" make up the largest region within which it is considered most appropriate and in which it is most "natural" to engage in talk. The residents think of these boundaries as coextensive with a particular style of speaking, which is characteristic of the community and to which its residents should conform. Definitions of neighborhood as scene, then, relate to native judgments about when to talk and ways of speaking, and both kinds of judgment are linked to a native view of place.

Every resident readily and emphatically identifies "the neighborhood" and defines it very insistently in terms of specific streets and blocks. Residents are equally insistent that they "know everybody around here"—that is, within the boundaries they perceive. Field observation and questioning of informants reveal that the boundaries reported vary considerably from person to person, and that the "we know everybody" assertion is not literally true. But the very specific definition and the insistent assertion suggest that a resident defines "the neighborhood" by reference both to physical setting ("around here") and to the particular people who make up his or her network of friends, associates, and acquaintances ("everybody") within it.

The physical boundaries of the neighborhood frame a scene for sociable interaction. For most residents these boundaries are the outer perimeter beyond which they do not socialize. In the course of my interviews of them, few Teamsterville men or women reported that they had participated in social events during the previous year with anyone who lives more than ten blocks from their home. Their reports of speaking practices, which observation confirmed in most cases, indicate a pattern of overt behavior, but what is more important here is that the reports suggest a local preference for talking within, not without, the perceived physical boundaries. Teamstervillers view the physical neighborhood as the largest scene within which talk is appropriately a focus of activity.

Within the physical neighborhood a Teamsterviller can be in the presence of people whom one defines as intruding into one's social world. The physical boundaries are therefore supplemented by social boundaries that define "everybody"—the roster from which may be drawn appropriate personae for talk. Specifically, the ethnicity and residence of a potential interlocutor—his or her social and physical place—are salient variables in decisions to mark an occasion as appropriate for speaking. A visitor to the neighborhood, if so bold as to intrude into semiprivate regions (which include, among other places, "the street"), must be placed by the resident in terms of ethnicity and residence before a conversation can comfortably proceed. Once a stranger is so located, talk might be relatively free, depending on the kind of person it is. "The hillbillies" and "Mexicans" live within the neighborhood boundaries, but do not, in the eyes of the long-term white residents, really "belong" there. These groups should, in the view of the people I studied, "keep in their place" by living elsewhere and socializing among themselves. They are not, as a rule, appropriate partners for talk.

Finally, there are those people who live in the neighborhood and whose ethnicity fits one of the traditional categories but whose ethnicity is different from one's own. Germans, Italians, Poles, and Lithuanians, among others, now talk to each other, but in the past these neighborhood groups had been relatively isolated from each other physically and socially, and there is still a sharp sense of difference between them. These persons include some people in the other groups in the term "everybody," yet they still can visualize an image of "the neighborhood" as people of like ethnicity sharing a street or block, and it is that scene in which talk most appropriately and naturally has its place.

The unusually strong relationship of social to physical place is no accident. In the nineteenth century Teamsterville's first residents established tightly segregated patterns of residence and association along ethnic lines. The residents, who were new or relatively new immigrants, settled in row houses on a block or street peopled by their countrymen, and ethnicity was a pervasive determinant of interaction, association, and residence. Today the patterns born of ethnicity are altered but not totally replaced. Even though a person's street address is no longer a perfect guide to ethnicity, many streets and blocks are still associated with a particular ethnic group. Parents still forbid their children to play in a particular place because it is an "Italian [Polish, etc.] block." Ethnicity and locality thus are at least practically interchangeable as organizing devices, criteria by which the Teamsterville resident selects from among the many social experiences available to him those which appropriately call forth speaking as a mode of activity (see Gans 1962, Suttles 1968).

In addition to locating occasions of speaking within the boundaries of "the neighborhood," Teamstervillers also locate on a scale of social worth the style of speaking they associate with the neighborhood. Awareness of their own speaking style as one distinct from others is reflected in their readily reported assessment, consistent across informants, that their speech is inferior to the Standard English of middle-class people—people who live on "the north side" (of Chicago), but superior to the speech of, respectively, "hillbillies," "Mexicans," and "Negroes." They respect and resent the speech of people who have a better control of Standard English than they do, are insecure about their own speech outside neighborhood contexts, and find reassurance in what they perceive to be the deficiencies of "Negro" speech. Thus Teamsterville judgments of locale, socioeconomic standing, and conformity to accepted standards of speaking are correlated—Teamstervillers see themselves sandwiched between the richer, linguistically superior whites and the poorer, linguistically inferior blacks who live to the south of Teamsterville.

Awareness of a linguistic norm and the concurrent belief that one's own speech is substandard can create what Labov calls "linguistic insecurity" (Labov 1966, p. 477). This in turn can lead to attempts at correction, even hypercorrection, the practice of speaking so carefully as to betray a deliberate attempt at compensation. Teamstervillers do not attempt or value correction or hypercorrection, and cultural interpretations linking speech behavior with native attitudes about social and physical place may account for suppression of attempts at change. On the one hand, the awareness of a linguistic norm that Teamstervillers do not measure up to serves to heighten a positive affective awareness of community patterns, providing a kind of unity in adversity, in which the local deviation from Standard English functions as a defining attribute of membership in "everybody around here." On the other hand, a resident who changes speech to be more like Standard English is seen as symbolically attempting to leave the neighborhood. The deviation from local usage is interpreted as an inappropriate assertion. Like other attempts at rising in the world, it is resented by those who do not make such efforts. One informant revealed a significant Teamsterville image when he described the neighborhood as a big crawfish barrel from which everyone tries to crawl out and in which everyone resents those few who succeed in reaching the top.

Teamstervillers believe that in order to maintain their status as one of the "everybody" they should not significantly modify their speaking style so as to deviate from local patterns. Changes in speech are easily noticed, so speech is therefore a means by which a person can signal a desire either to move upward on the social scale or to affirm a commitment to the norms of the present group. Teamsterville reactions to two prominent people provide a neat illustration of this dual possibility. Speech style is a principal factor verbalized in positive evaluations by Teamsterville teenagers of the television program "All in the Family," based on the lives of a New York City family that lives in a neighborhood much like Teamsterville. The day after Jean Stapleton won an Emmy award for her performances on the show, a group of Teamsterville girls expressed their strong approval of the show and the award. They were, however, keenly disappointed to learn that in real life Jean Stapleton talks differently from the character she portrays on television—she sounds "real sophisticated." On the other hand, a Teamsterville resident can succeed in the eyes of the world and yet not be resented by his neighbors. I asked one informant why it is that a particular local politician could be so successful and still enjoy the almost reverent adoration of his Teamsterville neighbors. The informant replied, in a tape recorded interview, "Well, see, he doesn't scare anybody because he speaks lousy English. I mean he has rotten pronunciation. And he has, y'know, he murders the

American language, the way most of us do, so we know he's one of us, he's just like us."

The same politician mentioned by the informant once sought, upon the recommendation of a political advisor, to undertake speech lessons from a professor of speech at Northwestern University. At the end of the first lesson, the politician said, "I'm sorry, Doc, if I talked the way you want me to they'd laugh me out of the neighborhood." (I am indebted to the late Glen E. Mills for this information.)

A college student, responding to a question about his own speech, spoke for himself and other Teamsterville residents when he said that he feels insecure in a university or other "middle-class" setting because he grew up in an "illiterate, poor neighborhood." The informant said he is reluctant to change his speaking habits because that would alienate him from his friends in the neighborhood. Few residents face the dilemma articulated by the informant, for they live their lives amid friends and neighbors who constitute the network of people known as "the neighborhood," and among these people speech is viewed as a resource for signaling one's similarity to his friends and for confirming his loyalty to them and their shared values. Thus it is that a Teamsterviller's sense of neighborhood is a lens through which he locates speech, socially, physically, and hierarchically.

"The neighborhood" is the most macroscopic concept that Teamstervillers use to distinguish places in general from places for speaking. They supplement their view of places for speaking with several other place concepts that "the neighborhood" subsumes. The most important supplementary concept is "the street," which as physical location refers to all outdoor areas in the neighborhood, but particularly to streets, sidewalks, and porches. "Everybody" participates in street life. A street is, however, considered primarily a man's rather than a woman's territory. Men spend more time in the street and have access to more of it than women do. It is used as a general setting for sociability among neighborhood residents. Although it legally is public territory, residents do not treat it merely as such; street territory as physical setting can be a scene in Teamsterville because people actively socialize there, and outsiders who walk or drive on sidewalks or streets often are felt to be intruding on at least semiprivate territory.

The nature of front porches, the physical design of the neighborhood, and the density of population facilitate the use of the street as a social setting. Porches are open and in most cases flush to the ground; they are small, usually about six feet square. One porch is near enough to another that neighbors can converse and at the least are mutually visible. People socialize in front of, not behind, their houses; they visit on front porches but not on back porches, perhaps because the latter look out on alleys and hold garbage cans. There are few back or side yards. A typical street has twenty-four buildings on one side (with a very small space between each building), each building has two or three flats (one flat per story), and flats house an average of 3.4 people. On one side of a typical block, then, there are about 160 people who are potential users of that block's porches, sidewalk, and street. There are about seven to ten people available for interaction in and around each front porch stoop.

An upper middle-class suburb contiguous to the northern boundary of Chicago is an instructive contrast to Teamsterville. There friends visit inside houses or in back yards where there is a patio, a large fenced yard, and a garden. Visitors are usually from outside a ten block radius. Only one family lives in each building, with an average of 2.95 people per household. A resident can enter his or her home by driving in the alley to the garage and walking from the garage door to enter the house by the back door, without exposure to neighbors. Adults do not socialize in front yards, and certainly not on front porches. In short, there are relatively few residents per block and they preserve privacy and avoidance patterns (Kitagawa and Taeuber 1963).

It is as part of the general physical layout that the street can be understood to be a significant setting in Teamsterville. Sociable speech is conducted in a relatively public region, the street, where people are available to each other because of the physical design of the community. Add to this the facts of population density and the relative absence of air conditioning, and one can picture people spilling out in the street in summer. When outdoors, people frequently congregate at porches and corners, and Teamstervillers share a view of what personae and what speech activity are appropriate to those two places.

"The corner" is an outdoor setting, at or near a street corner, which a particular group of boys marks as its regular meeting place and as its "turf," which is to say that a corner is the territory of boys or young men who are longtime friends and associates. For some men the neighborhood tavern becomes a surrogate for a street corner, so "corner personae" can include men of all ages beyond early adolescence with the scene shifting from corner to tavern in early adulthood. "The corner" in the broad sense is the principal scene where members of a group of males converse. Group members promote extensive sociability among themselves and define sharp boundaries between themselves and nonmembers. Accordingly, talk is an appropriate focus of activity "on the corner," but not elsewhere, and talk has value as social currency among corner personae but not with others.

A particular corner has social significance for a Teamsterville boy not only because that corner is where the boy's most important social activity occurs, or where he meets the group with which he has deep feelings of loyalty and identification, but also because there is more than a casual association of scene with personae. Youths express their group membership in terms of place references: they describe themselves as "Wallace [Street] Boys," "The Spirits of 32nd [Street]," "the 33rds." They write the street name on their clothing, and they paint the street name on neighborhood buildings (Kohl 1972). Accordingly, where a boy "hangs" influences how others see him and how he sees himself—it is a significant attribute of his personae. A boy feels at home, in the "right place," at his corner, and that has special significance in a neighborhood in which "keeping your place" both physically and hierarchically is an extremely compelling topos. Thus one boy summarized the corner's significance to him in saying, "Where you hang is your turf—you won it and it's yours."

One corner boy said that his group did not allow Mexicans to enter its turf but that others could pass through without incident. The boy's group does not define Mexicans as part of "the neighborhood," even though Mexicans live within the physical boundaries. This illustrates that a stranger's entry into another group's turf is considered a challenge to the claimants' control of their territory. Frequently such an intrusion prompts a fight. On the other hand, if a boy enters the turf of people he knows, even if he does not "belong" there, he is allowed safe passage because he is part of "everybody" around there. Thus, to walk only where one is known insures peaceful relations even with unfriendly groups. Because the presence of a stranger in alien territory can lead to fighting, residents value both staying where one "belongs" and knowing everybody.

Where a boy "hangs" is not only his turf but is also the social context he marks as most appropriate to speaking occasions. This association of speech with a particular context has significance for understanding the Teamsterville boy's outlook on speaking. At the corner, the boy acquires a highly developed appreciation for loyalty to and familiarity with his identity-matched fellows, and an equally sharp sense of the importance of the social and physical boundaries that insulate his group from outsiders. The corner boy's place for speaking is therefore relatively impermeable by interlocutors who do not share his background of meanings and experiences. On the other hand, the boy sees the world outside his place as a context not appropriate to activity that has speech as its focus. A consequence is a heightened appreciation for speech that (1) by its form emphasizes the boy's similarity to others in his group and sets him apart from those outside, and (2) is highly dependent for its meanings upon a context of shared experience. In short, the cultural meanings attached to places for speaking imply a preference for what Bernstein calls a "restricted" mode of speaking (in which the speaker does not make verbally explicit his or her meanings and in which speech does not serve as a mode for expressing the personal uniqueness of the speaker), and a relative deemphasis of what he calls speaking in the "elaborated" mode (speaking that is verbally explicit and serves to make public the unique motives, feelings, and ideas of the speaker) (Bernstein 1972; also see Whyte 1943).

Because women are denied full use of the street, they use front porches. The front porch of a house is not exclusively a woman's territory, but it has special significance for the Teamsterville woman. Although the street is in general a setting for sociability, not every means of participation in street life is sanctioned for women. In the local view, the woman's place is in the kitchen and the home, and the man's is in the street and the outside. Teamsterville men and boys report neighborhood boundaries as more extensive than those reported by girls and women. The negative sanction on certain types of female street interaction is reflected in patterns of child rearing. Girls are not allowed outside the home without permission. They are carefully supervised and must account for their whereabouts at all times.

Teamstervillers believe that strict control in raising a girl is the only alternative to overpermissiveness, which brings many negative sanctions. How, then, is a woman or young girl to participate in the social life of the neighborhood? The front porch serves as a link between street and home, as a place in which a Teamsterville woman can appropriately participate in social life. An adult woman, who had lived in Teamsterville all her life, reported that in winter she hardly sees anyone, but "in summer the whole block opens up" and everyone congregates on or around front porches.

"The porch" is a place at or near the front porch of a house, the physical porch usually being only a stoop or a few steps. "Everybody" uses the porch. It is a principal setting for sociability, particularly for young children and for women of all ages. Its use also facilitates a person's entry into neighborhood life, serving as a link between home and street. Although I had previously been aware of the front porch as a gathering place, and had participated in front porch conversation, its deep cultural significance first became apparent to me by accident. I asked an informant about who is and who is not socially active in the neighborhood, as a way of eliciting the characteristics of socially accepted people. The informant mentioned an attorney who was minimally accepted but not active in the round of block sociability. After several minutes of persistent but unproductive questioning about how the man could become more socially active if he so wanted, the informant answered with a note of exasperation and finality that the man could never be fully accepted because he did not have a front porch. Later work with other informants indicates that the front porch is used to extend invitations to talk and as a place for launching one's own participation in neighborhood social life. The consequences of having a front porch might appear negligible. However, an understanding of the function of the front porch in Teamsterville suggests ways of introducing oneself in the neighborhood, of initiating sociability, and of receiving such initiations from others.

FIELDWORK AS INTERCULTURAL COMMUNICATION

When a person seeks to understand speech behavior in a community whose culture is alien to him or her, the possibility of misunderstanding is high. Upon hearing that I was studying "communication in Teamsterville," a middle-class visitor to the neighborhood remarked, "There is no communication in Teamsterville." This outsider believed that because he heard little talk where he expected it, there was none. Richard Sennett, a student of middle-class mores and manners, wrote that when middle-class people want to feel they are socializing in a warm, personal way, they seek out "intimate and small places, the most powerful being their own homes" (Sennett 1970). Real entertaining is sheltered by the house walls and limited to those invited within.

Teamsterville's taxonomy of places for speaking suggests a very different model from that of middle-class or white-collar America. Teamstervillers have a strong appreciation for sociability in such "public" places as neighborhood, street, corner, and porch. Indeed, these are the kinds of places for speaking they value most. An implication is that one should discover where people talk in order to acquire anything but a culture-bound understanding of a people's speech behavior.

Teamsterville's criterion for marking a place for speech is different from that of some other communities. An upper middle-class living room is a place for talk, and men and women, adults and children, are appropriate personae for conversation there. Even relative strangers can be welcome; note that a host is anxious if a visitor does not participate in the round of talk and often a host deliberately encourages a reticent guest to speak. In Teamsterville, by contrast, the living room is not popular as a setting for talk. Rather, settings are popular, which exclude those of different sex or social position, and where outsiders would not be present to participate. In Teamsterville it is the presence of such identity-matched personae in a location traditionally set aside for sociability among them, to the exclusion of others, that marks a place for speaking. The search, then, should not end with the discovery of speaking locations but should uncover what, in the native view, makes a place fitting for talk.

In the present study the question of places invariably became, upon analysis, one of personae and of the scenes most appropriate for gatherings of particular personae. In other words, talk is not a focus of activity merely because of the setting. A gathering of Mexican and Italian boys on the same corner is an occasion for careful visual scrutiny as one group quietly passes through the other's turf, but to make it an occasion for talk would be to invite trouble. Similarly when an outsider walks into a corner tavern he changes the occasion from one of loud and frequent talk to one of near-perfect silence. On the other hand, a person comes to have a particular persona through participating in activity inextricably bound up with particular locales. One becomes part of the "everybody" by being from "around here." An adolescent girl can be excluded from the round of talk because she lives a block away from other participants in a conversation. A boy becomes a corner boy because he spends time on a corner and "his" corner is, to him and others, a significant aspect of his persona. The two schematic components—scenes and personae—were not in this study discretely separable. The outsider who uses situational components heuristically, as means for discovering a pattern in native judgments about talk, should be prepared to find that in accounting for cultural data in any given case, the components are interdependent.

Teamsterville data suggest that the major settings and occasions a people mark for speaking are important to understanding a culture pattern of speaking. It would, for example, be difficult to discern the significance of the front porch to Teamsterville ways of speaking if the investigator could not see its use and meaning as part of a larger pattern of setting and speech behavior in the community, a pattern that interrelates concepts of neighborhood, street, corner, and porch. Furthermore, discovering that pattern enables an investigator to explain symbolic behavior other than speaking which might otherwise be inexplicable. For example, Teamsterville place concepts were helpful to me in explaining one neighborhood practice that at first struck me as quite puzzling, the display of bowling trophies in funeral parlor windows.

A Teamsterville funeral parlor is, like a Teamsterville tavern, not so much an impersonal public setting as it is an intimate, familiar, private setting. It is not the setting for a brief service followed almost immediately by a trip to the cemetery; rather, there is a wake, which is attended by many people throughout the day and evening. A family chooses a funeral parlor along socially patterned lines, following the preference of their social circle within their parish. The funeral parlor owner is, in many cases, a resident of the neighborhood, a person who is an acquaintance, if not a social intimate, of the mourners. Thus the funeral parlor is a place for the meeting of friends and relatives as well as for the expression of sympathy.

For the funeral parlor, symbolic participation in the life of the street is an important rhetorical strategy, one aim of which is to create a scene appropriate to the funeral parlor's activities, and the display of a bowling trophy is a tactic in this strategy. The trophy faces *into the street,* not into the building, as is true of the small military figures that were, at the time of the research, displayed in many Teamsterville homes that had a family member in the military service. The funeral parlor businessmen and the residents display the trophies to people in the street, the front window serving not only as a boundary marker but also as a channel through which to announce locally-valued information, and through which to participate in the life of the street, a life whose focus is the expression of solidarity and of interaction with a close-knit peer group.

A bowling trophy in the window of a funeral parlor creates an effect wholly consonant with local patterns of symbolic expression of neighborhood solidarity. It is significant to local passersby. It communicates that the displayer values a popular peer group activity in the neighborhood, bowling, and that the displayer is therefore very much a part of neighborhood life. A bowling trophy in the window symbolically links the inside region of the funeral parlor with the outside regions of street and corner, and thus serves the rhetorical end of creating an impression that the funeral parlor is an appropriate place for its principal activity, meetings at which friends express solidarity and support. So viewed, as symbolic participation in neighborhood street life, the bowling trophy in the window is neither tasteless indelicacy nor queer custom, but a fitting display in its context. In order to see it thus, one must use the Teamsterville perspective on places for speaking.

CONCLUSIONS

When Teamstervillers look out on the world their perception of it is shaped by a finely developed sense of place. They see boundaries, social and physical, where others do not, and this vision serves as a major unifying perception in their worldview. The centrality of place in the cultural outlook is reflected in a strong concern for locating people in social-physical space; in a view of places as locales whose boundaries rightly enclose and shelter some people and deny entry to others; and in a pervasive concern that oneself and others know and stay in the proper place both hierarchically and physically.

Speech, of course, is an object of that worldview, and speaking as a mode of human experience takes on a culturally distinctive meaning when viewed from Teamsterville's perspective. Speaking is a focus of activity in social relationships and in physical settings that have sharp boundaries insulating the participants from interaction with those not matched to the relevant identity attributes. Speech is seen as an instrument of sociability with one's fellows, as a medium for asserting communal ties and loyalty to a group, and serves—by its use or disuse, or by the particular manner of its use—to signal that one knows one's place in the world.

One feature of "place" in Teamsterville is the settings in which the worldview locates speaking. These settings are significant not merely as physical locations, as the blocks and boundaries that define a neighborhood, as particular streets, or as the corners and porches that dot the streets. The worldview associates these places with certain people and thus "imbues the landscape with social meaning" (Bock 1969). These are the scenes in which speaking has a place in Teamsterville life, and these scene-personae configurations, because of the kinds of talk they invite, create for the resident of the community a cultural awareness of speaking. Thus by attending to the settings the community marks for talk, one can discover a lens through which to see not only the community's places for speaking but also the particular way in which its people understand that, in human affairs, talk has its place.

Chapter 3

MAYOR DALEY'S COUNCIL SPEECH

Chapter 2 presented an initial formulation of a Teamsterville way of speaking. It establishes a background against which chapter 3 is set. Chapter 3 examines a single speech event illumined through an application of previously formulated ideas about place and personae in Teamsterville spoken life.

The speech examined here is a particularly fortunate instance for cultural analysis. In it a bearer of Teamsterville culture replied to charges by an outsider that the speaker acted wrongly. The reply was intelligible and convincing to those who shared the speaker's culture, but not to those outsiders who in turn replied to the reply. Such an interplay of replies suits ideally an ethnographic inquiry because in it one can hear cultures being pressed into the service of explanation and justification. Such discursive events publicize cultural terms, provide opportunity to interpret culturally situated speech, and juxtapose the "otherness" of multiple codes of interpretation and action. Thus their analysis is ideally suited for the purposes of the present study.

THE SPEECH AND ITS RECEPTION

In July of 1971, the late Richard J. Daley, then mayor of Chicago, performed what might have passed as a thoroughly unremarkable act. He appointed a young, relatively inexperienced man, Thomas P. Keane, to the city's Zoning Board of Appeals. It was, on the surface, an appointment that would have aroused no public controversy, because young Keane (thirty-six years of age), although arguably light on experience, was eminently well qualified for paid civic duty in the Chicago of 1971: he had "connections" to people in high places. Not only was Thomas P.

Keane well connected (his father was Alderman Thomas E. Keane of the Chicago City Council), but his "connection" was well connected (the elder Keane was the mayor's close personal friend and chief political ally). Such conditions of network linkage had been, for many years, sufficient to assume that the Chicago city council would approve perfunctorily a mayoral nomination.

But by 1971 Daley's iron grip on Chicago politics had begun to loosen, if ever so slightly, as is revealed in the fact that the mayor's request to approve the young Keane did elicit a remark. Prior to the council meeting, Richard Simpson, a University of Illinois-Chicago faculty member and newly elected Chicago alderman had, in the political science class he taught, criticized Keane's appointment on the grounds of nepotism. And in the council meeting of Wednesday, July 21, alderman Simpson asked, "Why is it members of the same family get appointments in several sections of government?" The mayor responded with what the *New York Times* called a "wild outburst of temper" in a "five-minute tirade, striding back and forth across the council platform, his face purple with rage" ("Losing his Cool," 1971, Sect. IV, p. 5). That the triggering remark was made at all, and that it elicited such a vehement response from the mayor, suggest that Daley's iron grip on Chicago politics had loosened. But that his grip was loosened ever so slightly is indicated by the council vote, which was forty-five to two in favor of confirmation.

Studs Terkel, of WFMT-Chicago, tape-recorded the speech from the council gallery and, after playing it on his radio program, gave the tape to me. The quality of the recording is poor, but over ninety percent of the speech is transcribed here, with empty round brackets indicating inaudible or indecipherable sections. Newspaper reports were used to construct initially uninterpretable passages. Where such aids were used, the relevant passage is printed in italics, indicating my eventual hearing of the speech, not my unhearing faith that the newspaper report could substitute for observation. (That the newspaper reports are not reliable is indicated by differences in their reports of the speech's wording, in their discrepant reports of the event, and by apparent factual errors in reporting—the *New York Times* and the *Chicago Sun-Times* reported the speech's length as five minutes but my recording is timed at over eight minutes.) The entire speech was scanned, significant pauses noted, and the words were organized into lines as follows:

> A poem was written about sons. It goes something
> like this (   )
> "To press my lips against the fair
> Cheek or brow of my young sons,

So long I have stooped down . . .
But suddenly, today, to my surprise,
I find that I must rise on my toe tips
And reach up to kiss their fair lips

"These tall young sons, as straight
as any pine . . . can they be mine?
Soon I must leave, I must go . . . Soon I
know they will go
"But, Oh, I am so glad that I
Have had—
Small sons to stoop to
Tall sons to reach to
Clean sons to give
That other sons may live."

I hope the professor will give that to his classes.
Yes, sir.
I hope the halls of the great educational
institutes will stop
bein' places for agitation and hatred against this
government and this society.

And talk about the young people, with their cynical
smiles and
their failure and polluted minds . . .
(   ) that I made this appointment because a man's name
was Keane and he was the son of a famous member of
this
Council.
I made this appointment because I know Tommy Keane, the
boy that I appointed, since he's a baby and I know
his mother.
And Mike Keane wasn't called on this appointment, but
Adeline Keane, one of the greatest women that I
know not only in this city but in any city in the
United States.
A fine, Polish-American woman who raised a fine boy.
And should that boy be told by this professor or by any
professor that he can't hold office because his
name is Keane and she's his mother?
Wher're we goin' with this kind of a society? And

wher're we goin' with these kind of educators?
They're doin' these things to the young people of our country.
Let's start tellin' the truth. ( )
That appointment was never made at the request of Alderman Keane. ( )

. . . who's supposed to be the highest of vocations, a teacher if you will . . . dedicated to tell the truth. ( )
What kind of truth is that? What kind of education?
( ) You can heckle all you want

And let's look at the record of the University and what they're doin' to the minds.
Is this what they've told the students? That I made the appointment because his father is head of the Finance Committee?
I made the appointment because he's a fine young man and a decent Chicagoan. And for no otherwise.
Hypocrites and fakers. And that's what we have too much in the educational community today—hypocrites and fakers.
Afraid to tell and face the truth, *afraid to let the young people go into the combat of election contests.*
No, they want to stand behind the great university cloak and tell how wrong our country is, how wrong our society is . . . when they know nothing about it . . . and they refuse to take any steps to correct it, and haven't got the guts to make the charge on this floor what's wrong with this young man.
That's what's bein' taught . . . and it's a sad day, a sad day when we hear words of this comin' out of the University classes.
And he's not the only one . . . he's only typical of the large number that are in these universities polluting the minds . . .
The young . . . the young should know and they should know the truth . . . not be misguided and told by people who're making these statements without checkin' the record.
Am I to be criticized because I appoint a young man like Keane on the basis of nepotism when he doesn't know what nepotism is?

And am I to be criticized when I say and I don't care who it is . . .
( ) Some people have never had the burden of having a son that they could lean down to or a son that they could reach up to.
And it's sad that they haven't because if they had they wouldn't be talkin' this way.
And if this is the society in which we live . . . if we're afraid to appoint our sons or our nephew's son or our relative or afraid to appoint any member of our family, because of what. Fear . . . of what might be said? Not the truth . . . the fear.
Who creates the fear? Who creates these phony issues?
The very people we're talking about.
I say to you very practically . . . if you're a teacher,
God help the students in your classes if this's what's bein' taught to them. (loud applause)

There were four types of public response to the speech. One, substantive criticisms were expressed. Speaking on the floor of the Council, immediately after the speech, alderman Seymour Simon defended the colleges and universities, and the constructive role they played in criticizing the Viet Nam war (Golden 1971a, p. 5). At a press conference the next day, alderman Simpson charged that Daley's statements in the speech were "false and totally untrue" (Golden 1971b, p. 5). And the *Chicago Sun-Times* editorialized the following Saturday that Daley should be more open to the opinions of young people ("Mayor Daley's blood pressure," 1971, p. 15).

Two, there were several judgments made that the speech was a defective performance. It was characterized as an "outburst" (Golden 1971a, p. 1), a "tirade . . . the most emotional and physically florid exhibition they [observers] have ever seen" (Mayor Daley's blood pressure, 1971, p. 5), a "display of temper" (Schreiber 1971b, p. 1), and a "five-minute tirade" ("Mayor Daley's blood pressure," 1971, p. 5). Characterizations of the performance included assertions that Daley "reacted furiously" and "stormed" (Golden 1971a, p. 1), that his "voice rose and shook repeatedly" (Golden 1971a, p. 4), that he "exploded verbally," "strode red-faced up and down the rostrum," and was "shouting at the top of his voice" (Schreiber 1971a, p. 1).

Three, several observers, including both critics and defenders, went beyond mere characterizations of the act to propose psychological explanations of it. Alderman Simpson, in his news conference, read W.H.

Auden's "Epitaph on a Tyrant," which Simpson said "was not written about Mayor Daley, but . . . is apt." Immediately following its quotation of the poem and Simpson's comment about its aptness, the *Chicago Sun-Times* article that reported it quoted *A Reader's Guide to W.H. Auden* by John Fuller, which concludes that the poem is about Hitler and that "it is as though Hitler were seen as a puppet, not really responsible for the outcome of his moods" (Golden 1971b, p. 1). Daley's physician, Dr. Eric Oldberg, was quoted as saying that "Mayor Daley blew up this week because 'he's been working like a dog' and resented criticism from the university campus he helped create." The article reports: "Dr. Oldberg said Daley told him later, 'I'm not perfect. I'm human. Maybe I got excited'" (Miner 1971, p.1). City Hall observers were reported as explaining Daley's "increasing displays of temper in recent months" as the effect of a litany of troubles ranging from long days at work to administrative, political and personal problems (Schreiber 1971b, p. 1). All of these reactions interpret Daley's actions in essentially psychological terms, implicitly agreeing or disagreeing with the physician's statement that "Dick Daley isn't ready for the couch yet" (Schreiber 1971b, p. 1).

Finally, some observers found Daley's performance to be defensible. Daley himself is reported not to have been "contrite" (Miner 1971, p. 1). More positively, it is reported that after the speech Daley challenged criticisms with the statement, "The hell with it. I make my own appointments" (Schreiber 1971a, p. 1). His rhetorical question, "Should I appoint strangers?" (Schreiber 1971c, p. 1), was echoed in the statements of residents of Daley's neighborhood who, when I asked them about the event, said, "Who should he appoint, his enemies?"

The speech contains errors in style, logic, and pronunciation; it has lapses of topical coherence and structure; and it admits of glaring instances of disingenuousness. But these criticisms, and the responses quoted above, whether true or false, do not take the speech on its own terms, which is the task of the ethnographic interpreter. If one wishes to understand the speech, to know what was said in it, one must check the impulse to condemn it and one must go beyond merely psychological explanations. To understand its meanings and motives requires an interpretation grounded in ethnography, to which I now turn.

AN ETHNOGRAPHIC INTERPRETATION

At the time Daley gave the Council speech I was doing ethnographic research into Teamsterville speech behavior. Teamsterville is one of many small neighborhoods that make up the larger Bridgeport area, Chicago Community Area 60. The Teamstervillers lived a few blocks away from

Daley's home, and they considered him to be "one of us"—in part because, in their judgment, he maintained typical neighborhood speech patterns, had not moved out of the neighborhood, and exercised his power for the good of the neighborhood and its people. Teamsterville culture, as I recorded it, serves as the interpretive background for making sense of Daley's council speech.

In the earlier papers I posit that much of the meaning and force of Teamsterville speech ways can be understood in terms of two culture motifs, those of gender and place (Philipsen 1975; 1976a).

Gender is a prominent theme in much of Teamsterville spoken life, revealing a culture and a normative system that assign specific and well-defined functions to men and women. In this cultural scheme, men should be physical providers and rulers of the home, women should stay home and raise children. For men, the boundaries of the neighborhood—the limits beyond which they will venture daily for work and sociability—are defined to be larger than they are for women. Women are relatively tied to home and to boundaries of a neighborhood perceived to be physically smaller. Men, who must learn to assert themselves physically and economically, are trained to be aggressive and strong. Women, on the other hand, should be quiet, passive, docile, and supportive. But men who assert themselves run the risk of overstepping the boundaries of social and physical space, and these oversteppings, these excesses, can lead to troubles—to fights and failures. It is the place of women to do everything in their power to prevent troubles and, if they do arise, the woman should step in and correct them. For example, a Teamsterville boy says his mother will beg him not to fight, that sometimes fight he must, but that if he fights within his mother's sight or hearing she will intervene if the fight gets too rough (thus, one bitterly expressed resentment that the Irish, Italian, German, and Polish boys have toward Mexican boys is that the mothers of the latter do not look out their windows so as to be ready to check their sons' fighting—the Irish boy is at a disadvantage against an opponent who does not have someone in the background prepared to restrain him). Mothers and wives tend the home, maintain its cleanliness and order, and tend to the order of language and conduct as well. One may swear to, and in the presence of, a man, but the presence of a woman—particularly a mother—signals that one should refrain from profane speech.

Place is a second major theme played out in Teamsterville spoken life. When Teamstervillers look out on the world their perception of it is shaped by a finely developed sense of place. They see boundaries, social and physical, where others do not, and this vision serves as a major unifying perception in their worldview. The centrality of place in the cultural outlook is reflected in a strong concern for locating people in social-physical space; in a view of places as locales whose boundaries rightly enclose and shelter some people and deny entry to others; and in a pervasive concern that oneself and others know and stay in the proper place both hierarchically and socially. Teamsterville and the larger Bridgeport area, with its local streets, corners, and porches, is a culturally significant scene for those who live there.

The present analysis is sketched against the background of the previous articles. Here I shall focus on three aspects of Daley's speech: (1) its key symbols and symbol linkages, (2) the way the speech functions as a move in a speech episode, and (3) the code in which the discourse is grounded, a code of honor.

Symbols and Meanings

The manifest content of the speech emphasizes the specific and general actions of several agents, most notably the mother, Adeline Keane, the professor, and the mayor.

The opening poem announces a theme, which is later developed more specifically, that "mothers" raise "sons" to be "men"—that is, to take their "place" in "this society." Terms in double quotation marks are indigenous terms—taken from the speech—linked here in a statement that represents a Teamsterville belief and preference. To become a man in Teamsterville requires that one learn a complex code of demeanor and deference, that one learn to occupy his place in the world but also that one not reach too high. Men might be naturally grasping but it is the task of the community, and especially of mothers (who are assigned the cultural role of moral guardian), to train its members to be particular kinds of men with limits imposed on some appetites more than others. For example, one should not try to be something one is not, or something one cannot properly be, in the local scheme of things, but one should not fall below the potential of his social station—this is an intense version of the American respectability ethic mixed with a European sense of hierarchy. "Places" are assigned in society according to a known code of propriety—age, gender, and ethnicity being the key criteria in this code.

The code not only permits but prescribes a kind of social determinism by which who one is (socially) does and should count as grounds for where one can be located—where one lives, who one associates with, and how far up the social ladder one climbs. Thus, it is natural and appropriate that some might die that others might live, that some might lead and others might follow.

A good Teamsterville mother schools her son in this code, and Daley said in his speech that Adeline Keane had done this job well with her son Tommy. The mayor did not say, but it is part of the background understandings of Teamsterville culture, that he, Mayor Daley, is supremely entitled to make such judgments, and to make such appointments as he did in the disputed incident. From the Teamsterville community standpoint Daley's act was fitting—a "mother" had raised a "son" to take his rightful place in "this society" and Mayor Daley, who was less boss (as some critics called him) than king (in the local code), made the judgment by divine right.

The second major agent in the episode is Daley. His actions here, as when he appointed his own son to political office, can be understood best in light of a neighborhood belief and preference that men do, and should, act out of self-interest in their political and economic dealings. When seeking to control or regulate others, and when seeking to meet their own material needs, a Teamsterville man who acts altruistically is considered a fool and is morally suspect. Of course, the Teamsterville man and boy must be loyal to his fellows and to his relatives, and this loyalty extends to longtime friends such as members of the corner group. Men should help those who have close ties to themselves. There is, in the neighborhood, an intricate and approved system of social, political, and economic interdependencies and reciprocities. The Teamsterville code directs a man to maximize personal gain and the gain of those with whom he has close personal ties.

In appointing Tommy Keane, Daley acted so as to maximize the interest of himself and his colleagues. His public justification of the act was echoed by some Teamstervillers who later said about the incident, "Who should he appoint, his enemies? (laughter)." And there is the later statement by Daley in response to criticism over his appointment of his own son to political office: "If I can't help my sons, then they [his critics] can kiss my ass" (Kennedy, 1978, p. 254).

In Daley's view, and in the view of the Teamsterville community, a "man" had helped a friend by appointing the latter's "son." This is, in the local view, an unabashedly selfish, perfectly normal, thoroughly virtuous, even expected kind of conduct. It is, as I will argue later, not only permissible but preferred conduct, a way to be honorable.

Thus, from the speech community view, both Mrs. Keane and Mayor Daley had acted in ways that sustain and nurture "this society"—indeed, their acts in part constitute "this society." In order to appreciate fully the significance of the term "this society," it is useful to consider the action of another agent, "the professor," toward "this society," as that action is portrayed in Daley's speech.

"The professor" is one of the key symbols employed in the speech. It occurs structurally in the same place as do such related terms as "educational institute," "universities," "educational community today," and "university classrooms." Using "professor" here as the generic term, one can note two things. First, "professors" are assigned a typical way of acting—specifically, "professor" recurs as an evil agent polluting with untruths the "minds of the young people," so as to turn them against "this society." Second, "professor" is semantically opposed to "mother" and "father," the latter raising "young people" to sustain and strengthen "this society." Thus, the "professor" actively undermines the very "society" that the good "mothers" and "fathers" of Daley's acquaintance are trying to preserve. The "professor's" charge has become a charge against a "mother" and her "son," and thus against the life-giving principle of "this society," the latter being a god term in the Daley political code.

"The professor" is further maligned by Daley in culturally significant ways as (1) ignorant of the facts, (2) unaccomplished personally, (3) cowardly, and (4) naive. Taking (1) and (2) together, there is a unifying theme: Daley himself has accomplished much for "this society." He not only raised sons, but he governed the city in a way praised by many. Here Daley objected, as he had done before, that those who criticized him are on the sidelines; they are talkers, not doers. One is reminded here of the powerful phrase with which Daley's office titled his formal report about liberal/activist rioters and protesters at the Democratic convention in Chicago in 1968: *What Trees Do They Plant?* The question in the title invites the hearer to ask what the protesters had done to change or improve society in any tangible way. And it invites the hearer to ask, by way of contrast, what Mayor Daley and people like him had done for the society. The answer, of course, would contrast the apparent lack of tangible contribution made by the protesters and the objectively considerable contributions made in Daley's name.

The 1968 protesters had uprooted trees and attacked cherished tropes in Daley's "society." So too, "the professor" had "agitated against," but had not built anything tangible for, "this society." The professor is also pictured as unfit to make the charges he has made. According to Daley, the professor does not understand, does not try actively to "change anything," and does not have the "guts" to come to "this floor to make his charges." Rather, he stands/hides "behind the university cloak." A proper man, from Daley's view, would plant a tree, build a road, teach the young the truth, but would not overstep his bounds, and if he were to oppose a foe he must, according to the code, step into the open, lay down the gauntlet, and suffer the consequences of battle. He should not hide behind the "cloak" of the university.

The preceding analysis, with its emphasis on the importance of "sons," "society," "mothers," and "fathers" as god-terms, and with the contrasting terms of "professors," "pollution," and "agitation" as devil terms, from the Daley-Teamsterville perspective, tells us much about the meanings invoked in the council speech. Attention has also been focused on the links between these terms—"mothers raise sons" so as to take their rightful place in "this society." Furthermore, various radiants of meaning have been traced by examining the juxtapositions of various terms.

The Speech As Event

A complementary approach to interpreting this speech is to ask what kind of event this is. By examining the terms and their structural oppositions, but also by adding to these locally bound interpretations further, extratextual, comparative information, one can deepen this interpretation and thus make it fuller, more complete, and make the speech more meaningful.

A review of ethnography that deals with such countries as Ireland, Italy, and the state of Croatia in Yugoslavia, reveals that much of the new world social structure has its origins in that of the old world. The emphasis on positional social relations; on groups of age-, gender-, and locale-based ties; a sense of fatalism—all these strands of Teamsterville life and culture can be traced in part to the community's religious and national heritage. It is against this broad reading of old and new world ethnography of places and peoples similar to Teamsterville that I make the following speculative interpretation.

The interpretation grows from a reading of a particular ethnographic report from a segment of Daley's ancestral country. On an island a few miles off the northwest coast of Ireland, there has developed a socially structured event that has been described in detail by the anthropologist Robin Fox (1977). When there is an islandwide dance, and some of the men have become intoxicated, a specifiable, repeated sequence unfolds. One man insults another, and then the other returns an insult. This goes on for some time, until insults escalate to threats and these elicit invitations to fight with fists instead of words. There is a point of no return in the sequence—when one of the men takes off his cloak he is, in the local view, irrevocably committed to fight, and considered to be unable to restrain himself. A great show is made of the fact that the coat has been cast aside, and a ritualized process of the antagonist telling everyone he cannot help himself ensues. The friends of the two men try to restrain them, all in a very organized and routinized fashion, but the antagonists work very hard to put themselves in a position to fight.

The final point in the sequence introduces a safety valve. The men are irrevocably committed to fight, they could not back down now and still save face, but just at the last moment the mother of one of the men is brought onto the scene. She pleads with her son to stop, then pleads with her son's opponent to stop, and at that point the men agree to stop—cursing under their breath that the other would not have been allowed this rescue from certain harm had not my/your mother appeared to put a stop to it. They part company, all is well, and the community has allowed itself once more to release some tensions, all the while knowing the reliable safety valve is available for use.

This ancient—and contemporary—ritualized, agonistic sequence is uncannily like much of the conflict behavior observed among Teamsterville boys. And its surface form actualizes Teamsterville beliefs: men must fight, women do all they can to prevent it, and men fear and resent those "outsiders" whose mothers are not waiting in the wings to check a fight that threatens to get really serious.

The historical-cultural background provides a basis for further interpreting Daley's use of mother images and themes in his speech. On one level this is familiar stuff—a disingenuous exploitation of a near-universal symbol. Daley, here, might have been privy to Kenneth Burke's (1969) insight:

> Ideationally, a speaker might have to go through much reasoning if he wanted to equate a certain measure with public security. But if he could translate it imaginally into terms of, say, the mother, he might profit not only from this one identification but from many kindred principles of ideas which, when approached, in this spirit, are associated with the mother image (or mother principle, or idea of the mother). (p. 87)

Daley had, in the council speech, linked mother to public security or order in a way that illustrates Burke's point about rhetorical functioning of symbols. But to leave it at that would represent only a part—albeit a significant part—of the meaning and form in Daley's speech. In order to uncover more of the meaning in the speech, one must listen to this as a culture sui generis. In using the mother symbol, an ancient level of meaning is brought into play—the speech now becomes an episode in which the central figure is no longer a man but a man's mother. Subtly now, the listener can hear this sequence as one in which it is appropriate to stop fighting—the boys can and should honorably put their coats back on.

This is a social drama, an agonistic encounter, in which Daley has become a street fighter on a Teamsterville "corner," his corner, the Chicago city council chambers. "The professor" has dared to speak out on Daley's "turf," has dared to insult the lead corner boy, by challenging the corner boy's prerogative to rule his turf and to help those who occupy it with him. And yet, to the disgust of the street fighter, the challenger can "get away with it" by hiding behind the university "cloak." In effect Daley said, "If you won't take off your cloak, then be quiet and take your place on the sidelines." Daley's cloak was off, but he knew he would not have to fight, at least not, for now, very hard. Objectively, he was too powerful to have to fight; from the standpoint of his code, he was required to fight back, at least with strong words. The insurance factor was that a mother was—at least symbolically—present, and her presence made it not only possible but imperative that all of these boys walk away from the fight.

This, then, is not a "cockfight" (to use Geertz's celebrated occasion by way of contrast) but a street fight. This was not, again in Geertz's terms, "deep play" but "deep agony," in the sense of "agonistic," and it was "deep drama" as well. In order to understand the clash of codes that provided the bases for such deep agony for this drama, it will be useful to introduce a final line of interpretation, the third of the major themes I develop in making the total interpretation.

The Structure of Honor

In this street fight, as in many agonistic encounters in the contemporary world, the clash is not just over a specific issue but is a clash of codes as well. Specifically, I believe it is—at least in part—a clash spoken in the terms of the code of honor and the code of dignity. But here, too, as with the above analysis of the mother symbol, although these ideal types illumine much in the Teamsterville case, there is much that is culture-specific.

Paul Friedrich (1977) has argued, in his analysis of the "problem of Achilles," that there is a myth of honor that consists of a network of implications, which is reflected by an overt "idiom" or way of saying things. The structure of honor consists of a code component, with its implications of presupposition and enjoining, and of a pragmatic component, with its catalyzing and resolving aspects.

With regard to the code aspect of honor, Friedrich (1977) derives nine honor-linked values. Seven of these will be discussed as relevant to the Daley speech. *Power*, the ability to take from others; *wealth*, the accumulation of material goods; *magnanimity*, generosity, hospitality, and mercy to suppliants; *loyalty*, the caring for one's friends and relatives; and *precedence*, that one will seek desirable fortune for one's kind—all seem to cluster about a pole of politics and economics, and I shall refer to this as the instrumental dimension of honor. Daley was a powerful man, the highest human link in a hierarchy of "connections" whereby those in the larger neighborhood and a smaller kin group express their loyalty and magnanimity. An intricate system of "connections," whereby the less powerful appeals to the more powerful for aid, with the mayor at the zenith of the hierarchy, was well-known and appreciated in Teamsterville life. Connections was a familiar, natural, and approved idea and fact of life. And it was assumed that all would seek to maximize their gains and the gains of friends and relatives, but that those at a higher level would be magnanimous to suppliants. Everyone is not, and does not expect to be, treated equally in this system, but everyone is treated as generously as available resources—and due respect to position and rank—will allow.

A second cluster of honor-linked values includes a *sense of shame*, the inner feelings a person has in the presence of an audience that matters; *glory* ("kudos"), the fame that one wins in battle or contest; *courage*, the "moral fiber necessary to face other men in the struggle over desirable things;" *excellence* ("*arete*"), excellence in debate and war; and *piety*, reverence for the gods. These can be clustered around a pole of the moral-expressive dimension of honor. Daley did not arbitrarily make an appointment, nor did he merely help to make the system work efficiently. Nor did he, in spite of his disingenuous claim, appoint Keane "because he's a fine young man and a decent Chicagoan and no otherwise." Those were insufficient conditions for making the appointment. Rather, Daley awarded a spoil, a token kudo to his ally, something he and his friend had earned through their excellence and courage in the political wars. The appointment was a prize as well as the assurance that another puppet was lodged in the hierarchy. Having taken their spoil, Daley and alderman Keane can now stand up to a challenger, whom they scorn for having himself won few battles and for lacking the "guts" to face the mayor in public battle. In part, the professor is seen as unfit for the task because he lacks reverence (a proper sense of respect for "this society") and because he lacks shame (a proper sense of respect for this occasion and the mayor as audience).

In the *Iliad*, all of the honor-linked values are appealed to, but the catalyzing action is not a contest over political spoils and challenges to political power, but is a contest over the allocation of women. Sexual honor in Teamsterville certainly is important, but it is not the issue here, or in this event, as it was in the *Iliad*, where Achilles' concubine was taken from him. In the street-fight event, King Daley's right to exercise his power was challenged—he was attacked for appointing someone on the basis of power, magnanimity, loyalty, precedence, and kudos. Just as an abduction catalyzed an agonistic sequence in the *Iliad*, so a challenge to the king's political and economic power catalyzed one in the Chicago city council. Much of the council speech can be heard as a move in a ritual interchange—Daley has called for an apology, demanded that the professor humble himself by going back to his classroom to expiate himself by public confession of wrong thoughts and deeds. Daley's speech is a move in a game, a battle which, under the circumstances, he could not and did not lose.

This discussion of an honor culture has been designated to provide a coherent code and pragmatic context for interpreting the meanings in Daley's speech. This lays the basis for an insight into one kind of difficulty in intercultural understanding: the opposition of complex moral codes. One opposing, or at least different, code, can be labeled the code of dignity. Key values in this code are individuality, the sacredness of the person against the group, equality of opportunity, shared power, fairness, sense of self-worth, and inalienable rights to material well-being without the need to ask for it.

The making of an instrumental decision would be governed by a different system of values under the code of honor and the code of dignity. And the motive talk about such decisions would be different using those codes. The rules for negotiating controversies about such decisions, once made, are different in the honor and dignity codes. There is much in Daley's speech to suggest that he used a code of honor in making the appointment, and that his motivations and defense are expressed in an idiom of honor. His reply to his critics further reveals the implicit expectations that the pragmatic component of the structure of honor is being employed. The professor's challenge suggests that he would prefer that political decisions be justified and discussed with a code of dignity, and that such decisions be negotiated in the dialogic structures (question-answer rather than petitioning) appropriate to the structure of dignity. Whereas in the code of honor the favored form of negotiation is petitioning, in the code of dignity it is dialogue. Thus, one can discern in this agonistic encounter not only the clash of interests but the clash of ideas, of codes, of idioms, and of communal forms as well.

CONCLUSIONS

The contemporaneous reception of Daley's speech, as revealed in newspaper accounts of it, differs sharply from the interpretation of it produced here. Most of those accounts treat the speech as untrue in its substance, uncontrolled in its production, and untoward in its demeanor. I have tried to render the particular truth the speech expresses, the structure of motivation that prompted its utterance, and the sense of propriety it embodies. In order to do this I have both applied and further developed my previous formulation of Teamsterville culture.

The chief means by which my account of Teamsterville culture has been extended here is the use of a code of honor as an interpretive frame for hearing Mayor Daley's council speech, and it is that code to which I now turn. A productive way to dissect a culture is by uncovering its indigenous conceptions of "person," "society," and "strategic action." Taking that approach, the person in a code of honor is most fundamentally a persona, the bearer of a social identity, based on gender, age, lineage, residence, demeanor, and personal accomplishments. The proper relations among personae is expressed in a hierarchical social scheme; some personae are fit to govern others. A good society is one in which each person knows and enacts their assigned role and in the process attends to the ceremonial as well as the instrumental dimensions of social life. Expressive ratification of the social order properly implicates and reinforces another presupposition, that the society has a metaphysical and moral priority over the individual. Ideal persons in such a world discover their proper place, locate their persona within it, and act so as to reinforce this scheme, materially and ceremonially.

The code of honor, however, encompasses a world that is not merely static. Its pragmatic component specifies how individuals may act so as to alter prevailing social arrangements, and that too is a distinctively cultural solution to the problem of strategic action. The system can be exploited for more or less personal gain and adapted to personal motives by the petitioning and granting of favors, with the powerful obliged to be sensitive to the needs of deserving suppliants, the powerless enjoined to temper their appetites and to express their requests with deference. The system is also open in that access to roles is determined by achievement as well as by ascription, particularly by achievement in election contests. The system does not readily provide for individuals, acting alone, to assert themselves over and against the society. Rather, the permissible way to effect a change in existing social alignments is to act collectively, as with an interest group whose claims must be factored into the array of competing coalitions and groups or through victory in, as Daley said in his council speech, "election contests". "Connections," a theme discussed in my earlier papers, and "elections," a theme mentioned by Daley, are two approved means for social influence and accruing personal power. A third is that where there are differences of interest and values among powerful social groups, those groups should forge compromise agreements precisely to the degree that their mutual power, their interdependence, justifies concessions, but these are concessions granted owing to the power of others not to any desire to accommodate differences or to harmonize values. The code enjoins collaboration, but not "open communication," with outsiders.

Heard with the terms of a Teamsterville honor culture, Daley's speech can be interpreted as expressing its own truth, its own vocabulary of motives, and its own sense of propriety. What most distinguishes my account of Daley's speech from those of its critics is not differences in motive, personal involvement, and time devoted to its examination, but in the cultural terms brought to its hearing. How was such a hearing methodically produced? If there is a general strategy implicit in the interpretive method employed here, what is it?

First, general interpretive techniques were employed. Meanings expressed in the speech were diagnosed by locating terms that occur in structurally significant places in the text (such as "mother," "son," "this society," "professor") and by tracing the terms with which they are linked structurally and rhetorically. Then, the speech was situated in its generic event or episodic sequence, in this case a social drama, a discursive form in which key cultural standards of praise and blame are spoken. Finally, the speech was examined for whether a code of action is revealed in it, by searching it for an examined or narrated plot line in which virtuous acts are celebrated and base acts deplored (See Friedrich 1977; Philipsen 1987). With these techniques, the interpreter ascertains, respectively: What symbols are employed? With what is each symbol contrasted and compared? What episodic functions are performed and what kind of episode is this? What scenarios are sketched linking kinds of symbols to each other in permitted and preferred lines of conduct?

Second, extant cultural knowledge was used together with the general interpretive techniques. The culture themes of gender and place provided a conceptual background against which to place the structural linkages found among, for example, "mothers," "sons," and "professors." A previously formulated analysis of agonistic events on Teamsterville street corners provided an interpretive background against which to place Daley's speech as event, the event taking on the character of a street fight between two boys vying for "turf" and the respect due boys or men of some reputation in the "street." And Teamsterville accounts of manly action, supplemented by interpretations of the conduct of similar men in similar circumstances, provided the outline for delineating a code of honor against which to set Daley's council speech and to hear his performance as following a given system of principles. Thus, this study illustrates a general strategy for the interpretation of deeply cultured speech. The interpretive process employed here consists of combining insights gleaned from using general techniques of interpretation with insights gleaned from applying ethnographic knowledge relevant to the particular case in view (Gregg and Hauser, 1973).

One promise of ethnography is that, in revealing something about a culture that is alien to its readers, it can then be used to reveal something about speech that is ordinarily heard as culturally innocent. As a case in point, this interpretation of Daley's council speech, and the code of honor formulated for its hearing, can be juxtaposed to Bennett's (1985) proposed "code of good communication," which includes such prescriptions as that interlocutors subject themselves to an "unlimited interchangeability of dialogue roles," keep "language sensitive and accountable to human experience," and evaluate symbolic forms "for their expressed openness to transformation and change." These admonitions are at home in a code of dignity, which elevates to god-term status such terms as "equality," "experience," and "openness"; the code of honor would give privileged status, respectively, to "hierarchy," "tradition," and "precedence" (the quoted terms attributed to Bennett are from his paper; I have supplied contrasting terms faithful to Daley's culture). The point is not that Simpson, or Bennett, or Daley is objectively or morally right or wrong, but rather that the juxtaposition of their vocabularies of motives reveals each to be speaking in deeply cultured terms, and one important function of ethnography is to help us to hear just that.

In summary, this exploration into the "otherness" of a culture was undertaken by examining a speech grounded in the terms of that culture. The method of analysis, drawing from general interpretive techniques combined with extant cultural knowledge, has produced a reading of the speech that reveals that it was spoken in a code of honor indigenous to Teamsterville culture, and that this code provides a fuller conceptual context than heretofore proposed for understanding this community and its ways of speaking. Like many other ethnographic studies, this one reveals something not only about the culture it set out to examine, but as well suggests that other voices are likewise deeply cultural, and in this provides another illustration of the ideas expressed in a prefatory note to another public drama:

> In dramatizing the complex issue of power politics, *Julius Caesar* offers no easy solution to problems that are no less baffling to our own age. Many will find that this work is one of Shakespeare's most perplexing, for it is disconcerting when a play—or history itself—appeals to man's earnest desire to judge action in terms of simple, personal standards of right and wrong and then betrays and mocks his deepest convictions by suggesting that Power is better than Vir-

tue, that efficiency may be preferable to goodness, or that conscience may be dangerously inadequate in determining political action. (Rosen and Rosen, 1963, p. xxiv)

PART III

Speaking in Nacirema Culture

Chapter 4

"COMMUNICATION" AS A NACIREMA WAY OF SPEAKING

The materials that provided both the stimulus and the data for this chapter suggest that in some American speech about interpersonal life, "communication" carries localized and highly poignant meanings. The pervasiveness of "communication" in such speech, but more importantly the systematicity of its occurrence, its "compelling facticity" (Varenne 1977, p. 49), and the moral freight it carries for its users, make it an important term in an American symbolic universe and vocabulary of motives. This study is an ethnographic exploration of that term and of the discursive field in which it finds a place.

The basic move is to make problematic the meaning of "communication" in some American texts. We are interested, for example, in what is meant by "communication" in the statement made by a mother, who said in discussing her daughter, "She don't communicate with me anymore" (KIRO 1970) (earlier in the conversation she said she and her daughter do exchange routine information through speech); in an advertisement, placed in a business magazine, that includes the message ". . . if the listener doesn't show genuine interest and sensitivity to what's being said . . . the communication will fail" (Sperry 1980) (the advertisement attests to the importance of communication both at work and in homework); or in the description of a play by its director as being about "contemporary humanity's failure to communicate to reach love (Estes 1981). Consideration of these and other statements, in which "communication" is naturally embedded, has led us to ask, What differentiates that potent term "communication" from "mere talk," when Americans use it to discuss the quality of interpersonal life?

Our claim about the meaning of "communication" in some American speech is limited in two ways. First, we have not exhaustively surveyed American uses of "communication," but have described one field of discourse—interpersonal relationships—in which it has a localized sense; it has other senses in other fields of American discourse. Second, we do not claim that all Americans ever inhabit the field of discourse in which "communication" finds a place. We have, rather, uncovered and described the meanings and premises that give credence to *a* recognizable way of speaking that is part of the workings of the society in which we have situated our inquiry. It is the way of speaking itself, as a code or system of meanings, and not its social ecology, that holds our attention here.

In showing that a possible domain of everyday experience and its linguistic representation are cultural creations, we record and interpret a datum, an instance of humans creating and constituting a world of meaning in their own terms. That "communication" labels the academic discipline we practice is more or less incidental to the general point being made—that domains of everyday experience, such as communication, and the terms in which people make them intelligible to each other, such as "communication," are subject to human invention and coloration. Thus, in providing a glimpse into an American definition of "communication" we hope to show the possibility for scientific and critical insight that the cultural perspective (Schneider 1976) affords the student of speech behavior.

METHOD

Data for the inquiry were gathered, by both of us, during the course of one year of collaborative fieldwork, directed toward discovering a culturally patterned way of speaking in contemporary America. Our fieldwork took many forms, including the construction of in-depth life studies of several people, the analysis of everyday events and scenes, the collection and interpretation of assorted texts, and the reading of commentaries on American life (see Frentz and Farrell, 1976).

The core material for the project consists of case studies of communication in the lives of two women, each of whom was born and raised in the American Pacific northwest. Each case study is treated as a text constructed on the basis of (1) transcripts from several unstructured interviews, (2) a log kept by each woman for three days, describing, along a given format, the communication events in which she took part during those days (Zimmerman and Wieder, 1977), and (3) focused in situ observations of each woman's communication conduct. Many other texts were also examined, a few of which are interspersed throughout this report.

The principal case studies were given detailed interpretations with an eye to the role played by "communication" and related categories such as "self" and "relationship" in each informant's presentation of herself and her life. In the development of our observations into case reports, as well as in their presentation below, we deliberately mixed our readings of the lives studied and readings of other texts that constitute part of the life-world we and our informants inhabited, and with our readings of academic treatises (Berger, Kellner, and Berger 1973; Hsu 1963; Sennett 1976; and Varenne 1977). We consciously used our experiencing of these texts, considered singly and in juxtaposition to each other, to develop a grounded theory of "communication" as a cultural category in the speech examined.

Once the primary analysis was, for the most part, completed, we examined another set of cultural texts, transcripts of the Phil Donahue Show, which is a popular program shown daily on American television, and is the inspiration of a recent best-selling book (Donahue 1979). Each show selected dealt with the subject of interpersonal relationships, and each thematized "communication" as the remedy to all problems. These transcripts were examined for their general structure and content to test, and to articulate further, the theory initially grounded in life studies and anecdotal evidence.

A READING OF TWO LIVES AS AMERICAN TEXTS

Informant One

M is a 36-year-old woman, divorced, the mother of two daughters, ages six and eight. She has a degree in social work but has not worked in that field, and is presently not employed outside her home.

A key distinction in M's metalinguistic lexicon is that between "small talk," the speech of acquaintances, and "real communication," which is to her the speech of close friends in an intimate context (either face-to-face or by telephone). She sees persons as occupying a "personal space" (a term she used many times) that may or may not be penetrated by another person. "Communication" is, in part, this act of interpenetration. The expression "close friend" (the equivalent expression in Hebrew is "good friend") reinforces M's essentially spatial metaphor for "communication. "Close friends," people with whom M can talk about her problems, and who will listen sympathetically even if they disagree with her, are contrasted with other friends, with whom she associates mainly by "doing things together." When M says about a friend that he is "close" enough to hurt her, she implies that intimacy involves the highest of rewards as well as of risks, and the tension between the two is a source of interpersonal problems that persist after initial differences are overcome.

Much of M's biographical speech with us reports her frustration in meeting her need for "real communication." She feels her parents punished her for expressing herself, and she said as a result she was an (emotionally) "abused" child. M described her relationship with her ex-husband in similar terms. He continually "put her down" verbally as "a lousy person" and criticized her because to him, as she said, "an o.k. person does not have problems." His refusal to discuss her problems, which he said were intrapersonal difficulties, was for M the major source of distress in the marriage. She saw her ex-husband's attitude as one step more extreme and destructive than that of her parents in terms of her sense of self-worth. With the parents it was the verbalization of a problem, with the husband the very experience of one, that was unacceptable.

Thus "communication" was the substance of the major conflicts in M's life. In not being allowed to express herself in the way she felt she both needed and deserved to do, she felt she was disconfirmed as a person. The relationships M had, with her parents and with her ex-husband, lacked "supportiveness," the term she most often used to describe the nature of positively experienced forms of interaction.

Like many modern parents, M reports that much of her communication with her children stands in defiance of her own childhood experience. She tries to help her children "feel good about themselves"—she listens to them, answers all their questions, and provides detailed explanations and information about the world around them. A crucial function of parent-child communication, for M, is to help the child develop a "positive self-image." It is important to her not to have any "hassles" with her children in the morning before school, so that they do not spend the day feeling "what a no good person I am," which in turn makes them vulnerable to the inevitable "hassles" they encounter in dealing with others. To M the world is basically hostile, and one needs a "thick skin" to shield one from its troubles. She believes a "positive self-image" is such a shield, so that feeling good about oneself is a key to survival. A "positive self-image" can be achieved, according to M, only through "supportive communication."

The sense of problematicity that pervades M's experience of herself and of her world is in her view part of human experience in general. She inevitably attributes interpersonal problems to discrepant life experiences which resulted in irreconcilable personal differences. For example, she said her marriage could not have succeeded because she and her husband had different backgrounds; even if they had had similar needs, she said, they tried to meet them in different ways.

In the view we are explicating, human uniqueness makes "communication" both vitally important and highly problematic. If people are unique, the kind of mutual disclosure and acknowledgment entailed in "communication" provides a necessary "bridge" from self to others. But if people are unique, they also lack the mutuality necessary for achieving interpersonal meaning and coordination.

The resolution to the dilemma posed by human uniqueness is found in M's belief that the individual has the capacity to change through "communication." One source for new definitions of self is the communication by others about oneself. The moral imperative attending this possibility is to be "open" to the "feedback" others can supply. For M it is both natural and desirable that persons be continually exposed to and "open" to such a "rhetoric of conversion" in the interpersonal realm. Another source of materials for "personal growth" is the exercise of what is believed to be the innate capacity to choose what to be and become. We call the sense of moral obligation that attends this capacity "the imperative for self-definition." According to M, if persons are unhappy with themselves at a given time, they can and should change so as to maximize a sense of well-being. For example, she expressed strong disapproval of a man who would not quit a well-paying but personally unsatisfying job; she criticized him both because he would not change jobs and because he was not "open" to others' suggestions that he explore the possibility of change.

Thus, in the life and speech of M, "communication" derives its potency from the combined effect of the beliefs in personal uniqueness and personal malleability, and from the normative injunctions to be "open" and to define one-self continually. These beliefs and norms are predicated on a view of the self as continually changing and the concomitant experience of one's identity as shifting not only through time but also across roles and situations. With respect to the assumption of uniqueness, "communication" functions as the "how" of self, as the way to create and sustain a sense of personal identity by having it validated by another person. And, to the degree there is a tension between the demands imposed by the imperative to yield control for self-definition to others and the imperative continually to remake one-self, "Communication" is viewed as the dialectic of these opposing forces from which emerges a "negotiated self."

One of the fundamental tensions of that dialectic is the clash between the belief that persons continually change with the belief that each person has a "core," a unique endowment. M reconciles those beliefs by claiming that life experiences affect persons crucially, but mainly affect the external layers of "self." The core is affected only by a traumatic experience, or through the intervention of counseling, which M believes is the only way to solve difficult personal problems. She vacillates between an emphasis on either the fixed or fluctuating aspects of self in constructing an acceptable account of her life and world.

The belief that there is a personal core gives rise to a "rhetoric of naturalness." It was stated in so many words by the instructor in a workshop we observed on "effective oral presentations." The instructor said to students preparing to give a speech: "Be yourself, be natural." And, in describing the experience of giving a stilted speech, the instructor warned: "You actually become somebody else, you're not relaxed." Thus, the "work" of being oneself consists of shedding unnecessary impediments to the experience and presentation of one's "true self." It can also be the "work" involved in constructing a unified entity experienced (and presented) as one-self. For M this must be done against the background of a diverse and changing world. Thus she feels the need constantly to check her interpretations of events against the "feedback" derived from others through "communication." In this way she enhances her sense of reality: "Then I could deal with what was really happening and not what I imagined."

In conclusion, the study of "communication" in M's life became a study of the many ways she has tried, failed, and succeeded in building up a sense of "self," of the symbolic and interpretive code underlying this struggle, and of the way it has been played in several crucial interpersonal relationships.

Informant Two

K is a 25-year-old woman. She is single, holds a degree in business administration, and works in a health food store during the day and in a tavern two nights a week.

K frequently used the term "communication" in talking about herself, others, and life in general. As with M, all K's references to "communication" relate to its interpersonal function. This was of particular interest in that a great deal of K's talk referred to work settings, yet she made no reference to the instrumental function of communication.

K's self-image is explicitly linked to her view of her own abilities as a communicator, and she prides herself on her versatility as a communicator, saying she can communicate equally well with "a bum on First Avenue and the president of a corporation." When she expressed self-doubts concerning her worth as a person, these took the form of misgivings concerning her abilities as a communicator: "It's very important to me to communicate well with people . . . sometimes you are taken aback . . . you realize you are not so good at that . . . then you kind of humble yourself and realize maybe you are not this open person you thought you were. . . ." Being a good communicator and being an "open" person are near-equivalents in K's parlance.

"Open communication" is the phrase K reserves for her preferred form of communication, which is on a par with "really talking" for M. The former phrase encompasses both the notion of full mobilization of inner resources, so as to be able "to totally experience what is happening to me," as well as the notion of full utilization of the interactional opportunities posed by a unique other person. Thus: "I'm usually very open to conversation with our customers. I take advantage of the unique, unusual people that may pass through the door by verbally communicating with them."

K conceptualizes both the self and the other as resources, as potentialities to be exploited. "Communication" is the process by which this exploitation of resources is carried out. The industrial metaphor that underlies this way of speaking, whereby the person is seen as both the resource and the product of social life, is quite apparent. "Communication" thus becomes the production process, which in itself is both a resource and a product.

For K, the self continually changes in and through "communication." She invariably conceptualizes such change positively—as development, improvement, or "growth." Lack of "communication" implies more than lack of growth, but rather a sense of running in place, of stagnation: "Communication allows me to grow . . . it scares me to be stagnant." Through "communication" the experiences of self and other are merged and intensified: "The only way to get ultimate experiences is to experience other people through communication." Whereas M is concerned mainly with the supportive role of communication in validating self-images, M is at least as much concerned with the prior stage of constructing a self through "communication," so that the self as "communicator" becomes the paramount role with which she identifies. It is the most neutral and universal of roles, as in one form or another it applies to all social situations. In thinking of herself in these terms, K seems to mitigate the experience of multiple realities, and the ominousness of an open-ended identity.

Our second informant uses "prison-house" imagery to describe the noninteracting self. She described how, as an adolescent, she felt inhibited in her social interaction, although deep inside she knew she was "open" to "communication." She said she felt she had to "lock the extrovert inside this cage." Similarly functioning expressions are "outlet" and "escape into another," the latter describing "communication" as that process whereby one is emancipated from the prison-house of the noninteracting self. Of her family, K said: "Our family is not really an open family. You didn't just sit down and work out and talk about problems." She links this to a widespread shortcoming of people of her parents' generation, which consisted of "not communicating, not getting in touch with their children's feeling." K was able to "communicate" with her mother, who was her confidant. However, her father's unwillingness to engage in communication of the type she felt she needed, and thereby to legitimize it as the preferred way to conduct family affairs, had a detrimental effect on the way she experienced her communication with her family. Thus she described her communication with her mother in terms of refuge rather than of liberation: "In communicating with my mother, she was great and she took refuge in me because she could communicate with me and she couldn't with my dad, and he was so closed and she needed the outlet."

Although K said she knew her parents loved her, she also said she was very unhappy during her adolescence. The source of her distress was the absence of a forum accepted by all family members in which to discuss feelings, air differences, and examine divergent orientations. The communicative climate, which was marked by a lack of "open" interpersonal communication among all members of the family, rendered their family, as an integrative unit, less than satisfactory to K. K predicted that she would repeat some of the mistakes her parents had made in raising her, but, she insisted, "there are things I have learned, and that is that communication is important."

"Communication" is so important to K that the highest level of communication she recognizes is talk about talk. In the log she kept, K described the most rewarding communicative experience she had ever had, which occurred in the initial phase of what was to become an intimate relationship: "We sat for two hours at breakfast discussing each person's ability and method of communicating. We spoke on levels far beyond the normal chit-chat." The level of "normal chit-chat" seems to be the equivalent of the term "small talk" in the speech of M. Talking about one's communicative profile is, presumably, part of what M defined as "real talk." The purpose of this intense preoccupation with ways of communicating was to preillumine each person's mode of operation in the communicative sphere so as to be able to anticipate and thereby prevent possible "breakdowns" in "communication." As "communication" is the "how" of love, or the vehicle of intimacy, its inner workings should be studied and, one hopes, controlled.

In conclusion, the second informant conceives of persons much in the same way as the first: they inhabit a "personal space" which can be penetrated through the act of "communication;" each person is unique and this is a resource to be exploited for one's growth and development; lack-of-growth-through-"communication" equals stagnation, to the point of identity loss. The self is experienced as an event or is not experienced at all; one's identity is closely tied to one's view of oneself as communicator, which seems to be the generalized role of the person in this orientational system. Thus, concern with self-definition and self-validation is expressed as concern over one's own quality as a communicator. Like M, K is extremely concerned with having control over life, which she interprets as control over her communicative encounters. She is cheerful and pleasant with everybody, assuming that thereby she will secure a similar response to herself, and she engages in metacommunicative discussion as a form of "preventive treatment" in the interpersonal domain.

THE SEMANTIC DIMENSIONS OF "COMMUNICATION"

In the speech of our informants, and in the other texts we have examined in the course of our inquiry, there is evidence of two distinctive clusters of terms referring to communication. One cluster includes such terms as "real communication," "really talking," "supportive communication," and "open communication." "Communication," without an adjectival modifier, also can be included in this cluster when the term appears in the context of discussing "self" and "relationships." The other cluster includes such terms as "small talk," "normal chit-chat," and "mere talk." It is probably the case that neither cluster is exhaustively delineated here, but the present assignment of terms is defensible in the light of our field materials.

"Communication" and "mere talk" are differentiated on several semantic dimensions. The dimensions discussed below were derived from our readings of the lives of M and K, and of related texts in which "communication" was a key term. We tried to make sense of these various instances of the use of "communication" by submitting them to a kind of distinctive features analysis. The dimensions were thus derived inductively, based on scrutiny of the texts we collected and constructed (Seitel 1974). M and K, and the producers of the other texts we examined, use the dimensions *close/distant*, *supportive/neutral*, and *open/closed* to differentiate "communication" from "mere talk." In what follows, these dimensions will be defined, analyzed into finer discriminations, and applied to "communication" and "mere talk."

The first dimension identified, *close/distant*, suggests an essentially spatial metaphor. "Communication" is the medium for intercourse between those who are "close," such as "close friends" and intimates. Although the spatial metaphors of proximity and similarity are relevant here, perhaps of most relevance is the spatial metaphor of penetration. Specifically, "communication" is high on interpenetration of the interlocutors' unique psychologic worlds. To the degree that interlocutors make public what was previously private information about their unique self-image, *closeness*, one feature of "communication," is manifested. This is intimate speech, speech that penetrates psychological boundaries and barriers. "Mere talk," by contrast, is talk in and through which one "keeps his distance" or "stays at arm's length" from another. The content of this latter kind of speech is "everyday chit-chat," a content independent of the unique self-images of the speakers.

Supportive/neutral refers to the degree in which each interlocutor is committed to providing positive evaluations of the other's self. To engage in "communication," it is not necessary that one approve everything the other has *done*—the other's *actions*—but that one approve the other qua unique and precious individual. This is speech in which unconditional positive regard finds its natural home. The dimension does not contrast positive with negative evaluation, but the degree to which positive evaluation is relevant and salient. Thus, the polar opposite, manifested in "mere talk", is not negative evaluation, but rather is the absence of a commitment to, and the absence of the relevance of, positive evaluation.

A third dimension refers to the degree of *openness* manifested by the participants in the speech event. By openness is meant a willingness to listen to and acknowledge the other's presentation of self, to listen to and actively try to understand the other's evaluation of oneself, and to be willing to consider changing one's perception of self or the other, contingent upon the meanings that emerge in the speech event. This is the speech of emergent realities, of negotiated selves and the negotiated relationship. "Mere talk," by contrast, is considered the talk governed by a set of conventions independent of those that have been forged between the two interlocutors.

The three dimensional contrasts made above are formalized here to make explicit our emergent hypothesis about the mapping of the semantic dimensions represented by the native terms "communication" and its opposite, "mere talk." The analysis suggest that, for our informants, "communication" refers to *close*, *supportive*, and *open* speech between two or more people, and that it can be contrasted with "mere talk," which is relatively more *distant*, *neutral*, and *routinized*.

"COMMUNICATION" AS INTERPERSONAL "WORK"

Thus far we have defined "communication" by contrasting it with "mere talk." We further define it here by discussing its relationship to two other terms, which have emerged as salient for the interpersonal domain. An examination of "self," "relationship," and "communication," as they occur in our informants' speech, indicates that these terms label categories that together constitute a domain of meaning. In what follows we explore the key figure of speech, which makes that domain of meaning intelligible, and we articulate the key interrelationships among these terms. The purpose of these explorations is to deepen understanding of "communication" as a cultural category by examining it as one term in a larger "code of talking."

Our field notes yield the following observations about the words used in some American speech: people "work" on their "relationship" or make their "relationship work;" they "work" on "themselves" and on their "communication" together; "nervous breakdowns" within the person's mental machinery have been supplanted by "breakdowns" in "relationships" and "breakdowns" in "communication." Thus in the world of meaning constituted by the speech we have examined, "self," "relationship," and "communication" are things one can have and discuss, as well as take apart, examine, put together again, and make "work."

The figure that lends coherence to these three terms is the "work" metaphor. This is manifested in the use of "self," "relationship," and "communication" as objects of the "work" people do, as things which can be "worked on." It is also manifested in the notion of "communication" as the "work" necessary to construct a "self" and develop a "relationship." Although most of the metaphorical expressions used invoke the notion of a machine, there is an extension of the metaphorical domain to include other, not necessarily machine-based, industries. For example, people are said to "invest" in each other, but mainly in their "relationships"; people "contribute" to a "relationship," give one thing to it and take another. This secondary metaphoric domain is based on more organismic images, so there is talk of the "relationship growing," of "communication" being "alive," and of the "self" being involved in a continuous process of "growth."

Metaphors, as Fernandez (1972) states, "take their subjects and move them along a dimension or set of dimensions" (p. 47). In the way of speaking examined here, interpersonal life is made intelligible by moving it along the *work* dimension, and thus increasingly derives its validation from its ethos of performance. This is epitomized by the notion of "competence" that is so naturally applied to the interpersonal domain. Interpersonal life, which in some ways of speaking is associated with home and subjectivity (Kemnitzer 1977), has in the speech of our informants been made an arena for work and technique. To the first informant, a person can be judged by the quality of their "relationships," the second judges herself and others by the quality of their "communication." The "self," when it is discussed, is described in terms of its components; references are made to feelings, responses, and experiences, all of which can be "worked on," and not to the person as a whole. Both informants imply that interpersonal life is fundamentally an arena for work in which one's competence is the primary determinant of performance success.

People can be judged by many standards—their birth, blood, heroic deeds, or simply as intrinsically precious by virtue of their being alive. The way of speaking we have examined is notable for the emphasis it places on the competence to perform interpersonal "work." In this speech, "communication" competence would be a person's capacity for *close*, *supportive*, *open* speech in the discussion of—and thus in the "work" upon—one-self and one's relationships. Note that competence here is not an attainment, it is a capacity. Given the changing nature of persons and the moral imperative not to "stagnate," it is a capacity that is and should be continually put to new tests. Thus interpersonal life, in the terms of this communication code, is a life of unrelenting work in which one's competence is ever newly applied and newly tested.

If the conceptualization of the interpersonal domain as an arena for "work" creates great demands for effective performance, it also provides a way to mitigate a sense of personal responsibility for one's interpersonal difficulties or failures. Our informants attributed family problems and divorces to the absence of "communication" and to the reluctance of people to "work" on their "relationship" or their "communication." If "the relationship" can be made responsible for some aspects of human conduct, then the burden of the "self" is eased. Thus when "communication breaks down," and "the relationship" does not "work," both parties can still be "o.k." Such a way of speaking helps to mitigate the discomfort that attends difficulties or misconduct and thus enhances the state of "feeling good about oneself," which is the ultimate goal of interpersonal life as here conceived.

Given the importance of effective interpersonal work in the way of speaking formulated here, we could expect that highly routinized procedures have been developed for doing that work. Such procedures have been codified in our discussion of the "communication" ritual to which we turn next. Here we turn from a metaphor supplied by our informants, that of "communication" as "work," to one supplied by us, that of "communication" as "ritual."

THE "COMMUNICATION" RITUAL

Throughout this chapter we have noted that the people we have studied do not consider all talk to be "communication." Nor is all interpersonally oriented talk experienced to be as satisfying and liberating as "communication" implies for the informants. A more specific set of expectations has evolved concerning the episodic sequence referred to by the native phrases "sit down and talk," "work out problems," or "discuss our relationship." We call such a sequence the "communication" ritual. It functions as ritual as it is the culturally preferred way to reaffirm the status of what the culture defines as a sacred object—the definition of "self" as experienced by any one of the participants, usually the one who initiates the sequence.

In what follows we outline the basic ingredients of the "communication" ritual in terms of several components of speech events as discussed by Hymes (1972). The purpose of this outline is to point to a general mold, not to provide a recipe for communicative encounters. Obviously, each enactment of the ritual, each token of the general type, will deviate from it one way or another, but this general account captures the essential ingredients of the ritual as we understand it. The following of Hymes's categories were used for the description: topic, purpose, participants, act sequence, setting, and norm of interaction.

Topic

The topic is problems arising in one's experience of one's "self" and one's world. Both "self" and world must be defined by each individual, but these definitions must also be validated by others. The simultaneous awareness of personal uniqueness and the demand for intimacy and mutual validation is a continual source of problems, which are experienced as interpersonal rather than intrapersonal. Thus, their solution naturally calls for "communication," and this is not accompanied by a sense of imposition, because the others will consider the problems their own, too. Turning inward and brooding over a problem is not considered a step toward its solution. Hamlet, if he were a member of this culture, would have tried to sit down and talk things over with his family, or at least discuss his problem with Ophelia. "Communication" seems closely related to this sense of problematicity, and it seems that the term "fun," as in "having lots of fun together," is reserved to the description of lightheartedness and well-being in the interpersonal domain (in which "communication" is not "fun" but "work").

Purpose

The purpose of the ritual is to resolve the sense of problematicity that one or more of the participants experiences, by affirming participants' identities and engendering intimacy. In a "talk show" recently shown on American television, which dealt with death, one of the participants said the purpose of the sequence she advocates is for "people to relate to each other in a positive way around a difficult issue." This captures much of the purpose of the "communication" ritual, and indicates that it is not a problem-solving session in the regular sense that participants have a specific problem that can be overcome and resolved. Rather, participants are expected to face whatever problem emerges, in a dignified way—that is, through talk of the supportive variety. The person who refuses to face problems by discussing them is felt to be "copping out," to be relinquishing control over life, and thereby that person becomes unwholesome.

Participants

Participants are (potentially) all the persons considered by the initiator of the ritual to be intimates who will not be imposed upon by discussion of the "problem," as they consider it, in part, their own. For a primary unit such as a family to be considered well-functioning, all its members have to be committed to the communication ritual on a symmetrical basis, so that the enactment of the ritual is surrounded by a climate of legitimacy.

Act Sequence

There are constraints on the way the episodic sequence labeled the communication ritual can proceed. The structural constraints that seem to govern its unfolding are: (1) Initiation: a member of an intimate pair initiates the sequence by announcing the existence of a personal problem, which can be "worked out" only through "communication" with other members of the primary group. The initiator suggests that they "sit down and talk about it." (2) Acknowledgment: the addressee(s) acknowledge the problem, its legitimacy as an interpersonal concern, and its relevance to the other members of the primary group, by indicating their willingness to enact the sequence. They disengage themselves from other activity, and make ready to render the discussion of the problem the focus of their attention. They "sit down to talk." (3) Negotiation: the problem is formulated, its ingredients examined from as many perspectives as possible, and its implications for the initiator and the other participants in the ritual are studied. The initiator does a great deal of the self-disclosing, and the other participants' behavior is marked by empathic listening, nonjudgmental comments, and noninquisitiveness. The initiator's attitude is that of openness both to feedback and to change. (4) Reaffirmation: the need for this phase seems to derive from the potential effect on the negotiation phase, in which discrepant positions, needs, and interpretations between committed individuals are brought into relief. At times a compromise on the substantive level is not possible, and at all times the discord is threatening on the relationship level. It is this threat that the reaffirmation phase seeks to mitigate.

Setting

The setting in which the ritual is appropriately enacted is one in which talk is accepted as the focal activity, in which interlocutors have privacy, and can be fully immersed in each other.

Norm of Interaction

When persons experience a problem related to their sense of identity or to their functioning in the social world, they should initiate the "communication" ritual. Conversely, a person who is approached by an intimate concerning a problem the latter experiences should reciprocate by helping him or her to enact the communication ritual. The norm calling for enactment of the sequence is very powerfully felt, to the extent that it loses its formative status of the "how" of love and the "how" of self, and becomes the only indicator of their very existence. In this orientational system, not having a problem is interpreted as suppression or reluctance to face the problems one "must have" by virtue of being "alive" in the world today. A state of nothing in particular happening in one's life—no change—is experienced as dullness and deadening boredom, and longterm relationships are particularly vulnerable to it. As one of our informants put it, the comforts of a longterm marriage and its habitual structure prevent one from searching for a higher awareness of "self" and "relationship." This kind of probing is made possible and legitimate in enacting the ritual, so that for some people the absence of the ritual becomes the problem. This can be a tangled issue when partners disagree about their commitments to enact the ritual with each other. Unlike any other disagreement, this one cannot be remedied through "communication"—an attempt to do so would be a de facto enactment of the "communication" ritual. The gripping force the norm can have was indicated on two occasions when people with whom we discussed this project at length, a few days later, in the context of discussing their lives, expressed the strong belief that "communication" is important, and that one should "sit down and talk." The ethnographic smile that lighted our faces did not jolt them into "hearing" what they were saying. When it was pointed out explicitly, they noticed and concurred.

Finally, we speculate that the intensity of the preoccupation with the kind of speech found in the "communication" ritual stands in sharp contrast to the communicative requirements of nonintimate encounters in this society, where the ruling injunction seems to be: "Thou shalt exude well-being." Our first informant commented on this bitterly, saying, "If I am mad I don't care who knows that I am mad," and she described herself as a social misfit in this regard. The second informant seemed rather compulsive in following this injunction, pointed out that she took care not to burden others with her problems and, by so doing, secured a similar behavior toward herself. This, it seems to us, puts an added burden on interpersonal relationships in primary groups or dyads. They become the only source of personal validation, given the strong proscription against self-exposure in nonintimate settings. The "communication" ritual, then, is so terribly important not only because it allows the expression of the "how" of love and the "how" of self, but also because it is the only place to find them.

Having defined "communication," situated it in a larger code of meaning about interpersonal work, and formulated the episodic sequence by which such a work is most naturally performed, we can make sense of "communication" (as it appears in some American speech) in a way we could not have done before. Thus we conclude by turning to a brief examination of a communication event that has a prominent place in American life. We turn to an examination of a television show witnessed daily by a large number of Americans and in which "communication," as we have formulated it, is very naturally and poignantly spoken by the participants.

ON BEING "IN TOUCH" WITH PHIL DONAHUE

The Phil Donahue show practices and preaches the "communication" creed we have described. At the studio in Chicago, Phil Donahue and his guests "sit down and talk." They discuss interpersonal problems that many Americans would not talk about in the privacy of their homes, and the voice travels across America: "What you need is communication." Indeed, to be fully "in touch" with Phil Donahue, one must also be in touch with the "communication" ritual and the meanings to which it gives expression.

Phil Donahue, it will be noted, does not deal with insoluble problems in his broadcasts; he deals with problems that *seem* insoluble to the people "out there" who are enmeshed in them. To his guests, these are problems they have solved. Underlying these shows is a rhetoric of conversion. It is not the person who beats his wife and cannot stop—it is the ex-wife batterer—who is invited to the show; it is not the person who is struggling with his sexual identity but the person who has come to terms with it that we see. It is they who have a message to convey, and the message is: "I could change, you can too."

The Phil Donahue show marks off a world of talk where the "real stuff" is brought to light; emotions are thematized and simplified by being abstracted from conduct and experience ("today's show deals with jealousy"). The climate is generally supportive (when it is not, Donahue chastises the audience); interlocutors openly "share" their feelings and views; the phenomena dealt with are provocative and problematic, such as children who "divorce" their parents, husbands who beat their wives, couples who agree to have extramarital affairs, and so on. The specific topic is not of concern here, the point is that anything can be a problem if so perceived, and any problem can (and should) be overcome by enacting a version of the "communication" ritual. A statement to this effect by one of the participants in the show that dealt with parents' and children's rights was as follows:

> Okay. Well, I think what Lee is talking about here is that she felt that she wasn't getting an adequate forum at home to discuss her problem. . . . This first woman that spoke was saying: "Well, we could have talked it out, and if the child didn't want to go that's fine." But many of these cases come up when there is just no communication at home. Now Cindy here went to court to have herself declared incorrigible and taken away from her parents. And she said there were long stretches of time when her parents just didn't talk to her at all, let alone have a basis for communication.

The except, which is representative of many others taken from Donahue shows, illustrates the high value assigned to "communication" by Donahue participants, and implies awareness and belief in the efficacy of the "communication" ritual. The healing value of communicating about problems is attested by the mother of a woman who, through her childhood, had been sexually abused by her father. Like many other people on the show, she feels her message to the public has a missionary value to it, and it involves a call for "communication": "I'm here to support our daughter and to offer help to people who have had the same thing happen to them who will understand. But mostly, that things can be worked out, and as a family you can learn to communicate, you can learn to overcome what has happened." On another show, dealing with marital infidelity, a couple who had overcome the "problem" described their newly found intimacy. The wife said: "The communication we have now is so different. I trust his honesty, he'll answer any question, won't become vague . . . doesn't say, 'put it behind you, forget it.'"

In line with the view that problems are always to be solved in an interacting context, guests whose problems are thematized often appear with some of their intimates—potential participants in the "communication" ritual. The clearest example we found was the above-mentioned show on incest in families, where the sexually abused daughter appeared on the show with both parents (who were in silhouettes). This appearance, like all others, was a postconversion one, so that given the episodic structure of the ritual, the normative expectation is that by following the "communication" ritual in which they all had taken part (and to which they testified), their relationship could be fully reaffirmed. It was interesting, therefore, to note that the daughter, who appeared to us to be angry with her father, worked so hard to contain her anger; anger was out of place in the "script" implicit in the Donahue show, which presupposes a sequence that ends with a reaffirmation phase.

The special rhetorical effectiveness of the Donahue "communication" shows is due to the iconicity of its form and its content: Donahue does what he says, and he says what he does. He both embodies and calls for the possibility of personal conversion. He capitalizes on his standing as the archconvert who has learned that women are persons too, and that if you have a problem you must not keep it to yourself, but "sit down and talk about it."

In response to an obstinate caller, who refused to see the light, Phil Donahue expressed the injunction that underlies his show, and seems to underlie interpersonal ceremony in private life as well: "We are not asking you to change this culture but we can ask you as an adult to step back and look at what you are saying." This seems very much like the ethnographer's task—to step back and look at what people are saying, Phil Donahue among them (see Carbaugh 1988 for a fuller treatment of the Donahue show from a cultural perspective).

CONCLUSIONS

By interpreting several instances of American speech, we have constructed a way to hear the term "communication" that renders its use in that speech intelligible and illuminating. We have found that in the field of discourse in which "communication," "self," and "relationship" cooccur, "communication" refers to the speech that manifests mutual self-disclosure, positive regard for the unique selves of the participants, and openness to emergent, negotiated definitions of self and other. Such *close*, *supportive*, and *open* speech is the artful "work" required to follow the contradictory cultural injunctions, "be yourself" and "be the self you want to be," while simultaneously conceding to others part of the control for self-definition.

Thus "communication" is a culturally distinctive solution to the universal problem of fusing the personal with the communal. In the ideology in which "communication" is a pivotal term, affirming oneself in and through a process of social interaction is the highest good. But this is always problematic. Each person is unique among persons—that is, different from all others due to differential life experiences—and each person is malleable—that is, subject to change due to personal will and changing definitions supplied by others. Given human uniqueness, the interpenetration of life worlds is always necessary for understanding another person and thus validation of another's self-image is always problematic.

Given human malleability, such interpenetration holds the promise of the kind of interpersonal speech that fosters the favorable conditions of growth and change, and failure to expose oneself to such experiences is tantamount to denying one's full humanity. Thus, the achievement of commonality with others and the construction of a sense of self are always problematic, but "communication" is the process in which the problematicity is relieved, or at least "worked on." "Communication" is the solution to the problem of "relationship" (love) and of "self" (personhood). In terms of overcoming personal differences, "communication" functions as the "how of love," the primary vehicle and constituent of a "relationship"; in terms of constructing and validating a "self," "communication" is the "how of self."

Given the cultural meaning and ideational context of "communication," as delineated here, it should be no surprise to find that "communication" has its quintessential place in the ritual we have described. Like other rituals, the "communication" ritual, by its very enactment, thematizes that which is problematic for its performers, and constitutes, in its enactment, the solution to the problem. Just as prayer thematizes as problem one's separation from God, and solves it through ritual acts of obeisance to a deity, so the "communication" ritual thematizes the reality of human separation and solves it through acts of obeisance to the coconstruction of selves in and through "communication." Thus the "communication" ritual functions to reinforce the unspoken consensus underlying intimate life—an agreement to be *close*, *supportive*, and *open*, and its performance thereby implicates and insinuates performers in a world of meaning and morality, which gives credence and legitimacy to "the relationship." It is this constitutive power of the ritual that makes the fact or the possibility of its performance so poignant.

If various types of cultural performance, such as everyday and public dramas, are "dialectical dancing partners" (Turner 1980), then our readings of the everyday lives we have studied should help us to understand the meanings underlying some more public dramas. For example, for us, the Phil Donahue Show was made intelligible in the very terms and tropes that color the speech of M and K. Just as a reading of Phil Donahue's autobiography suggests a striking parallelism between the structure and the content of his program and of his life, so his show simultaneously reflects and provides "a rhetoric, a mode of emplotment, and a meaning" (Turner 1980, p. 153), which articulates with the ideals espoused by M and K. But the dramatic metaphor fails us here. It is more apt to say that Donahue and company communicate in evangelistic tones. Following a public display of "communication," they endorse it and preach it, apparently to a fervently appreciative audience. That we could find so prominent and so plausible a public use of the code we formulated suggests, not that it is universal in America, but the discourse that uses it is *intelligible to* many Americans (Hart, Carlson, and Eadie, 1980).

So, we have, as Donahue exhorted his viewer to do, stepped back and looked at what some of the people in this country were saying. We found that a "wholesome adult" in the ideology studied looked suspiciously familiar—he is his own ethnographer. The difference between the ethnographer and the reflective person who can deal with his problems through "communication" is further minimized if we accept Ricoeur's (1977) dictum that the aim of ethnography is to reach an understanding of the self via an understanding of the other. Our study of American "communication" has led us to think of ethnography less as a journey into a foreign land or culture, and more as a journey into a no-man's land, which is neither the territory of the self or of the other. As every Israeli child who was taken on that mandatory fieldtrip to the border knows, one cannot risk more than a few steps into unsettled territory. In doing so, however, one becomes aware not only of the existence of the other's territory, but of one's own, and of the concept of territory in general. The ethnographer, like the careful tourist, pays his tribute to the border at designated spots, but the border stretches and winds between these spots as well, and it is in this unmarked territory that the "person" searches for a sense of personal meaning. The "communication" ritual provides members of the social world we studied a context comparable in import to the ethnographic encounter for the ethnographer, but the sign, if any, would say "exchange station" rather than "border." Thus, despite the excessive territorial metaphors, we hope this study does not read as an exercise in cartography, that we have been able not only to delineate some of the scenery in that stretch of no-man's land, in that area of heightened consciousness in which our informants told their stories and we made our interpretations, but that we have been able to convey as well a sense of possibility for ethnography as perspective and method in human communication.

Chapter 5

JOANNA KRAMER'S IDENTITY CRISIS

In his paper, "Social Dramas and Stories about Them," Victor Turner drew attention to the interdependence of public myths and personal stories. The former, widely available to the members of a society, provide interpretive and rationalizing materials for the everyday stories that speakers tell each other in small groups, or that individuals themselves use in their private musings about their lives. For example, Homer's *Odyssey*, a story of absence and return, displays a system of meanings and motives with which individuals can tell and make intelligible their own story. The disparate, seemingly incoherent, fragments of a life can be given some kind of story line by a teller who draws from the *Odyssey's* interpretive and justificatory resources. It is not only that public myths inform personal stories but also that the intelligibility of the former derive, at least in part, from their consonance with the latter. For example, Homer's *Iliad*, a story of Achilles' wrath over the abduction of his concubine, which is told in terms of power, wealth, loyalty, shame, and piety, is intelligible only to the degree these concepts have some counterpart in the personal lives of those who hear the myth. Public myths that, according to Turner, develop rhetorical traction and semiotic sense, are those whose terms and tropes resonate with the existential condition of their hearers.

Turner's thesis about the symbiotic relationship of public and personal stories is of particular value to anyone who wishes to ascertain a society's common culture. Myths, particularly those about the catalysis and resolution of agonistic conduct, are forms that display a culture's interpretive and rhetorical resources. By listening to and interpreting a society's myths, one can learn what meanings, motives, and story lines are intelligible and persuasive in that society, in that a myth, expressed in the form of a story, reveals a code. Furthermore, the code elements used in a public myth or a personal story have heuristic value, in that insights gleaned in the interpretation of stories at one level can suggest particular insights into what is expressed at the other level. Finally, the convergence of terms, tropes, and story lines, across public and personal stories, provides evidence to judge that one has found elements of meaning and justification that are parts of a *common* culture. That is, where an investigator finds convergence, in the discourse of a given society, across its public and private stories, there is an opportunity for finding evidence about the contents of, and the consensus on, a cultural code.

In chapter 4 Tamar Katriel and I formulated a cultural code with which to interpret the situated meaning of "communication" in some American speech about interpersonal life. In this chapter I develop further the formulation of that code. This is done by the analysis of ethnographic materials not treated in the earlier work, specifically the analysis of a public myth, one that converges strikingly with many of the personal stories Katriel and I heard and recorded during our fieldwork, and was received as a discourse of compelling facticity by a large segment of the American people, at the time our fieldwork was conducted. The interpretation here of that myth will enable me to develop further the articulation of the code we formulated earlier and thereby to illustrate and instantiate my thesis that the convergence of public myth and personal story has heuristic value to the student of a culture.

The novel-film *Kramer Versus Kramer* (hereafter KVK) tells a story that was extremely popular, plausible, and emotionally compelling to its contemporaneous audience. Whatever its artistic merit, KVK is a significant cultural artifact of American intimate life circa 1980. The film version received an Academy Award as the best motion picture for 1979, an award widely believed to be an index of commercial and popular success. Reviewers in several major magazines and newspapers asserted that the film portrayed accurately the concerns and motives of contemporary intimate life, saying the film should be put in a time capsule to reveal to future generations something about the way life was in the New York City of 1979; that it was a truthful film, and that it accurately expressed "the way we are now." In addition to the reviewers' explicit claims that the film is "realistic," "true," and "accurate," there is implicit in their essays the sense that they find KVK to be a very believable story in terms of its treatment of motive and story line; there is nothing puzzling about it to them. And it was not only a plausible but a poignant tale, one that gained national notoriety for the emotional response—open weeping—that it routinely elicited from its audiences. The following popular reviews were examined: Canby (1979), Geduld (1980), Hatch (1980), Orth (1979), Rich (1979), Schlesinger (1980), Simon (1980), Westerbrook (1980).

The part of the story I examine includes these events and their telling:

1. Joanna left her husband, Ted, and her young son, Billy.
2. During Joanna's absence, Ted and Joanna were divorced. Ted was given custody of Billy, with no contest by Joanna, and Ted began the process of caring for Billy in Joanna's absence.
3. After fifteen months of absence, Joanna returned. She asked Ted to give her custody of Billy, but Ted refused. Joanna sued him and convinced the court to grant her custody.
4. Having been given custody, Joanna decided to allow Ted to keep Billy and so the boy stayed with Ted.

According to Varenne, a French ethnographer of American culture, there is only one inviolate rule in contemporary America: "parents are not free not to take care of their children" (Varenne 1977: 5). Joanna's abandoning Billy violated this rule, a violation all the more serious because she is Billy's mother. That Joanna did this, and what its consequences would be, create the tension that give KVK its dramatic life.

During Joanna's absence, Ted's metamorphosis from uninvolved father to an aggressively attentive single parent was accomplished. In America from 1970 to 1978, the eight years preceding the film version of KVK, the number of single men who cared for their children increased by 136 percent (Rich 1979:77). During this time there was a flowering of lay and professional interest in the role of the father, with an emphasis on fathers becoming involved in the care of their children and in sharing domestic tasks with mothers. Ted's new role was a comedic resource that the film (more than the novel) exploited, and provided the means for showing Ted's "growth" from relatively traditional to a more 'liberated' man.

Joanna's abdication of her role as mother and Ted's embrace of his new role as father provided emotional backdrop for the key agonistic scenes of the drama. When Joanna returned to New York and sought to regain custody of Billy, the American viewer alternately cheered for Joanna, as she broke with convention to "assert" her "self," and for Ted, as he "grew" into a new identity. A dramatic conflict was created over whether Ted or Joanna should have custody of Billy. The tension was exacerbated precisely because both Ted and Joanna had "grown." Ted had become less involved in his instrumental, and more involved in his expressive, roles; Joanna had broken from conventional role expectations to "work" on her "self." Thus, both Ted and Joanna had become "competent" to raise Billy, even if they were so "different" from each other as to make their reconciliation as a couple impossible. And even though their lack of "communication" had caused their "relationship" to fail, they now might come together again as new "selves" who were more "competent" at "working" on their "relationships."

How did Joanna persuade the audience, and the court, to excuse her violation of the rule proscribing abandoning one's child so that she now could be given custody of him? For this task, she used a rhetorical argument grounded in the value system of her audience. When she was married to Ted, she suffered from conditions that caused her to lose a sense of "self." Her "self" had been so harmed that she could no longer be a "person," let alone a good wife or mother. What were these conditions that caused Joanna's breakdown? What actions did she take to overcome her difficulties?

First, consider the *causes* for Joanna's breakdown. She claimed that one of two conditions was necessary for her emotional well-being (her sense of being a "person") to be maintained. One was the freedom to pursue a career. If Ted had allowed her to take a job outside the home, it would have provided the opportunity for personal development not provided in her role as wife and mother. These "stifling" circumstances had debilitating psychic consequences for Joanna. She could have endured this deprivation of opportunity, though, if a second condition had been met: if Ted had spent time with her talking through the problems imposed by her emotionally constricting role. But Joanna was denied both of these conditions. This denial was the catalyzing condition for Joanna's decision to flee her home and abandon her child. Like Achilles, who had been injured as a "man" because his woman had been taken from him, Joanna was injured as a "person" because her "self" had been hopelessly undernourished and restricted from "growth."

Second, the story reveals the conditions for resolving Joanna's troubles. During her absence, Joanna went to California. She met a man with whom she "communicated" about her problems. In and through this process she reconstructed her sense of "self." Like Odysseus, Joanna went to a land where the sirens could minister to her; for Joanna, the land was California and the ministry was "communication." The absence and the "communication" prepared Joanna to return to New York City, where, like Odysseus in Ithaka, Joanna endured a difficult trial. She returned to New York to reclaim her entitlement, the privilege of caring for her child.

Like Odysseus, it was necessary for Joanna to prove herself worthy of the prize that awaited her upon her return. Ted had blocked her efforts to regain custody of Billy. The state of New York, which ordinarily would grant child custody to the mother rather than the father, had to be convinced that Joanna, who had abandoned her child, was now "competent" to be a parent. Joanna's account, her explanation of her past conduct and her claim that she was now sufficiently self-possessed (as to be competent) to raise a child, convinced the state of New York. But ultimately, Joanna did not accept her prize; rather, she let Ted keep Billy. If the reader/viewer had expected the ritual of resolution to include reconciliation, the viewer was disappointed. Joanna's triumph ended when the court declared her "competent," when she won her battle for custody.

That the court, Ted, and the audience, found this account to be plausible requires explanation. A woman had left her husband, not because he did not provide adequately for her material needs, not because he was cruel, not because he beat her, not because he was unfaithful to her, but because he insisted that she stay at home and tend their home and child, and because he pressured her to accept this role, and because they had, as she said, "differences" of temperament, interest, and psyche. She had left her child, not because some cruel twist of fate had required her to do so, but because she had sufficiently lost her sense of being a "person" that she was not able, in her view, to care for him properly. These terms and motives are not everywhere intelligible and reprehensible. Joanna's parents tried to understand her, but even they could not reconstruct from her discourse a reason they could understand and affirm. There is direct ethnographic testimony indicating that many men and women in many societies would find Joanna's vocabulary hard to understand, her reasons unpersuasive (for example, Komarovsky 1962). How Ted and Joanna, their friends, and the court could honor Joanna's account can be explained by saying that they used a code to hear Joanna, a code that enabled them to find in her story the words to establish knowledge and belief. That code underlies what I call a myth of dignity, to whose formulation I now turn.

In *The Homeless Mind*, Berger, Berger, and Kellner (1973) point to the emergence of a new conception of personal worth, which has in the past century or so come to have a privileged place among the god terms of humankind: a conception of *dignity*, the worth possessed by any person by virtue of being alive. Dignity is a function of one's "intrinsic humanity divested of all socially imposed roles or norms" (p. 89). By contrast, honor, a term that Berger et al. oppose to dignity, refers to one's individual worth as measured by one's place in society, as mother, father, teacher, ruler. Dignity, on the other hand, pertains "to the self as such, to the individual regardless of his position in society" (p. 89). This view of persons and the basis for assessing their worth implies what Berger et al. call an implicit sociology and an implicit anthropology. "The implicit sociology views all biological and historical differentiations among men as either downright unreal or essentially irrelevant. The implicit anthropology locates the real self over and beyond all these differentiations"

(p. 89). The chief virtue in this view is that "self" be allowed to "grow," to develop into that idealized potential that is a person's birthright, but that the forces of "society" have retarded through socialization. The cardinal sin is to restrict one's own or another's "self" from "growing" by treating it in terms of some socially assigned category.

There are, in this view, evil forces in the world, and they are invariably social in origin. It is "society," with its rules and conventions, that threatens to repress or retard the development of "persons." It is "society" that originally shaped and twisted the innately free, spontaneous, and creative self. A "person's" great life task is to free one-"self" from the constraints of "society" sufficiently as to "grow" continually. A crucial ingredient in this process is "communication," in which one both affirms and negotiates "self" in and through speech with others. "Communication" is a process in which "growth" is facilitated, and in those cases of severe repression or retardation, the communication ritual is a necessary antidote or curative process.

Having briefly outlined the code of dignity, its terms will be defined and applied to Joanna's story. Perhaps the most prominent term in the code is that of "persons" or "self." In this code, the "self" exists, is important, and is more important than "society." Moral energy is properly directed against "society," which constrains and threatens the "self." Joanna complained to Ted that neither working nor talking with him had suffocated her as a "person," a claim that reveals Joanna's reification of "self." When Joanna told Ted "a woman has to be her own person," she spoke in terms of the reality and the importance of "self." She further affirmed this when she said about her friend, Linda, "she's a person," because she has a job (Corman 1977, p. 27). Ted's refusal to respond to Joanna's complaints as legitimate created a condition for Joanna of "emotional confinement" that seriously injured her sense of "self." The "mental anguish" of not being able to work outside the home might have been alleviated if Ted had been "open" to hearing about Joanna's interests and problems (Corman 1977, pp. 215–16).

Ted's sin was that he treated Joanna as the incumbent of a socially ascribed role, that of wife and mother. He wanted her to perform a very traditional role, to stay home and care for Billy. Furthermore, he tried persistently to convince her that she should bear another child. Both of these issues were points of contention between them. In both instances, Ted's sin was in not treating Joanna as a differentiated individual, in not being "open" to hearing Joanna's unique needs and ideas, in not being attentive to Joanna's "selfhood" or "personhood," in insisting that she perform a stereotypical, conventional role.

The significance and moral status of "self" in this code is evident when Joanna's account of her conduct is juxtaposed to that of others' accounts using another code. One informant, whom the author interviewed as part of a study of American marriage codes, said that although he and his wife seemed to be deeply incompatible, they would never divorce because their religious beliefs prohibited them from altering their marriage vows. In that informant's code, the sanctity of marriage is more important than the sanctity of selves; in Ted and Joanna's code, the opposite is true. For Joanna, the society, or tradition, are less important than the self. At least, the particular care given the "self" in this story is that each self's unique, inner potential is more important than is shaping it to conform to an external moral code.

The "self" can develop from a state in which its true nature and potential are stifled or repressed. Such development is "growth," and the "self" is not healthy if not "growing." Whereas in another code the emphasis is on status rather than process, in the dignity code the moral imperative is always to "grow." This is justified in part by the belief that "persons"/"selves" have so much potential for development that it is unfortunate at best, immoral at worst, for them not to "grow." In part its justification is that "society" is an ever-present danger to "persons," and thus "working" at "growing" is a necessary process for healthy selfhood.

A crucial way in which the "self" grows is to exercise "choice." A "person" is assumed to be healthy when it can, and does, "choose." To be deprived of "choice" is to be deprived of personhood. "Choice" is crucially important to persons because in its exercise "growth" is fostered. Whereas in some codes the individual has a duty to make wise choices for the social good, in the dignity code the person has a duty to make choices true to its "self's" unique potential.

Joanna's chief complaint about Ted was that he restricted her "options" and thus her capacity for "growth." Joanna had difficulty being a wife and mother, she later argued, because Ted had stifled her as a "person." The lack of "choice" stifled her "growth," which "smothered" her "self," which made her "incompetent" as wife and mother. When Ted cut off Joanna's "options," she did the only sensible thing to do, if one subscribes to the sorites expressed above—she fled. When she returned, and set about to reclaim Billy, she cited "Ted's "growth"-constricting acts. She also expressed, through her boyfriend, that she "really chooses this now" (Corman 1977, p. 201)—that is, to regain Billy's custody. Whereas previously "choice" had been denied her, she was now able to "choose," and because she "chooses this now," one could believe that she is "competent" and restored to health. The theme of "growth" is also expressed in Ted's metamorphosis. When Joanna left him, Ted's friends encouraged him to seek therapy because it would help him to help him-*self* to "grow" (Corman 1977, p. 63). Later, when Ted's case was presented for keeping custody of Billy, it was said in Ted's favor that he had "grown" because of his child-rearing experiences. Thus, "growth" through "choice" is necessary for one-"self" to be healthy and "competent."

That selves can and should "grow," and that "choice" for them is both important and problematic, is congruent with another proposition of the dignity code, that "selves" are fundamentally "different." Individual "difference" in this code refers not to biological or social difference, but to inherent uniqueness in feeling, temperament, attitudes, and values. When justifying divorce, for example, the "differences" between partners is a prominent and intelligible rationale. When she was first contemplating leaving home, Joanna told Ted, "We don't have anything in common. Nothing. Except for the bills, dinner parties and a little screwing" (Corman 1977, p. 45). Joanna's complaint was that only economics, sociability, and sex hold them together. What she feels but does not say is that they do not have a deep, rewarding psychic compatibility and this is a fundamentally important deficiency to her. For Joanna, their inability to experience common interests, feelings, and perceptions is deadening. This inability is more important to her than the other conditions, which might bind them, including the shared function of managing and caring for a household or the vows they once had made.

Selves that are stable, passive, and common can, presumably, coordinate and align easily with other selves. Selves which are in 'process' (actively defining themselves) and unique should find common action with others to be difficult or at least challenging. Whereas in an honor or dignity code persons are pressured to play specified roles, which fit together into a unitary social performance, in a dignity code moral energy is directed to the "relationship" more than to "society." A "relationship" in this code refers to the highest, the most valued, form of human connectedness; it refers to a negotiated and negotiable system of agreements or commitments between people. "Relationship" is reified in the dignity code such that one can speak of relationships rather than persons failing in the efforts of people to live well with others. This effectively diverts responsibility from "selves" to their "relationships" as the locus of blame for failures.

"Relationships" are a function of "different" "selves" making "commitments" to each other. A "commitment" is an active, intentional expression or a state of intention to pledge oneself to have a "relationship" with another. When the U.S. Constitution states "We, the people, in order to form a more perfect union," it speaks in a version of this code. The statement implies that an active agent deliberately creates a social union. Hervé Varenne uses this statement to reveal, in American speech, a manifestation of the American code. In some other cultures, he cites the cultures of France and India, "society" or union is taken for granted as something over and above individuals and not contingent for its existence upon the intentional acts of persons (Varenne 1977).

"Relationship" and "commitment" are directly talked about and thematized in KVK. A substantial part of Joanna's defense was that it was not she, but her "relationship" with Ted, that failed. When Ted's lawyer challenged this claim, contending that she had been, and still was, incapable of sustaining a "relationship," she wept and confessed that this was true. In the film, Ted nonverbally signaled his agreement with Joanna that it was the "relationship," and not her "self," to which blame should be attributed. Attribution for failure was directed outward to a social creation, to the "relationship," and not inward to the individual's character or to a "person's" actions. "Persons" are not evil, but they can have bad "relationships." If "persons" are evil, it is because they have not diligently "worked" on their "relationships," not because they are evil as "persons." It is important not to cast blame on the individual "self." Ted was praised for having such a good "relationship" with Billy. When Ted's neighbor and friend was asked why Ted should be allowed to keep Billy, she, in a tearful outburst, pointed to their (Ted's and Billy's) "relationship." Joanna's lawyer criticized Ted because he had difficulty in sustaining "relationship" with women.

A crucial issue in the story is whether Joanna can "commit" herself to Billy. There is little talk of "duty," except by Ted's and Joanna's parents. In this code, "commitment" to one's spouse or child is not to be taken for granted, not conceptualized as a given; rather, it is something that is contingent and precarious. Thematizing "commitment" as contingent opens the possibility that one might never achieve "commitment," that one's "commitment" might wane, and the corresponding importance to take preventive measures to ensure that one's "commitment" does not weaken. In another code of marriage and family, commitment is not thematized; it is taken for granted that if one is legally married or the legal guardian of a child, that one has an irrevocable and unquestioned duty or responsibility to the spouse or child. This responsibility derives, in large part, from the "society," the norms of which prescribe responsible conduct. Whereas in the KVK code, responsibility is contingent upon the act, and the continuing action, of a "person," in some other codes, "society" (convention, tradition, the ancestors, the group) prescribes responsibility or duty.

The conception of "persons" and their proper relations with each other, which this code thematizes and affirms, is one in which individual "selves" have the empirical possibility and the moral imperative to exercise their capacity for "choice," and if they do so they will "grow." It is "growth" that frees the individual "self" from its socially induced "incompetence" and frees it to develop its unique potential. Such a process of development enables the self to "commit" itself to interpersonal "relationships." These "commitments" are real, but always perilous, because of the continuing possibility that inherently "different" selves will "grow" in divergent directions. "Relationships" are perilous not only because they are contingent but also because if the parties "grow" they can diverge and the "relationship's" demands would constrict one or both of the "persons" in it.

"Communication" is a god-term in some American speech because it is the process by which one discovers one-"self," facilitates "growth," informs "choice," manifests "commitment," and "works" on "relationships." The absence of "communication," in a life or a "relationship," is, in this code, a sufficient condition for impairing "growth" and thus personal health. To impede communication is to threaten the highest good, "self," and the preferred form of sociation, the "relationship." "Communication" is the solution to the problem of "relationship" (love) and of "self" (personhood). In terms of overcoming personal "differences," "communication" functions as the "how of love," the primary vehicle and constituent of a "relationship;" in terms of constructing and validating a "self," "communication" is the "how of self."

"Communication" is thematized as a resource and a problem in KVK. When Ted told a friend that Joanna had left him, the friend explained the problem by saying "You should have communicated," to which Ted replied ruefully, "It's too late now" (Corman 1977, p. 63). Just as a "relationship" can fail because of a failure to "communicate," so too can a "relationship" or a "self" be reconstructed in and through "communication." Thus, Joanna's process of "self"-reconstruction was accomplished primarily through "communication" with a man she met in California. One night, as he later told the story to Ted, Joanna spent the entire night expressing her feelings. This same man came to New York with Joanna for her trial and he tried to intercede for her with Ted. When he and Ted met, he told Ted that "you two don't communicate," as warrant for Ted's lack of any right to hope to reclaim Joanna's affections.

Ted was guilty of refusing to enact what Katriel and I call the "communication ritual," an episodic sequence in which persons "sit down and talk," "work out problems," or "discuss the relationship." It functions as a ritual as it is the culturally preferred way to reaffirm the status of what the culture defines as a sacred object—the definition of "self" as experienced by any one of the participants, usually the one who initiates the sequence. For some people—Joanna—the absence of the ritual becomes the problem. This can be a tangled issue when partners disagree about their "commitments" to enact the ritual with each other.

Ted had refused to be *close*, *supportive*, and *flexible* with Joanna. He had not been *close* in that he had not disclosed his feelings to her and he had not listened freely to her self-expressions. He had not been *supportive* of her in that he had refused to treat her as a "person" rather than as a role and thus had not supported Joanna's "self." He had not been *flexible* or *open* with her in that he was unwilling to enter into a process of talk in which his definitions of reality, including his definition of his "self" and their "relationship," would be subject to emergent redefinition.

Ted's refusal to "communicate"—to engage in *close*, *supportive*, *flexible* speech with Joanna—had created problems for Joanna in her sense of "self." Ultimately, it was Ted's refusal to deal with *this* problem that was the catalytic condition for withdrawal and abandonment by Joanna. Put differently, in Katriel and Philipsen's terms, Ted had refused to enact the "communication" ritual with Joanna. To so refuse her thus created an even more insurmountable condition, one that Ted could never repair, but which could only be resolved by Joanna's acts of separation and abandonment. Her healing came, then, through separation, "communication" in exile—a kind of liminal state, and a triumphant return in which she forced public ratification of Ted's evil and of her right to take away Ted's child. Joanna's court victory was symbolic and not material: she did not keep the child, but her claim, that Ted had destroyed her self, was honored in her victory in court. Thus, from this perspective, there is an answer as to why Ted and Joanna could not reconcile and why the court's judgment as symbolic act, rather than the actual return of Billy to Joanna, completed the resolution process.

In this interpretation I have attempted to construct the underlying code of the myth of dignity. It is a code that has as its key terms "self," "choice," "growth," "difference," "relationship," "commitment," and "communication." The code stresses the primacy of the "self" over "society" in the human scheme of things, and posits that "choice" is necessary for "selves" to "grow," a condition necessary to combat the retarding forces of "society." Social union is always problematic, but can be achieved, even if always contingently, if "selves" make "commitments" to "relationships." These "commitments," like the "relationships" they constitute, are contingent, the product of human intention, and thus "communication" is a vital process by which "relationships" and the "selves" that make "commitments" are continually "worked on" and allowed to "grow." Anything, or anybody, thwarting these processes is evil and must, ultimately, be vanquished for good to prevail. It is in these terms, and with these motives, that Joanna Kramer's tale is told.

PART IV

Speech Codes

Chapter 6

SPEECH CODES IN TWO CULTURES

The British sociologist Basil Bernstein (Bernstein 1972) has formulated a subtle and powerful theoretical approach to ways of speaking. Based on his studies in contemporary England, he has raised the possibility that, within the same society, there can exist different social groups or social classes whose communicative practices differ in important ways. His way of putting this is that there are many possible types of communicative codes, ways of using language and other communicative means. The use of these ways is highly sensitive to the socioeconomic background and the situational context of speakers and hearers. In particular, he has applied his approach to the study of middle versus lower working-class groups in contemporary England, arguing that speakers in these groups make systematically different use of, and differently value, ways of speaking, even though they speak the same language.

For Bernstein, ways of speaking are expressed as coding principles and their realization. In his scheme, coding principle is a rule governing what to say and how to say it in a particular context; its realization consists of various concrete communicative practices. An *elaborated coding principle*, for example, directs the speaker (1) to use novel, complex, and diverse linguistic means to communicate individual intent; (2) to emphasize the communication of unique personal meanings; and (3) to adapt to the unique personal circumstances of listeners. A *restricted coding principle* directs its speakers to rely relatively less on verbal expression of intent to signal meanings, relying more heavily on (presumed) shared context; to emphasize the expression and continuing ratification of shared understanding among interlocutors, such as their gender or status.

Bernstein never claimed that there are only two coding principles or that any social group or class uses only one. He did claim, however, that specifiable socioeconomic conditions would influence the degree to which the members of a social group or community would differentially use and value such codes. And his empirical work contains evidence that speakers from the English middle class were more predisposed to use and appreciate elaborated coding, and those from the English lower working class were more predisposed to use and favor restricted coding, although neither was confined to only one in all circumstances.

Bernstein has been much misinterpreted and much maligned, particularly by those who read him as saying more than he intended to say, or did say, about class differences. It is not my purpose here to review or defend Bernstein's program. I have drawn attention to it here because it helps to introduce fundamental questions about the communication process: whether there are different speech codes, what they are, and how they influence spoken life.

The papers presented in chapters 2 through 5 of this book were inspired, in part, by Bernstein's thesis. Like Bernstein, I too set out to examine speech codes. But I proceeded differently. In the first place, I asked what codes might be found to be employed in particular speech communities. Bernstein had hypothesized that, under specified circumstances, certain speech behaviors would be more or less prominent than under other circumstances. Mine was a more exploratory approach then Bernstein's. I examined worlds of talk to learn what the codes of speaking there are. Second, I started from an ethnographic, rather than from a sociological, linguistic standpoint, as Bernstein has done. Mine was a search, in each of two worlds of discourse, for a system of concepts, premises, and rules pertaining to communication. Bernstein's emphasis was on abstract coding principles; mine was on speech codes for their own sake. I was concerned with particular, culturally situated conceptions, premises, and rules about communication.

The results of my inquiries are presented in chapters 2 through 5. Now, having presented these ethnographic reports, I shall comment on the speech codes expressed in them and on how these codes function in the constitution of personal and social meanings. These codes are systems of symbols and meanings, about the cultural domain 'communication'. They consist of resources for talking about and thematizing spoken life in particular contexts. One of the findings of these studies is that such systems are not only about communication, but are as well about what it means to be a person, how persons are and can be united in social relationships, and how communication can be and is used to link persons as social beings. Thus, they provide, for their users, a distinctive way of being, saying, and hearing.

The particular codes were presented in the ethnographic chapters. Here I step up the ladder of abstraction to formulate more general versions of the codes of which the Teamsterville and Nacirema codes are particular expressions. The codes I formulate in chapter 6 overgeneralize and oversimplify the more particular codes from which they have been abstracted. But what they lose in particularity they gain in generality. This permits me to formulate in general terms two contrasting codes of persons, society, and strategic action. This formulation provides a framework for interpreting spoken life in the communities I have studied—that is, it provides a resource for analysis and interpretation. Indeed, these more general codes have already been used in the interpretation of Mayor Daley's council speech and Joanna Kramer's identity crisis. Here the underlying formulation used in those interpretations is made more explicit. The Teamsterville and Nacirema cases are particular, ethnographically based instances of more general speech codes. I have labeled these general formulations the codes of honor and dignity. In what follows I explicate the bases of these codes, in general, and then show how the Teamsterville and Nacirema cases are particular instances of the more general types.

THE CODE OF HONOR

"Honor" refers to the worth attached to individuals by virtue of their attained social identity, as that identity is found to be valued in a particular community. It is concerned with the persona as built up out of heritage, residence, and valorous past conduct. Discourse spoken in a code of honor prejudices the talk—and the hearing of talk—in favor of treating individuals as social categories and in favor of treating society and social groups as organized hierarchies of social identities. Communication, in such a code, is considered the means by which socially different people coordinate their activities and cognitively similar people link themselves to each other.

The anthropologist Julian Pitt-Rivers formulates honor as "a nexus between the ideals of society and their reproduction in the individual" (1966, p.22). This suggests that what is considered honorable varies with the particular group. To be warlike in ancient Greece was valorous and thus honorable. To be pacific in a Quaker community is valorous and thus, there, it is honorable.

Although what is considered honorable can vary from community to community, there is a core to "honor" and the core concerns the person as a member of society. The usage of "honor", since the sixteenth century, has several senses, including reputation, the reward of virtue, obligation, and respect. These senses refer to the individual as a social being. Reputation is the estimation in which a person is held by a community. Reward of virtue suggests the person receives favors for conduct that conforms to the rules of a group. Obligations are tied to responsibilities one has to others. And respect refers to admiration or deference bestowed upon a person by others. From the Latin *respicere*, "looking back", it suggests the reading by others of a person's past conduct and the deference paid to the person based on the quality of that conduct. Each of these senses suggests an appreciation of the legitimacy and force of a particular community's ideals, history, and practices as they bear on and constitute the life of the individual.

The concept of honor is illustrated in Homer's epic poem the *Iliad*. The story centers around Achilles, a young warrior chief of the Achaeans, an ancient Greek tribe that was engaged in a fierce and protracted struggle with the Trojans. Agamemnon, who was king of the Achaean city Argos and who outranked Achilles, seized Briseis, the girl whom Achilles had taken as a prize in the defeat of a captured city, and whom he had come to love. Achilles, enraged at the abduction of his concubine, thereupon refused to return to battle. This was a refusal of great consequence for the Achaeans, because Achilles was their greatest warrior and they were caught in a war in which the presence or absence of a single great warrior could mean the difference between victory or defeat. The poem presents a series of scenes in which Achilles' compatriots, one after the other, appealed to him to return to battle. He stubbornly refused their appeals, as he did, eventually, Agamemnon's lavish offerings of reconciliation. Achilles returned to battle only after his dear friend Patroclus was killed by the Trojan Hector, whom Achilles successfully sought out to kill as revenge for his friend's death.

Insanity and irrationality have been invoked to explain the apparently excessive measure of Achilles' wrath and the apparently excessive stubbornness of his refusal to return to join in battle with his comrades. Paul Friedrich has advanced the alternative hypothesis, that although Achilles' words and deeds are "headstrong, verbal, and arrogant" (p. 281), they "seem normal in terms of . . . the presuppositions and enjoinings of Iliadic culture" (p. 303).

Honor is at the heart of the culture in whose terms Achilles' words and deeds can be understood as sane and predictable. The values of that particular culture can be organized into two clusters. The instrumental cluster includes power, wealth, magnanimity, loyalty, and precedence. Loyalty, the caring for one's friends and relatives, is a value that emphasizes one's interrelations with others, particularly with others with whom one has longterm blood ties. Precedence, the seeking of desirable fortune for one's kind, emphasizes ties to one's kin or fellows. Both values concern the relation of the individual to specific others, including others to whom one did not choose to be related. Another instrumental value is kudos, that which one wins in battles and similar contests. Achilles had taken Briseis as his property, his prize for victory in battle. She had become to him not only kin but a symbol of his name and his accomplishments. Agamemnon, supposedly a loyal comrade to Achilles, took not only Achilles' prize possession, but in taking Briseis he also took from him his very honor—and thereby he robbed him of his sense of personal well being, his integrity.

A second cluster of honor-linked values is expressive. This cluster includes a sense of shame, glory, courage, excellence, and piety. Piety refers to reverence for the gods. Here there is an emphasis on hierarchy, on the individual as lower than something or (someone) else. A sense of shame "signifies the inner feelings of a person in the presence of someone, an audience that matters" (p. 293). For Achilles there is a great sense of debasement because his injury is sustained upon the public stage of the warrior community. He was a man who was slighted in front of his fellows, a man who, occupying center stage in the life of the community, was, in effect, disrobed and humiliated upon that stage.

These comments about Iliadic culture help explain how "the violence and extremity of Achilles'' response is 'sane' precisely because what he is responding to touches the taproot of his integrity, and the code by which he has learned to live and die, and by which he does in fact live and die" (Friedrich, p. 295). They reveal something about an honor code, a code that makes salient such valorized concepts as wealth, loyalty, precedence, and a sense of shame. Achilles lived in a public world in which one's integrity, one's sense of well being, is intricately bound up with one's public identity.

There are three attributes of honor that are illustrated vividly in the case of Achilles. One is that honor is based not merely on individual accomplishments or attributes but on the complex refraction of these through the lens of society. A second is that honor is a possession of the individual and a person can have more or less, can accumulate or spend, can gain or lose, his or her store of it. A third is that, for the individual who subscribes to an honor code, gains or losses of honor have fundamental consequences for the individual's sense of personal integrity.

In his classic study of American society, Alexis de Tocqueville makes a distinction that reveals another attribute of honor. He differentiates "simple notions of right and wrong which are diffused all over the world" (p. 242) from a "peculiar rule founded upon a peculiar state of society"

(p. 243). To illustrate the distinction, he wrote: "It is the general and permanent interest of mankind that men should not kill each other; but it may happen to be the peculiar and temporary interest of a people or a class to justify, or even to honor, homicide" (p. 243).

A literary illustration of de Tocqueville's point is found in the discourse surrounding the actions of the conspirators in William Shakespeare's *Julius Caesar*. The conspirators, "all honorable men" in the speech against them, killed the emperor Caesar because, they said, he had become too ambitious for the general good of Rome and the only way to curb his power was to murder him. For Brutus, who loved Caesar, as did many others of the conspirators, this was a soul-wrenching act, one committed only after much casuistry, along the following lines:

1. Caesar had been a good and noble Roman.
2. Caesar had been a friend to Brutus, and to the other conspirators.
3. Killing is wrong.
4. But the well-being of Rome required Caesar's death.

Killing, an evil act ordinarily, was the honorable act, in Brutus's mind, because it served the interests of the state. It was, as the conspirators rationalized it, the honorable—although painful and distasteful—thing to do. At least for Brutus, here the honorable action was counterpoised to the personally pleasing or generally ethical thing to do (Welsh, 1975).

What is emphasized here is the fundamentally conservative idea that other virtues can properly be relegated to the preservation of a particular society. The polis, the political community, is taken to be a desirable end because it is the existence of (a particular) society from which all other goods flow. As bad as killing might be, for Brutus and his fellows a murder was justified if it helped to preserve the stability of the republic. This illustrates a fourth attribute of honor, that it reflects an appreciation of the republican virtue of being a person whose conduct sustains the existence of the community.

These attributes of honor are further illustrated in the modern novel *The Virginian* by Owen Wister. The hero of this novel, throughout referred to not by name but as "the Virginian," is a cattleman who has come to the Wyoming territory before the turn of the century. He is shown there as a man of rhetorical sophistication, one whose power with words is as pronounced as his physical prowess.

There are several episodes that reveal this to be a book in which honor has a special importance. The Virginian's early skirmishes with the outlaw Trampas are among the most celebrated in American literature, including the scene that produced the line, "When you call me that, smile . . .", showing the Virginian to be a man of reputation whose person must be treated with respect. His close friend could call him "a son of a ———," but the stranger Trampas, when he addressed him with that appellation, was answered by the Virginian's now famous warning. It is, too, a novel that affirms mythically the salience and truth of fundamental differences among men, and between men and women. Among men differences of genetics and breeding translate into differences in character. Between the Virginian and Molly Stark Wood, the schoolteacher whom he courts, there are displayed differences in temperament and talent, which he attributes to their difference in gender. These differences, far from being the object of scorn, are thematized and celebrated in the novel.

Nowhere in *The Virginian* is the idea of honor more poignantly exploited than in the final confrontation between the hero and Trampas. Trampas had, over several years, repeatedly tried to best the Virginian, who had patiently but firmly kept his disreputable antagonist at arm's length. But on the eve of the Virginian's wedding, Trampas spread a rumor throughout town that the Virginian was a cattle thief. In a drunken stupor, Trampas twice challenged the Virginian to a duel, which the Virginian refused; but upon the third issue his resolve to join the duel was sealed.

The Virginian's decision is a complex one. It shows the principle of honor operating importantly. This is first foreshadowed in Wister's description of the Virginian's reaction to hearing, in the company of some twenty of his friends, about Trampas's slanderous claims: "Perplexity knotted in the Virginian's brow. This community knew that a man had implied he was a thief and a murderer; it also knew he knew it" (p. 400). Having resolved to fight Trampas, the Virginian faced a trail even greater than the gunfight that was to ensue later. This greater trail was the confrontation between himself and his fiancée. Molly, who personifies the pacific, domesticated Easterner, urged the Virginian not to fight. As with Achilles, the Virginian's friends had appealed to him, to avoid the gunfight with Trampas, but Molly's appeals were more vehement, coupled with a threat to break their wedding plan if he should go through with the duel.

The Virginian's decision to fight, resisting Molly's appeals, is based on honor. There are two dimensions to it. One is the hero's sense of self-esteem grounded in his perceptions of his fellows' perceptions of him. He said to Molly, "What men say about my nature is not just merely an outside thing. For the fact that I let 'em keep on sayin' it is a proof I don't value my nature enough to shield it from their slander and give them their punishment. And that's being a poor sort of jay" (p. 410). Like Achilles, the Virginian felt the slight as something that disturbed his very sense of integrity. For the Virginian, the accusations, made in public, pierced the membrane of his persona, intruding into his very self.

The second dimension, closely linked to the first, but distinguishable analytically, is the Virginian's sense of living his life on a particular scene. His initial justification to Molly, of his decision to fight, was expressed in a statement given additional significance by its brevity and its elliptical content: "I work hyeh. I belong hyeh. It's my life. If folks came to think I was a coward—" (p. 409). What Trampas had said about the Virginian, and who had heard it, and in this particular place, the Virginian's town—all of these combined to make his response to Trampas a matter crucial to the maintenance of his very integrity, his sense of wholeness as a person.

The Iliad and *The Virginian*, far removed from each other in space and time, each tell the story of a hero whose words and deeds can properly be understood as governed by a code of honor. From the standpoint of Achilles and the Virginian, other men's words about them and actions toward them were interpreted, were constituted, as one kind of meaning or another, through the application of a coding principle. Agamemnon's seizure of Briseis is a deed that for Achilles, counted as the very piercing of his soul. The loss of Briseis, and the fact that another man could take something dear from him, were facts whose significance to Achilles can only be understood by understanding that Achilles' sense of integrity was intricately bound up with his standing as a man who owned, and was identified with, Briseis, and as a man whose reputation should have protected him from the virtual assault on self that Agamemnon's seizure of Briseis constituted for him. From the Virginian's standpoint for Trampas to say the words he did, in the company in which he said them, in the town in which they were said, was to act in such a way that, for the Virginian, could only be interpreted as fundamentally consequential for himself. Given the Virginian's code of honor, Trampas's utterances constituted acts whose force could not be ignored if the Virginian were to continue to try to enact his role in the very scene in which his sense of self, his personal integrity, was constituted. Just as a code of honor constituted for Achilles and the Virginian what their antagonists' deeds would count as, so too such a code specified, in these instances, what words and deeds Achilles and the Virginian must perform in order to restore their sense of integrity.

These examples show particular variants of the more general idea of a code of honor. That more general idea consists of the following. First, in an honor code, the individual is conceived as a role or character, a persona. Who an individual is is defined not by unique feelings, needs, and attitudes, but by social attributes—whatever social attributes are relevant and salient in the person's particular community.

The essence of a person is constructed out of such social features as gender, lineage, achievements, and age. What characteristics and achievements are judged honorable varies across communities. The honor a person possesses is calculated by reference to some particular standard, the standard of the Achaeans, for example. Honor is not something that proceeds from the individual's interior to stamp itself upon the public; rather it is the product of social judgments that penetrate the skin and constitute the person.

Second, society, in such a code, is existentially and morally prior to the individual. Society existed before the individual. Life is a preset stage and persons are merely players who make a brief appearance in a drama that preceded, and will go after, them. The person makes a brief appearance in a never-ending drama. And that drama is more important than any single character who struts about the stage for a particular moment. The scene's the thing; men and women are only players.

Third, communication in such a scene functions to coordinate interpersonal activity, to allocate individuals to their places in the scheme of things, and to reinforce the social order as hierarchically organized. Given that the fundamentally important attributes of individuals is not their uniqueness, communication is relatively unimportant as a vehicle for signaling intentions or idiosyncratic messages. As strategic action, communication takes the form of petition, whereby the less powerful appeal to the more powerful. It can also take the form of direct action, particularly physical action.

The code of honor, as delineated here, is closely related to the rhetorician Richard Weaver's conception of a conservative rhetoric. His idea was to formulate the bases for thinking up and formulating arguments designed to move hearers to right belief and action. It consists of three key premises. The first is the premise of *hierarchy*, that some things are better than others. The second is *memory*, that the way to judge what is best is to interpret the lessons of history to discover what has been effectively put in place and what has produced right conduct in the past. The third is *status*, the idea that each person has a proper place in the world and that the most satisfying condition for an individual is to find the place that history assigns one and to live one's life in it. Persuasive communication, in such a rhetorical system, consists of making appeals, grounded in historical precedent, designed to persuade people to realize their highest potential given their proper station in life. A code of honor, with its emphasis on social identity, place, and precedent, is congruent with such a conservative rhetoric.

A Code of Honor and Teamsterville Spoken Life

An auditor of Teamsterville speech cannot help but feel instructed in the vocabulary of honor: "around here," "neighborhood," "the Spirits of 32nd," "the 32nd Girls," "my corner," "he's not really from around here," "street," "Italians," "Polaks," "Mexicans," "connections," and "City Hall" are among the pervasively occurring items in Teamsterville parlance. Talk in Teamsterville is filled with references to place, with references to social identity. Place of residence, gender, and ethnicity are focal concerns in any Teamsterville conversation. These are attributes by which people are defined and placed. The individual in such a world is a persona, a social identity composed of a bundle of roles. Whether one's conduct is judged fitting is properly determined by a consideration of whether that conduct is an appropriate enactment of those roles.

Achilles' own sense of personal integrity was inextricably bound up with the reputation and well-being of the women related to him. In this sense, Briseis became more to him than a material possession, as Achilles came to love her and came to consider her his kin. His honor, in part constituted by his relation to Briseis, was thus enhanced by his possession of her and damaged by her abduction. So too, for a Teamsterville man, his reputation, and thus his sense of well-being, is constituted by the public perception of females linked to him by blood or marriage. Analyzing the particular cultural code used in Teamsterville, the status of a woman linked to a man is directly linked to his own status. If she is sexually permissive, talks too much, or lacks in personal appearance, any of these directly reflects on the man and thus, in turn, directly affects his honor.

I have already shown how various verbal attacks on female relatives create a situation in which the Teamsterville male feels he must act aggressively in defense of the female (or, more precisely, in defense of his ostensible ability to protect or control her). Here I would like to apply this particular aspect of the Teamsterville honor code to another Teamsterville communicative practice. On several occasions I drove groups of Teamsterville boys and girls on long outings. The personae in these trips consisted of myself as driver and three or four adolescent girls and three or four adolescent boys. The girls and boys knew each other well, as might be expected. Indeed, they were, for the most part, lifelong friends who had always lived within a few blocks of each other and who, at that time, were central figures in each others' lives.

During these trips there was a continually repeated series of insults and taunts the boys directed at the girls, the substance of which centered on the likelihood or actuality of various states of uncleanness among the girls. For example, there were repeated taunts about the possibility of maggots on various parts on the girls's bodies, particularly orifices and underarms.

Although I had extensive experience in working with gender-mixed adolescent groups of a similar economic level, in several cities, I had never before, nor have I since, heard teasing that, to my ears, was so persistent and so offensive. And although I cannot approve the conduct, I can report that, apparently, it was not considered outside the pale of decency among members of the particular groups.

Thinking back, it is instructive to consider this pattern of interaction from the standpoint of a code of honor. I say "pattern of interaction" because it was repeated conduct and because it involved not just the boys' teasing acts but also the girls' acts of defense and counter-challenge. One interpretation of the patten is that it reflects a focal concern of Teamsterville life, specifically the concern that a woman associated with a man have a reputation for virtuous conduct. The protection from permissive contact with the parts of a woman's body associated with her sexuality was crucial to her reputation and, by extension, to her man's honor. Of course, a girl was not likely ever to have flies or maggots covering her mouth. But through teasing her about that possibility, the Teamsterville boy taunted and warned the Teamsterville girl about the importance, to him, of her state of purity and through his taunts he expressed which parts of her body it was important to keep "clean."

The girl whom a boy teased was, in his eyes, a friend and potential romantic partner or mate. It was important to the boy for such a person to have a virtuous reputation. If she were not virtuous, and linked to him, his honor would be diminished. Likewise, if she were too talkative, she could create a scene in which he felt obligated to defend her honor. For the boy, whose integrity was intricately bound up in the reputation of women-associated ideals, it was important to him to communicate to her what he perceived those ideals to be and, perhaps more important, to communicate to her how important the ideals are to him.

Another illustration of the honor code in Teamsterville concerns the community standard for appropriate speech style. Chapter 2 includes examples of individuals who took care to see that their pronunciation and spoken grammar did not deviate too much from the Teamsterville standard, a standard that Teamstervillers themselves believed to be inferior to the style they heard used by people from some other parts of the city or on television. This general pattern is illustrated further in the lives of several Teamsterville young people I interviewed. These were young people who had grown up in Teamsterville and who had left the neighborhood to study at a prestigious private university. One, a woman who had gone on to graduate school, expressed her concern that she not sound too well educated when in the neighborhood because her interlocutors there would judge her to be an undesirable person who tries to appear better than others. It was she who told me about the metaphor of the crawfish barrel, in which everyone tries to crawl out but devotes more effort to preventing others from crawling out. This applies not only to conspicuous consumption but to conspicuous refinement in speech as well. A second example is a young man who felt that, when on the campus of his prestigious university, every time he spoke he sounded like a stupid person. He said that, in the campus setting, he sounded stupid and uneducated to himself and he believed others heard him likewise. On campus, he struggled to mask his speech style or to avoid speaking. In "the neighborhood," however, it was a 'badge of honor' (my phrase) to sound like "everyone" from "around here."

These examples illustrate sharply the idea of honor. There is a standard of value, which an individual can reach in greater or lesser degrees. That standard of value has a social locus and pertains to public conduct. And the individual derives a sense of who he is by virtue of refracting his own conduct through a social lens; his inner sense of self-definition and sense of well-being are determined by this refraction. The social not only prevails over but, at least in part, also constitutes, the personal.

This process of social refraction applies not only to the individual's achievements or acts, as with speech style, but also to features of his persona over which he has no control, such as the acknowledged virtue of his female relatives. He does not choose all his female relatives or where he was born or what his nationality is. The same applies to the woman, who does not choose, for example, her father and brothers, and thus does not control completely the honor she achieves through ascription. But who a man is, or who a woman is, is determined in part not only by what he or she does but by who he or she is, by birth as well as by behavior.

Mayor Daley's council speech, the act as well as the text, is an instance par excellence of a cultural expression grounded in a code of honor. Throughout the speech Daley refers to "this society" as an organism made up of different sorts of people, each of whom plays his or her well-defined part. Some men lead, others follow; men lead, women nurture; women raise boys to become men who will take their rightful place in society; those persons who try to be something for which their birth or attainments do not fit them violate the hierarchical order of society;

speech is used to reinforce this order and to help fundamentally different persons act together, when they must, but not to bring them closer together as individuals.

Several elements of the code of honor are displayed in the speech. Society is reified as a powerful and hallowed entity ("this society"). "Society" is thematized as an organism made up of many interdependent parts. These various parts are arrayed in a hierarchy of importance, but the implication is that even though some are higher than others, all are important in their way. Distinctions made on the basis of age, gender, and nationality are fundamentally legitimate and useful (these are matters of ascription); distinctions made on the basis of differential achievements—the relatively scant accomplishments of Alderman Simpson contrasted to the greater accomplishments of Mayor Daley for "this society"—are emphasized. As event, the speech functions to reinforce the existing social order through expressions along the expressive dimension of honor.

A general conception of a code of honor has been outlined and examples drawn from classic literature presented. This provided a background against which to set Teamsterville communicative practices. Although the culture of the Teamstervillers is not exactly that of the Achaeans and the culture of the Virginian is not exactly that of Achilles or of Richard Daley, certain broad themes have been extracted from these cultures and developed here to construct and illustrate an ideal type of a speech code. Such a code, in general, thematizes the individual, society, and communicative action as a resource for linking individuals socially. The code of honor, in particular, addresses the individual as a persona playing a role against the backdrop of history and community, with communication functioning to link such individuals in hierarchical relations such that social knowledge can be brought to bear in guiding individuals to play out the roles which their history fits them for and to which their achievements entitle them. The use of such a code, it has been shown, regulates the messages by which persons link themselves into social relations and constitutes the meaning by which persons construct the realities of their lives.

THE CODE OF DIGNITY

Dignity refers to the worth attached to individuals by virtue of their being a person. It is concerned with the person qua person, as someone who is made up of unique feelings, ideas, and attitudes. Discourse spoken in a code of dignity prejudices the talk—and the hearing of talk—in favor of treating individuals in terms of their "intrinsic humanity divested of all socially imposed roles or norms. It pertains to the self as such, to the individual regardless of his position in society" (Berger, Berger, and Kellner, p. 89). A concern with dignity does not merely deemphasize a person's social roles but also positively emphasizes the uniqueness and legitimacy of each person's cognitive and affective world. This uniqueness makes communication important as a resource for elaborating individual intent, taking the role of the unique other so as to understand her or him, and of forging negotiated understandings and agreements between persons who are fundamentally different from each other cognitively and affectively. The capacity of communication to signify and reinforce social differences is deemphasized, even deplored, in the code of dignity.

The *Oxford English Dictionary* lists several senses of "dignity," including "the quality of being worthy or honourable," "honourable or high estate," and "nobility or befitting elevation of aspect, manner, and style." These senses share with "honor" an emphasis on the worthiness of a person deriving from qualities of the person. The last sense, with its reference to manner of conduct, suggests a difference between dignity and honor. To the English-hearing ear a "dignified demeanor" is a happy expression but an "honorable demeanor" is not. Likewise, one can pledge "on my honor," to carry out a task, but not "on my dignity," although one can pledge to carry out a task in a dignified manner. "Dignity" suggests respect deriving from the individual's manner of action, rather than from achievements and precedence.

Some uses of "dignity" quoted in the *Oxford English Dictionary* suggest further that it has to do with an inner quality of a person, as that quality is manifested in outward demeanor. The *Oxford English Dictionary* quotes these lines from Wordsworth's "Yew-Tree Seat":

> True dignity abides with him alone
> Who, in the silent hour of inward thought,
> Can still suspect, and still revere himself,
> In lowliness of heart.

And it quotes Sir H. Taylor in *Statesman* (xv, 107): "It is of the essence of real dignity to be self-sustained, and no man's dignity can be asserted without being impaired." The first of these quotations implicates the idea that dignity is an inner quality, the second that it is an inner quality that influences the manner of outer conduct. In this regard dignity is the reverse of honor—in dignity the inner quality determines the performance, in honor the social judgment of performance determines the person's inner experience of self.

A person can act, but can also be treated, with dignity. This is the giving of respect to the person. To what aspect of the person is this respect being paid when that person is treated with dignity? To honor a person is to pay respect to that person's accomplishments and social identity. Dignified treatment pays respect to the person's inner quality. One is entitled to respect precisely because one is a person. Although persons vary in their inner qualities, in the dignity code they are valued because of the fact that they consist of an inner core of dispositions, attitudes, and feelings that properly, in this code, constitute the essence of the person. Some theologies enshrine the person with dignity, for example, as a "child of God," but the secular version is equally pointed, in its emphasis on the irreducible value of the individual person.

The ideal of dignity informs the use of, and attitude toward, names and personal address, and these provide useful illustrations of the concept. A surname links a person to a family history and to particular parents, and thus can in part constitute one's persona. A given name can be given by parents and it, as well as a surname, can be associated with a person throughout a life. A name, thus, places a person and is part of his or her social identity. Also, whether a name is used to address or refer to a person, or whether a title is used, are governed by and express the speaker's estimate of the social identity of the person named or addressed. All languages include linguistic resources by which such social placement is accomplished, by which social status or position is signaled. An exemplary resource is address by *Title + Last Name* ("Mr. Jones") versus the use of *First Name* ("John"); the former is called an "honorific".

Given the tie of honorifics to an idiom of honor, one might expect that in a code of dignity the socially expressive use of names and distinctions in address would be objects of scorn. That this is true is recorded in many historical instances of change in social norms regarding personal address. In the European languages in which there are two forms of the singular "you" as a term of address, such as the French *tu* and *vous*, one form (generically labeled the *T* form) is characteristically associated with situations of informality and intimacy; the other form (generically labeled the *V* form) is associated with formality and is a signal of social distance or respect. Social difference is most sharply expressed by an asymmetrical pattern of address, in which one person says *T* to the other and the other returns *V*. For such languages as French, German, Italian, Russian, Swedish, and Norwegian there is evidence that, over the past two centuries, there have been dramatic changes in the use and acceptance of the *V* form and of the asymmetrical pattern. To varying degrees, and in varying circumstances, the societies in which these languages are prominent have shown a dramatic turning away from the *V* form and the asymmetrical pattern, a turning away that has explicitly been linked to the rise of social ideologies asserting the dignity of all persons. These ideologies emphasize that all persons should be treated as equals and therefore that some persons should not give the informal (and less deferential) *T* form to others who are expected to return the more deferential *V* form. For example, one visible and audible aspect of the French revolution of 1789, in which the ideal of political equality was asserted, was the move to discard the use of *vous* (the "you" of social difference) with universal *tu* (the "you" of equality).

A related illustration is drawn from the movement to change conventional ways of naming. Hamblen presents a complex and sophisticated argument to show that in Western society The Married Woman's Name—"Mrs. Donald Spencer"—expresses a wife's subservience to her husband, whose name she uses. Hamblen's essay on The Married Woman's Name concludes with a statement that "the customary married woman's name has become a shabby linguistic symbol which needs to be discarded to free individuals and society from any left-over power which it may have" (p. 255).

Hamblen's argument and the wisdom of her conclusion are not the issue here. Rather I am concerned to read her statement as a text written in the terms of the dignity code, and thus to use her text as an illustrative resource. To this end I will not examine her argument itself but will examine the value terms—symbolic expressions of good and bad ends—that she employs in advancing her argument.

Her call for discarding The Married Woman's Name is based on the claim that the practice expresses, promotes, and reinforces three undesirable aspects of marital relations in contemporary Western society. Her quarrel is with the externally (historically and socially) imposed (1) status differences, (2) division of labor, (3) and differences in power, obtaining between husbands and wives, which are implicated in the married woman's name. Each of these aspects concerns social difference. The wife is lower in rank and prestige than the man is, and this is symbolized by the fact that she takes his name. The division of labor is arbitrarily determined, with the husband assumed to be the giver of life and the wife assumed to be but the vessel through which his progeny are transmitted, thus the children take her husband's name. And the man is the more dominant or powerful member of the pair, and thus his name is extended to her, not the reverse.

In her exposition of the argument, Hamblen uses many evaluative terms, phrases, and expressions that reveal her use of a code of dignity. Some of these are used as devil terms, including "societal role," "social stratification," "rigid categories," "old criteria—age, sex, family membership." Use of The Married Woman's Name expresses and reinforces these ends and Hamblen treats these ends as self-evidently undesirable.

These are, of course, some of the very terms of an honor code; they are terms of role, hierarchy, and social categories. They are undesirable to Hamblen, apparently, because they are opposed to several god terms or expressions of desirable states in a dignity code; these include: "an identity nurtured from within rather than imposed from without," "individual talent and initiative," "autonomous," "choose to live together," "independent identity," and "unique personal history and set of goals for the future." These include such key terms of an honor code as individual, choice, autonomy, and uniqueness.

Hamblen's critique of The Married Woman's Name convention takes direct aim at the scenario or life script implied in and reinforced by the naming practice. This scenario constitutes, of course, a powerful source of identity for both men and women. It provides a clear answer to the questions of what ends one should aspire to reach and what steps to take to reach those ends. That answer derives from a reading of the past, in general, as the source of the basic lines of the scenario. It derives as well from the particular biographies of the parties, in that, for example, the woman takes on a particular new identity when she stops using her birth surname and takes the man's surname for her own—she sheds an old identity with a particular meaning in her social world and she takes on another identity with its own meaning in that world.

It is precisely such scenarios that a code of dignity opposes. In such a code the individual's identity is not properly constituted by the unique and precious inner qualities that she or he possesses. This is, as Hamblen wrote, an identity "nurtured from within" rather than imposed from without. And the person links to other persons as one who autonomously chooses to do so in arrangements arrived at not through precedent but by negotiation.

In this chapter I have treated the code of honor as a speech code by showing how it thematizes the person, society, and strategic action. A parallel formulation can now be presented for the code of dignity. First, in the code of dignity, the person is quintessentially a unique self rather than a bundle of social roles. The person is who he is by virtue of his inner qualities. It is a violation of nature, as well as of morality, to try to suppress the development and expression of those unique inner qualities because it is these qualities, and their expression, that in large part constitute the individual as a person. For example, for a woman to take her husband's name as her own imposes on her unique self an externally defined role. This is an evil thing, in this code, because it impedes the development and expression of the woman's essential identity, the identity built up from her unique personal potentialities and goals.

Second, the individual person is existentially and morally prior to society. Society is built up from individual acts—"you are the community," as one advice-giver wrote, using the vocabulary of dignity. And society is less valuable than the individual. As the economist Milton Friedman pointed out in the introduction to his classic book, *Capitalism and Freedom*; when John F. Kennedy said, in his inaugural address, "Ask not what your country can do for you; ask what you can do for your country," he implicated a fundamentally un-American premise, that is the purpose of the individual is to serve the state, and not the other way around. It is, of course, a statement whose terms are properly provided by a code of honor, not by a code of dignity. In a code of dignity, the drama is less important than each individual player; the scene exists as a setting for individual performances.

Third, communication in such a scene functions to express, and interactively ratify, individual self-images and expressions. As strategic action, communication takes the form of dialogue, a form in which unique, independent selves negotiate shared realities.

The code of dignity, as delineated here, is closely related to the rhetorician Richard Weaver's conception of a modern rhetoric (Weaver 1964). It consists of three key premises, which can be counterposed to those he formulated for a traditional rhetoric. The first is the premise of equality (as opposed to hierarchy), that all things (for example, unique individuals' inner qualities and potentialities) are of equal value. The second is presentism (as opposed to memory)—that is, that when choices among alternatives must be made, the deliberations should be made on the basis of what is wanted now, and what appears likely to work in the here and now. The past is not consulted as an important source of wisdom to guide human action, and precedence is not given conventional ways of ordering human activity. The third is process (as opposed to status), the idea that each person's proper activity in life is continually to search for and continually to reconstitute one's identity, continually making and remaking one's person. Persuasive communication, in such a code, consists of making appeals grounded in situational expediency regarding immediate wants and desires, as these are assessed through a process of open communication (dialogic negotiation). A code of dignity, with its emphasis on the unique attitudes and aspirations of individuals, is congruent with such a modern rhetoric.

Weaver's three premises are clearly illustrated in the discourse about the married woman's name as a symbol expressing and reinforcing an undesirable social arrangement. Reasoning from the premise of equality, one would argue against the husband or wife being more powerful than the other, and one would argue against an arbitrary imposition of a division of labor. Reasoning from the premise of presentism, one would argue against using tradition as a guide for defining marital arrangements. And reasoning from the premise of process, one would argue in favor of social arrangements that maximize individual opportunities for persons to change their identities during the course of their lifetime and, by implication, to change the character of their relationships with others.

A Code of Dignity and Nacirema Communication

An auditor of Nacirema speech about "communication" cannot help but feel instructed in the vocabulary of dignity. The individual, the self, communication, relationship, growth, and choice are among its god terms.

The cases of M and K are illustrative. Each complained about her "relationship" with another important person in her life. M's complaint was that her husband would not "communicate" with her—that is, would not engage in close, supportive, flexible speech with her—and that this void in her life prevented her from realizing her full potential as a partner in the marriage. K's concern was that her father would not engage in "open communication" with her, that he would not reveal his innermost feelings to her, and would not enter into dialogue in which his own identity was open to negotiation through a process of communication. K viewed her father's reluctance to engage in such talk as limiting not only his own "growth" as a person, but as limiting her own capacity for developing herself through her relationship with him.

The use of "relationship" in this code reveals much about dignity as it is conceptualized here. The code treats interpersonal "relationships" as organic and potent. A "relationship" can grow, thrive, survive, and die—it is organic. And it can cause a husband and wife to fail in their marriage or cause a parent's life with a child to be unsuccessful. Both M, as discussed in chapter 4, and Joanna Kramer, as discussed in chapter 5, attributed the failure of their marriages to their "relationship"; it was, they claimed, not the individuals, but the "relationship," that failed.

The reification and personification of "relationship" in a dignity code does important cultural (interpretive) work for its users. First, it provides a resource for explaining an important phenomenon, the failure of a marriage. And it does this without any necessary recourse to positing a defect in the inner qualities of person. Thus, all parties can, in their discourse, be "supportive" of the selves of persons who are partners in a marriage that has failed—the selves are "ok," to use the Nacirema vernacular, even if the "relationship" was not.

If the individuals failed at all, it was a failure to "communicate." The failed marriage is attributed to a defective "relationship," which is defective because of insufficient "work" done through "communication." In this parlance, there are not bad husbands, bad wives, bad parents, or bad children, there are bad "relationships."

Here an important difference between the codes of honor and dignity is manifested. In the former, there are established, transpersonal, and transsituational rules governing how to perform the role of spouse or parent. One can be a bad parent or bad spouse by violating those rules. In the dignity code, these social rules are less important; they are replaced by the injunction: use "communication" (close, supportive, flexible speech) to "negotiate" the "relationship." The negotiation of relationship requires the give and take of both parties to create a set of relationship-specific rules that enable two ("unique") persons to act together or be with each other in some creative (created) way. The moral failure, in this code, is to fail to do the "communication."

When they are defined by a historical precedent with contemporary motive force, roles, such as husband, wife, or father, provide for their performers a script for enacting the role. They delineate what to do and how to do it, and these injunctions provide as well a basis for evaluating performances. One complaint about Nacirema life is that such scripts are not as readily available to Nacirema code users as they have been in other times and places. De Tocqueville hints at this when he writes, "Among a democratic people poetry will not be fed with legends or the memorials of old traditions. The poet will not attempt to people the universe with supernatural beings, in whom his readers and his own fancy have ceased to believe, nor will he coldly personify virtues and vices, which are better received under their own features. All these resources fail him; but Man remains, and the poet needs him no more" (pp. 80–81).

Although there is more than a grain of truth to de Tocqueville's statement, this does not mean the Nacirema is a person without myth. The formulation I have given of the dignity code suggests that it can provide its users with considerable dramaturgical and mythic resources to use in guiding and interpreting their life performances. Joanna Kramer's story (chapter 5) is a case in point. During the year that we elicited M's story (chapter 4), of a marriage that failed because of a lack of "communication," Joanna Kramer's story, in the film *Kramer Versus Kramer*, was being told more frequently, and with greater emotional impact, than for any other story being told in M's society. Joanna Kramer is not a supernatural or superhuman figure. But she faces a situation that, in the code of dignity, is fundamentally problematic. And she responded to that situation in a culturally plausible way, employing a prized resource, "communication," as the means for facilitating her "growth" as a "person."

CONCLUSION

The codes of honor and dignity are general formulations of the nature of persons, society, and strategic action, which were derived from a consideration of well-known concepts of society, established meanings of these concepts in everyday speech and in academic jargon, and historical and literary examples. Teamsterville spoken life exemplifies a way of speaking expressed in a code of honor and Nacirema spoken life exemplifies a way of speaking expressed in a code of dignity.

Whether the two types of speech code presented here, codes of honor and dignity, can be shown to have a more general application than given here—that is, that other culturally distinctive codes can be subsumed under one of these two types—is beyond the scope of this presentation. The localized codes have been juxtaposed to and subsumed under the more general formulations here in order to interpret further the ethnographic cases of speaking examined in this book. In particular, the interpretation has helped to show more sharply how speaking, and the speaking people make about speaking, reveals cultural codes about the activity to which they refer and how these are codes of persons, society, and strategic action. Such a showing as has been provided here helps to set up the remarks presented in the concluding chapter, which follows.

Chapter 7

SPEAKING CULTURALLY

In introducing chapter 1, I declared that I had set out to describe Teamsterville and Nacirema cultures in order to learn something about speaking as a radically cultural medium of communicative activity. This intention belied two interrelated beliefs, (1) that there is something about speaking that is important to lives and societies, and that (2) whatever that importance is, it has something to do with culture. The studies that followed chapter 1—the ethnographic reports in chapters 2 through 5 and the comparative analysis in chapter 6—have presented empirical findings and interpretations from which I now draw general conclusions about the uses that people make of a medium and about the significance that medium has for them.

Several years ago Peter Farb wrote a book entitled *Word Play: What Happens When People Talk* (Farb 1972). When people talk, Farb proposed, they play a kind of game, whereby they pursue ends by making a series of moves, all the while following the rules of the game. In this book I have presented two cases, which suggest, indeed which support empirically, the claim that the game of talking is fundamentally—radically—cultural. That claim can be expressed as the following thesis: *The rules of the speaking game, the object of playing it, and its meanings to its players, all of these are contingent upon the culture(s) the interlocutors use to play it with in particular times and places.* Chapter 7 is devoted to the development of that thesis.

The thesis as formulated suggests that conceptualizations of speaking as culture-free should be replaced by conceptualizations of speaking as culture-rich. Culture-free conceptualizations include all those treatments of speaking that do not pay explicit attention to the fact that the ends and means of speaking are culturally contingent. A culture-rich conceptualization would provide for the possibility that what speaking is, how it is organized, and what values it has to interlocutors, are matters of local definition. In the remainder of this chapter I develop four principles that are consistent with, and that in part constitute, a way of thinking about speaking as culture-rich. These principles, grounded in the studies presented in this book, are articulated here to suggest some of the ways that speaking is, fundamentally, speaking culturally.

The central focus of the discussion to follow is the concept of speech code. Each of the four principles is stated as a generalization about speech codes—that is, about historically transmitted, socially constructed systems of symbols and meanings, premises and rules, pertaining to communicative conduct. The concept of speech code was selected as the central focus of the discussion because in each of the data-based chapters—that is, in chapters 2 through 5, the exposition ranged over a wide variety of human experiences and meanings, but in each case a common element could be found—that all of these particular findings and interpretations could be shown to implicate a code, some system of meanings about communicative conduct. Furthermore, in chapter 6 the concept of speech code provided the organizing basis for comparing, contrasting, and characterizing the diverse and distinctive meanings and experiences that provided the basis for the empirical chapters. Thus, in this final section of the book, and in this final chapter, I state the conclusions of this project in terms of its emergent central concept.

THE CULTURAL DISTINCTIVENESS OF SPEAKING

The preceding chapters have presented studies drawn from two cultures, the culture of Teamsterville and a mainstream American culture, here called Nacirema culture. In Teamsterville and Nacirema cultures, it has been shown, speaking is thematized, but thematized distinctively. In these two systems, speaking is assigned different purposes, valued differently, linked to distinctive cultural themes, and conceptualized by a different metacommunicative vocabulary.

This point can be expressed no less sharply because Teamsterville and Nacirema speech codes are each expressed in the same language, English. Each of these codes draws from the same language a distinctive set of terms and notions. And each makes of the same terms something distinctive. "Communication," a quintessentially Nacirema *symbol*, is certainly part of a Teamsterville lexicon, but "close, supportive, flexible speech," a Nacirema *meaning* for "communication," is a meaning not active in Teamsterville talk about talk. "Neighborhood," an important symbol in Teamsterville culture, is certainly also part of the Nacirema symbolic repertoire, but the sense of "neighborhood" as a culturally defined place for speaking is not a prominent part of Nacirema sensibility.

Likewise, there are contrasting Teamsterville and Nacirema premises and rules about speaking, such that one can think of two distinctive speech codes built up from the same linguistic codes. The "same" linguistic code provides the basic symbols from which such contrasting orientations can be constructed as the Teamsterville notion that "children should be seen and not heard" and the Nacirema notion that "you can't keep a child quiet at the dinner table."

The finding that each of these cultures thematizes speaking in culturally distinctive ways is consistent with the large number of ethnographies of speaking that are now available for comparative analysis (Philipsen and Carbaugh 1985). In study after study, drawn from languages and cultures from throughout the world, have come data that support the proposal, here formulated as Principle One, that *wherever there is a distinctive culture, there is to be found a distinctive code of communicative conduct.* These studies show cross-cultural distinctiveness in terms, semantic dimensions used to define those terms, metaphors, premises, and rules, pertaining to 'speaking'.

The Nacirema term "communication," with its dimensions of *close-distant*, *supportive-neutral*, and *flexible-closed*, suggests a useful point of contrast. Other speech codes, for which semantic dimensions for 'speaking' terms have been reported, include that of the Afro-American peasants of St. Vincent in the West Indies, a code that makes prominent the semantic contrasts *sensible-senseless* and *polite-impolite* as dimensions for characterizing acts of speech (Abrahams and Bauman 1971); that of seventeenth-century New Englanders, in which a *controlled-uncontrolled* contrast is prominent (St. George 1984); and that of the Haya, in which *substantial-insubstantial* is prominent (Seitel 1974). The available literature suggests that for each cultural system of speaking there is a distinctive system of such semantic dimensions, which in part constitute the domain of 'speaking'.

Another way the cultural particularity of speech codes is manifested is in metaphors for 'speaking.' Again the juxtaposition of "communication" to other codes is instructive. Katriel and I found the "work" metaphor—as in, "'communication' is the 'work' which is necessary for a 'relationship'"—to be a cultural resource for conceptualizing and interpreting Nacirema speech. Speech codes in other cultures have a metaphorical theme, which ramifies through the domain of 'speaking.' The Haya, for example, conceptualize the domain of speaking in terms of an "alimentary process" metaphor (Seitel 1974). The Chamula (Gossen 1974) and seventeenth-century New Englanders (St. George 1984) conceptualize speaking in terms of a "heat" metaphor, which has different meanings in each case.

As it is with symbols and meanings, so it is with premises and rules. Consider Walter Ong's proposal, quoted in chapter 1 of this book, that speaking links individuals in social relationships. He writes: "Because in its physical constitution as sound, the spoken word proceeds from the human interior and manifests human beings to one another as conscious interiors, as persons, the spoken word forms human beings into close-knit groups" (Ong 1982, p. 74). Ong's statement reveals a premise about speaking that emphasizes the interior of the individual as the starting point and source of experience of communication. This is, of course, a deeply cultured model, one whose evocation might be quite stirring to the Nacirema ear. But regardless of whether Ong's model is objectively true, the ethnographic literature suggests that other cultures implicate other premises.

For example, Michelle Z. Rosaldo's (1982) ethnography of speaking among the Ilongot in the northern Philippines, an "oral culture," portrays a people whose understanding of speaking deemphasizes the individual speaker as the intentional initiator of spoken meaning. The Ilongot's understanding presents a model of speaking as something quite different from what Ong proposes—individuals are, in the Ilongot code, already wedded to each other in unbreakable bonds of sociality, and speaking is merely a manifestation of that connection. Rather than proceeding from the interior of the person outward, speaking—and the meanings it embodies—originates outside the person.

Verschuren (1989) has conducted an 81-language survey of what he calls "language action verbs," such as "to speak" or "to say." He discovered that in all 81 languages there is a vocabulary item for the word or words that can be glossed as "to speak" or "to say." Seventy-seven of the 81 languages include a word for the English "to talk." But beyond that, there are many differences across languages as to what notions of linguistic action can be expressed in the language. Verschuren's finding that "to speak" is a linguistic universal suggests that in all cultures 'speaking' is thematized in some way. But in the Teamsterville and Nacirema cultures, and in many others in the ethnography of speaking literature, it can be seen that this linguistic universal is but a starting point for thematizing speaking, a point from which each language and culture takes its own distinctive course.

THE MATTER OF TALK

What do speech codes thematize? What is their substance? Of course, they are about speaking, but what, one might ask, is the substance or matter of speaking, as this is illumined by the study of speech codes? The thematization of speaking in Teamsterville and Nacirema cultures reveals a distinctive code of self, society, and strategic action. These codes, historically transmitted, socially constructed systems of symbols and meanings, premises, and rules, about communicative conduct, are at once codes about the nature of persons, about the ways persons can and should be linked together in social relations, and about the role of symbolic action in forging, sustaining, and altering such interpersonal linkages.

This can be expressed as Principle Two, *a speech code implicates a culturally distinctive psychology, sociology, and rhetoric*. A speech code does not provide simply an account of coding, decoding, and encoding, as neutral processes sealed off from other aspects of culture. Rather, such a code implicates a view of what a person is and of how persons are constituted, of the particular kinds of social relations that persons can and should enter into, and of the appropriate and efficacious symbolic resources available to interlocutors for constituting themselves as persons in social relationships. This was shown in detail, for the Teamsterville and Nacirema cases, in the comparative analysis in chapter 6.

Principle One points to difference across speech codes, Principle Two to the substance of such codes. These two principles can be joined to comprise the following elaboration of Principle Two: *speech codes are distinctive thematizations of the ends and means of social action*. Each implicates a distinctive conception of what goods humans should aim to secure, how to secure those goods, and how to judge efforts to attain them. For example, Mayor Daley's use of a Teamsterville speech code, as his use of it was described in chapter 3, shows him affirming an end of enacting a tightly prescribed, socially defined role, and doing this in and through communally sanctioned modes of action. Joanna Kramer's use of a Nacirema speech code, as her use was described in chapter 5, shows her affirming an end of pursuing individualistic goals, and doing this in and through "communication."

A speech code, as a culturally distinctive "social rhetoric" is part of a common culture that can provide individuals with a kind of practical knowledge about what to feel and what to do (Scruton (1979). It provides a system of meanings and beliefs that provides answers to questions about ends to seek, as well as answers to questions of the proper and efficacious means for achieving those ends. In particular, a speech code provides a system of answers about what linkages between self and others can properly be sought, and what symbolic resources can properly and efficaciously be employed in seeking those linkages (Philipsen 1987, 1989).

The matter, or substance, of speech codes is, by this account, interpersonal life, if that term is construed broadly. And the general point is woven through the literature of the ethnography of communication. Hymes suggested, in the early formulations of the enterprise (1962, 1964), that communication can be thought of as a metaphor for social life, and that as communication (including speaking) is thematized and enacted distinctively across cultures, and across speech communities, so cultural thematizations of communication and speaking should reveal a culturally distinctive code of interpersonal meanings in particular cases.

In a review of several ethnographies of communication, produced in response to Hymes's call for such studies, Carbaugh has shown how Hymes's proposal has been supported empirically in particular cases. Carbaugh's focus is on cultural terms for talk, such as "communication." His finding is that in all the cultures he surveyed, such terms are parts of larger codes of personhood, society, and strategic action. As Carbaugh has written, of cultural terms, "Persons use cultural terms for talk as a way to speak directly and literally about words and as a way to talk more metaphorically about interpersonal relations, social institutions, and models for being a person" (1989, p. 113).

THE MEANINGS OF SPEAKING

Principle One refers to the distinctiveness, and Principle Two to the substance, of speech codes. Principle Three refers to the use, or function, of speech codes. It is concerned with the part that speech codes play in the process of communication.

It has long been assumed that whenever interlocutors speak with each other, they potentially create shared meaning. They do this, for example, by referring to experience in such a way that the interlocutors can find common meanings in the use of language. It has long been assumed as well that users of language, and of other media of communication, not only express and interpret communicative acts in terms of what is being said—or talked about—but also in terms of what is being done (Austin 1962). Attention has been drawn to such "actions" performed in speaking as 'persuading', 'entertaining', 'uniting', 'chatting', 'conversing', and so forth.

Principle Three is that *the significance of speaking is contingent upon the speech code used by interlocutors to constitute the meanings of communicative acts*. The Teamsterville settlement house worker who talked with unruly boys to discipline them and to influence their future conduct was interpreted by Teamsterville boys to have been unmanly, because, in such circumstances, he *spoke*. From the settlement house worker's perspective, his acts of speech were gentle but firm administrations of discipline and the benign exercise of adult power. That Mayor Daley spoke in the council and that he spoke in the way he did meant one thing to Teamstervillers and another to those who did not control the Teamsterville code. The different meanings are expressed directly in the comments that Daley's various hearers made about the speech. What these acts, of the settlement house worker and of the mayor, respectively, were—that is, what they counted as for the interlocutors involved—was in each case contingent upon the speech codes used to constitute the meanings of the acts.

"Constitute" is used here with deliberate cognizance of its use in the speech act theory of the philosopher John Searle (1976). That theory holds that there is a definite range of what can be done, what acts can be performed, in speaking. And it holds that what a given speech behavior counts as is determined by the universal conditions necessary and sufficient for a behavior to count as, for example, a promise, a command, and so forth. Searle is concerned with a set of philosophical possibilities and the logical requirements for an observer to say that one of these possibilities was realized in a given utterance. For example, Searle posits that it is possible, in an act of speech, for the speaker to make a promise; and that a promise is made if and only if certain conditions are fulfilled. In uttering, for example, "I will take you to the cleaners tomorrow," certain conditions must be met for the locution to count as a promise (for example, the speaker must think the hearer wants to go to the cleaners or else the utterance might count as a threat rather than a promise). If a speaker said, "I will take you to the cleaners tomorrow," and all the logical requirements were met for classifying the utterance as a promise, Searle would call it a promise even if the speaker and the hearer called it an expression of sorrow. Searle would say, I believe, that although the utterance was mistaken as an expression of sorrow, a promise was indeed made, because the conditions for making a promise were met.

To propose that speech codes are used by interlocutors to constitute speech acts as meaningful says something different from, but not necessarily in conflict with, what Searle says about speech acts. My move here has been to interpret what interlocutors, singly or jointly, experience their speech acts and interactions to be. To Searle's set of logical possibilities this adds, in particular instances, a further component of the speech act or of spoken interaction, and that is what the interlocutors experience the meaning of their acts of speech to be. These meanings are such outcomes as "communicating," speaking "like a man," speaking in a way that is "supportive," and speaking "like one of us." Although Searle's system might be perfectly adequate to determine the conditions under which an observer can say that an utterance counts as a directive or a promise, it is through knowledge of particular speech codes that the observer can hear and interpret such experienced meanings as those I have instanced here.

Cultural types of acts and cultural meanings do not necessarily meet any philosophical or logical criteria, only the criterion of shared significance among interlocutors. The cultural formulation of these acts and meanings might have its own logic but that is not necessarily the logic of the philosopher of language. The Nacirema term "communication" illustrates these differences between the philosophic and the ethnographic accounts of speech acts. "Communication" is a Nacirema term that, in some contexts, refers to "close, supportive flexible" speech. To say that "we are really communicating" requires that interlocutors engage in spoken interaction that is highly disclosive, in which the interlocutors are supportive of each other as unique persons, and in which both parties are committed to the possibility of negotiating their perceptions of self and other. This is not a philosophical or a philological account of what conditions must be present to say we are "really communicating"—it is an observer's formulation of what some interlocutors take "really communicating" to be.

The implication of Principle Three is that generalizations about the meanings of speaking to those who participate in it must be qualified in that each culture provides a distinctive system of resources to use in constituting acts of speech as meaningful. Such a generalization is found in Ong's chapter, "Some Psychodynamics of Orality" (Ong 1982). Ong contrasts how orality, or speaking, is considered or thought of differently by people who live in *print* cultures or in *oral* cultures. But I have shown here that there is not just one "psychodynamics" of orality. The Teamsterville and Nacirema cases, along with the larger body of data in the ethnography of communication, suggest that the "psychodynamics" of orality are particular to each system, that in each case there is a distinctive system of terms, semantic dimensions, metaphors, rules, and premises available to interlocutors to constitute the meanings of speaking. The finding of cultural distinctiveness in speaking provides an understanding of speaking as an activity. Its meanings, phenomenology, or psychodynamics must always be established in the particular case. It provides an understanding of speaking as meaningful in ways that can only be fully grasped if they are grasped in the terms of a particular culture.

The question, What happens when people talk?, is thus reconfigured here as, What do the interlocutors interpret—or experience—themselves to be doing in speaking? And the answer is: it depends. It depends upon the speech code they use to constitute—to construct, to define, to interpret—their communicative acts. To the extent this claim is true, and the claim is consistent with the data arrayed in this book, then the meaning of speaking is always, at least in part, a function of culture.

CULTURE IN SPEAKING

The book began by quoting an utterance. At every turn it has been concerned with auditing utterances and interpreting their significance to those who make and hear them. In many instances, I have interpreted instances or collections of instances of speaking that, upon first hearing, sounded culture-free, or at least culture-neutral. For example, in the early part of Teamsterville fieldwork, when I heard neighborhood people talk about "the neighborhood," "around here," or "connections" I was not aware that they were speaking terms that, although they are common English words, are also code terms in Teamsterville culture. Likewise, when I first listened to Nacirema parents say that "communication" is vital to the parent-child "relationship," I did not hear such expressions as deeply cultured. The data-rich experience of auditing and interpreting Teamsterville and Nacirema speech has suggested Principle Four, that *the terms, rules, and premises of a culture are inextricably woven into speaking*. In this book, a special application of this principle has been made to speech codes—that is, to cultural systems of symbols and meanings, premises and rules—pertaining to communicative conduct. In each of the data-based chapters attention has been given to particular ways that *elements of speech codes are woven into speaking*. In what follows, I identify four ways this is done.

Patterns in speaking. In chapter 2, for example, I used the organizing frames of participants, setting, ends, and topic, taken from Hymes's (1962) scheme, to examine who talks to whom, in what settings, toward what ends, and about what topics, in order to learn fundamental aspects of a Teamsterville speech code. Such central categories in Hymes's scheme as speech event, components of speech events, and functions of speech events, provided a way to organize many separate instances of spoken behavior into a culture pattern that could be, and was, tested against further events and validation by local consultants. The use of Hymes's framework enabled me to hear, in the stream of Teamsterville behavior, a culturally distinctive pattern where initially I heard no culture pattern being implicated.

It was by applying these categories that I was able to hear the Teamstervillers not simply as speaking but as speaking in culturally organized ways. For example, it was only by applying the framework that I was able to appreciate that one never merely speaks in Teamsterville but that one always speaks as the bearer of a culturally defined social identity—that is, that if one is male one always speaks as a man, as that category is thematized in Teamsterville culture. The local pattern for speech behavior, as well as the local commentary upon behaviors that do and do not fit the pattern, comprises ways that Teamsterville speaking invokes and implicates a culture. That is, one way that culture is woven into speaking is that interlocutors pattern their speaking in culturally distinctive ways.

Metacommunicative vocabularies. A second, immediately obvious way that culture is woven into speaking is in the use of a culturally distinctive metacommunicative vocabulary (and other talk about talk). When, for example, I asked a Teamsterviller about who his preferred interlocutors are and he replied by saying they are people from "around here," he used a culturally distinctive term, one whose meaning was different from that which I supplied prior to studying Teamsterville culture. When a Nacirema talks about the importance of "communication in a relationship," cultural terms with very particular definitions are being used—and are being displayed. The studies presented in this book show interlocutors using freely such words and thus revealing themselves to be users of a culture.

The rhetorical invocation of metacommunicative vocabularies. Applying a methodological principle articulated by Kenneth Burke, that one should not merely compare "verbalizations . . . [but should] also correlate the situations behind them" (Burke 1965[1954], p. 183), suggests a third way that interlocutors weave culture into speaking. In all the data-based chapters, I have attended to how speech code elements are expressed in the naming, interpreting, explaining, evaluating, and justifying of communicative acts. If, following Burke again (1950) one thinks about utterances as addressed to some hearer for a persuasive purpose, one can hear—or at least interpret—interlocutors as using speech code elements to serve rhetorical ends.

For example, that the Teamsterville man told the settlement house worker that a man should hit rather than counsel an errant child is an example of invoking a cultural rule to justify a particular course of action. K's statement, in chapter 4, that her father's discourses with her did not constitute "communication," contains an instance of using a term from a speech code to characterize spoken activity and thus to evaluate it. In these instances, a speech code element was used to do more than simply to designate something; it was used to interpret, to explain, to justify, communicative conduct. Such utterances reveal their speakers to be speaking in the terms of a culturally distinctive speech code.

The use of metacommunicative vocabularies in culturally distinctive forms. Cultures are not unordered arrays of elements, displayed without pattern or form. Some elements of any culture are more important than others in terms of their significance to the interlocutors who use them; some cultural themes ramify more widely throughout a cultural system and throughout the lives of those who use them; and some elements of a culture are expressed more prominently than are others. The studies presented in this book suggest that a fourth way to hear the articulation of speech code elements is to listen for the use of them in three communicative forms whose structure enables one to notice the cultural significance of the symbols and meanings, rules, and premises displayed in them. Those forms are totemizing rituals, myths, and social dramas. Each will be discussed to show how its use reveals interlocutors weaving speech code elements into their speaking in particularly significant ways.

All routinized episodic sequences—known, repeatable ways of structuring an interaction event—entail the use of cultural ways of speaking and interacting. All episodic sequences do this because they are routinized—stereotypical, predictable—and because their routinization marks some aspect of shared practice. Greeting rituals are an example.

A *totemizing ritual* (Turner 1988, pp. 161–63), a particular type of ritual, is a structured sequence of symbolic actions, the correct performance of which pays explicit homage to a sacred object of a group or culture. Thus a totemizing ritual is routinized but it also is a particularly poignant (meaning-full) ritual. There are two ways cultural poignance is manifested in totemizing rituals. First, they are infused with the expression of emotional content such as anger, frustration, joy. Second, the referent of the situation—the sacred object of the group—is made explicit. Nacirema greeting rituals are highly structured. But the "communication" ritual, a totemizing ritual, is highly structured plus it is infused with emotional content and it includes explicit references to things taken as sacred—that is, selves, relationships, and communication. To participate effectively in a totemizing ritual entails speaking and interpreting with particularly important terms of a particular code.

All stories, which string together cultural symbols in meaningful sequences of activity, potentially implicate cultural content. *Cultural myths*, a special kind of story, make key elements of a cultural code particularly salient. A myth is a story of some type of person who confronts a type of problem and responds effectively through the use of some type of action or resource. A cultural myth is a story that, in the telling, provides its hearers with resources for interpreting their own experiences and for telling their own stories in ways intelligible to them and their interlocutors (Hannerz, 1969; White, 1981).

Joanna Kramer's identity crisis, discussed in chapter 5, is a story in which a type of person (a woman, a mother) confronts a problematic situation (a husband who does not "communicate" with her) by taking a journey upon which she meets someone who will "communicate" with her and thereby she restores her sense of "self." Such tellings provide a form in which the cultural richness of speaking is revealed.

A third communicative form in which significant cultural symbols are made salient is the social drama. In the *social drama*, someone invokes a moral rule in challenging (criticizing) the conduct of another. In the next step of the sequence, a reply, consisting of a repair, a denial, or the like, is made to the challenge. The reply is either honored or dishonored, with the consequence that the offender either reintegrates with the group, or alienation or schism has been revealed. In this process of invoking rules and replying to rule invocations, code elements are pressed into service. They are pressed into service in a form that, like rituals and cultural myths, provides not only for the invocation of the code element but also for the discursive coratification of its legitimacy by the interlocutors. In this way, interlocutors deploy significant code elements and their "discursive force" is revealed in and through how their use either does or does not have force for the interlocutors.

In replying to Mayor Daley's council speech, Alderman Simpson criticized Daley's conduct, and in so doing he invoked the terms of a speech code. Daley's reply was condemned by some editorial writers in New York City and Chicago newspapers and by Simpson, and was praised by some Teamstervillers. Like the accusation and the defense, the condemnation and praise involved the use of codes to justify the speakers' positions. In the process of accusation, justification, condemnation, and praise, the force and scope of rules and meanings are discursively spoken and tested and, thus, are made salient by and to participants and observers.

Interlocutors organize and interpret spoken activity in ways that can be detected by the application of such frames as participants and setting. They express and articulate meanings about speech in their use of a culturally distinctive metacommunicative vocabulary. They seek to accomplish things by invoking elements of a speech code. They participate in rituals, mythic tellings and hearings, and social dramas, forms of discourse infused with the elements of a culture. In all these ways, and this is an illustrative but by no means an exhaustive account, speaking is revealed to be richly woven through with the resources of a culture.

The principle that culturally distinctive speech codes are woven into speaking complicates the ambitions of those reformers of communicative practices who propose that all rhetorical uses of language be made "sensitive and accountable to human experience" (Bennett 1985). If by "sensitive and accountable to human experience," Bennett and those he follows mean a kind of respect paid to the common wisdom that has grown out of a life of a people and has figured in that people's sustaining discourse across generations—in that case, I would have no quarrel with the proposal. But if it means what I take it to mean, if it expresses a principle of plain representation, a doctrine of designativist clarity, a belief in the sanitizing of discourse, then the studies presented and comparatively juxtaposed here suggest that the proposal is hopelessly idealistic.

It is hopelessly idealistic because it ignores that speaking is laced through with cultural prejudices and particularities. For example, the very phrase "sensitive and accountable to human experience" itself contains terms that express a prejudice. "Experience" refers, in this use, to the individually apprehended and interpreted meanings derived from events in one's life. As such, it can be contrasted with "tradition," "the *common* sense," "convention," and so forth. "Experience" refers to something that resides in, and is constructed exclusively by, the individual; "tradition" refers to something that, at least in part, resides in the communal wisdom.

The point is not that "tradition" is superior to "experience" as a guide to human action. Rather the point is that when Bennett insists that being "sensitive . . . to experience" is a requirement of "good political communication," he is not invoking a term that is politically or morally neutral. He invokes a term that finds a happy place in a code of dignity, just as Mayor Daley's council speech is sprinkled with the terms of a code of honor.

This point takes on particular importance when interlocutors are sensitive to the ideological or political undertones that can be found in social and communicative practices. It is easy to hear, in the speech of one side or another in some dispute, that the other's speech reveals them to be prejudiced, interested, and partial. By reporting here on two ways of speaking, by showing each to draw from and express a code of speech and society, I have complicated discussions in which one side accuses the other of speaking in terms that are ideologically colored. Both sides are, in the light of my discussion, speaking in subtly coded terms. For example, when the voice of dignity and the voice of honor, to take but two examples, meet, or clash, neither side necessarily speaks in bad faith, but each speaks with a different faith, a faith that, more often than not, is implicated in the terms and tropes in which it expresses its arguments.

The positive contribution that this analysis makes to such disputes is not to provide a method by which voices can reconcile their differences. Rather it provides a language and a spirit that interlocutors can use to hear themselves and others for what they are—that is, to hear speech as deeply cultured—and, thus, to hear speakers as such. The terms of that language are, on the one hand, persons, society, and strategic action, and, on the other, code, community, speech situation, functions of speaking, and speech act. The values these terms take, in particular instances, are cultural values and thus must be discovered in each particular case. The spirit in which these terms are to be taken is that acknowledging that the distinctive values terms take in particular instances are, indeed, distinctive, not amenable to preformulation.

Thus, the political scientist's preachment, quoted initially in chapter 3, to "keep language sensitive and accountable to human experience" (Bennett 1985) is read, here, as hopelessly idealistic. Language, it has been shown here, particularly when pressed into the service of socio-rhetorical ends, is fundamentally spoken in the distinctive terms of a speech community. Speaking is inextricably speaking culturally.

CONCLUSION

In chapter 1 I told the story of my dinner companion who implied—or so I thought—that speaking is a matter of little significance in lives and societies. In chapter 1 I proposed that the studies to follow would suggest that speaking is filled with significance, but in ways that can only be known by inquiring into the particularities of experience and the particularities of the speech codes that interlocutors use to shape and interpret their experience. I have, in this final chapter, presented a thesis and four principles that begin to articulate that position.

To summarize, I have argued from the data presented here that speaking is a radically cultural medium of human communication. Four principles, stated in terms of the concept of speech code, have been formulated as specific expressions of that thesis. I have argued that:

1. Everywhere there is a distinctive culture, there is a distinctive speech code.
2. Speech codes implicate a culturally distinctive psychology, sociology, and rhetoric.
3. The significance of communicative acts is contingent upon the speech codes that interlocutors use to constitute those acts.
4. Speech codes are inextricably woven into speaking.

The first of these principles points to the existence of speech codes, to the fact that cultures provide distinctive thematizations of speaking. Quite simply, I have argued that with regard to any given culture, if there is something in that culture that pertains to speaking—if there are symbols and meanings, premises and rules pertaining to speaking—then that something differs across cultures. The second principle posits something about the substance of cultural thematizations of speaking. I have argued that speech codes inevitably—in all cases—implicate a kind of social theory or social rhetoric.

Principles One and Two are grounded securely in the empirical literature of the ethnography of communication (Philipsen and Carbaugh 1986; Carbaugh 1989; Verschuren 1989). The Teamsterville and Nacirema cases, which are part of that literature, provide some of that support. Given the amount of the empirical support for these proposals, it is unlikely that future research will lead to their empirical disconfirmation.

Although it is unlikely that these generalizations will be disconfirmed empirically, it is possible that they could be reformulated in the light of new evidence or in the light of a reanalysis of extant data. For example, it might be that, even though there are differences across speech codes, there is a specifiable range of such codes. It might be that a large number of such codes can be subsumed under a small number of types, and that these types will correlate with specifiable social and cultural circumstances. It might be, for example, that the types represented by the codes of honor and dignity can be shown to subsume a wide range of cases.

Principle Three points to how speech codes work in the process of communication. It suggests that the particular sense that interlocutors make of communicative acts is contingent upon the speech codes they use in interpreting those acts. This, too, is an empirically grounded claim and is one subject to empirical disconfirmation. One rival claim is that there are kinds of speaking that are, to the interlocutors who experience them, the same everywhere, and thus not contingent for their meanings upon the speech codes available to particular interlocutors. The data of the ethnography of communication, including the data of the Teamsterville and Nacirema cases, provide many instances consistent with Principle Three, but there is a good deal of speculation and interpretation involved in inferring this principle from these data. This is a principle that merits further empirical study, particularly empirical study that pits my proposal against the possibility of universal principles of interpretation (see, for example, Rosch 1987).

Principle Four points to the site of speech codes, to where they are used and thus to where they can be found—in speaking itself. In arguing that elements of speech codes are inextricably woven into speaking, I am again making an empirical claim—a claim grounded in observations and a claim subject to empirical disconfirmation. It is possible that there are kinds of speaking that do not carry within them elements of a speech code—that is, that speaking is not necessarily a carrier of culture. Furthermore, it is possible that certain types of speaking are particularly rich in the use of code elements, a possibility proposed in systematic terms by such scholars as Silverstein (1979) and Wierzbicka (1986). This is a topic in which there is considerable progress to be made through the analysis of new ethnographic material and through the reanalysis of extant data. Nonetheless, given the materials presented in this book, it seems unlikely that new data or the new interpretation of extant data will lead to a picture of speaking as something fundamentally innocent of cultural penetration.

Taken together, these four proposals—about the distinctiveness, the substance, the function, and the site, of speech codes—suggest something true of the significance of speaking. They suggest that in all times and all places, the significance of speaking is something important, but important in distinctive terms in each case. They suggest that speaking, one of the principal activities through which a common life is constituted, is something that, for all its universality as a human activity, is fundamentally and radically particular in its human significance.

At one level, the theory of speech codes that I have proposed here—as expressed in the thesis and the four principles—points to certain fundamental truths about speaking. At another level, it suggests ways to inquire into the particularities of speaking in particular cases. In this sense, the theory has value not only as a claim about general properties of speaking and communication, but also as a kind of heuristic or investigative perspective in the study of particular cases of spoken life. Principles One and Two, for example, perform a kind of enabling function for students of human communication, in that they hold the promise that whenever one sets out to study the communicative conduct of some particular moment or milieux, that it is likely one will find there some distinctive substance with regard to speaking as medium of communicative activity. Principle Three suggests that when one turns to situated acts of speaking that these will embody—for the participants—particular senses of meaning and social experience. And Principle Four not only suggests a generalization about speaking, but its development in this chapter reveals a system of maneuvers one can deploy in the delineation of distinctive codes of speaking. Thus, the findings of these studies suggest not only that speaking is distinctive in particular cultures, but they suggest as well some of the interpretive resources available to students of speaking for doing the work of investigating and interpreting the codes of speaking with which particular lives and societies are constituted. Given the point of Principle One, life presents seemingly limitless opportunities for the study of such socially situated, culturally distinctive ways of speaking.

Although the studies in this book are designed simply to address a particular empirical and theoretical question—how speaking is a radically cultural medium of human communication—it has been my aim to produce answers that might bear suggestively on some of the central themes of the discipline of communication studies. Thus, I conclude by making a few such suggestions.

Communication studies is centrally concerned with how interlocutors achieve common understandings. The studies presented here emphasize that the media interlocutors use in a communicative situation are not merely carriers of signals. Their use itself is a source of situated meaning; the fact that someone speaks, or does not, or speaks in a particular way, or does not, are matters of interpersonal significance. Interlocutors bring to the construction (the production and interpretation) of communicative acts the use of culturally distinctive speech codes, codes that function in two ways. First, a speech code makes available to interlocutors a culturally distinctive system of terms, scenarios, and premises with which to produce particular communicative acts. Second, they make available a system of resources for interpreting communicative acts. Thus, speech codes could be shown to play a vital constitutive function in the production of interpersonal meanings. This should have important implications for learning about cross-cultural encounters and the meanings produced in them (see, for example, the work of Gumperz and his associates—Gumperz 1982a, 1982b) as well as for encounters in which cultural differences are not pronounced (the 'basic' communicative situation).

Communication studies is also centrally concerned with how interlocutors use symbols to facilitate cooperative activity. As with the construction of communicative acts, so do speech codes figure prominently in the persuasive-coordinative function of communication. First, a speech code names and conceptualizes the ends and means of achieving coordinated action, and it does this in a culturally distinctive way. Second, a speech code provides a system of enjoining and legitimating premises to which interlocutors can appeal in justifying their conduct or in grounding appeals to others to act. Thus, speech codes could be shown to play a vital coordinative function in social life. This has important implications for understanding how, in general and in particular speech communities, the process of living and acting together is accomplished communicatively.

In addition to these communicative (referential) and persuasive-coordinative (rhetorical) functions, communication studies is concerned with a communal function. Here the concern is with how the use of language and other symbolic resources serve to create for interlocutors a sense of shared identity. The studies in this volume show interlocutors expressing culturally distinctive senses of shared identity. They also point to speech codes that provide culturally distinctive resources for performing this function. For example, how an individual expresses a sense of membership or communal identity is specified very differently in a code of honor and a code of dignity, the former emphasizing the use of speech to express one's place in a hierarchy (one's social distinctiveness) and the latter emphasizing the use of speech to express one's unique psychological contents (one's psychological distinctiveness). Here again, speech codes could be shown to perform a crucial function in the activity of interpersonal linking, particularly at the level of individuals identifying symbolically with a group, tradition, or community (this is worked out more fully in Philipsen 1987, 1989; and see Eastman 1985).

With regard to all three of these functions—the communicative, the persuasive, and the communal—the present studies suggest not only that interlocutors must bring to bear distinctive resources for performing these functions in distinctive situations, they also suggest some of the ways that these distinctive resources can be discovered in particular instances. Given that elements of speech codes are inextricably interwoven into speaking, it is to speaking that the student—or practitioner—of communicative conduct can turn to discover local knowledge about the ends and means of communication. Knowledge of speech codes, and knowledge of how to study them, such as is exemplified in the data-based chapters and made more explicit in the exposition of Principle Four in chapter 7, should prove invaluable as a resource for figuring out, in particular situations, what the local (situated) resources are.

Finally, communication studies is concerned vitally with a critical understanding of the activity of communication. That is, communication can be thought of as something in which the work of the world gets done and this can be treated unproblematically, as something that is, is good, and is to be studied so as to make it work more efficiently or more effectively. Knowledge of communication processes, from this view, is valuable because it facilitates communication, cooperation, and communal identification. The critical perspective in communication invites attention to the ways in which social inequalities are expressed, reified, and reinforced, and in turn invites students of communication to examine critically these ways. The studies in this book, by juxtaposing two very different speech codes, and by doing this in a way that has tried to treat each code on its own terms, without, I hope, making gratuitous negative or positive judgments about either, should contribute to one's ability to think through critical judgments about speech codes and the ways of life they represent. They contribute, precisely, in this way: by examining two such different ways of speaking as the Teamsterville and Nacirema cases, each of which embodies a code, it makes it difficult to privilege one of these as neutral or unprejudiced, and the other as coded or prejudiced. I have tried to suggest not only a perspective but also a language for examining communicative conduct as coded and therefore to hear not only a Mayor Daley but also a Joanna Kramer as speaking culturally. The capacity to hear various speakers, those who are close to as well as those who are distant from one's own prejudices, as speaking culturally, seems to me to be a precondition for any kind of intelligent hearing and intelligent practice of communicative conduct.

References

Abrahams, R., and Bauman, R. 1971. Sense and nonsense in St. Vincent: Speech behavior and decorum in a Caribbean community. *American Anthropologist*, 73, 762–72.

Albert, E.M. 1972. Culture patterning of speech behavior in Burundi. In Gumperz, J.J., and Hymes, D. (eds.), *Directions in Sociolinguistics: The Ethnography of Communication*, pp. 72–105.

Austin, John L. 1962. *How to do things with words*. Oxford: Oxford University Press.

Basso, K. 1970. "To give up on words": Silence in western Apache culture. *Southwestern Journal of Anthropology*, 26, 213–30.

Bauman, R. 1972. The La Have Island general store: Sociability and verbal art in a Nova Scotia community. *Journal of American Folklore*, 85, 330–43.

Bauman, R., and Sherzer, J. (eds.), 1974. *Explorations in the Ethnography of Speaking*. Cambridge, England: Cambridge University Press.

Bennett, W.L. 1985. Communication and social responsibility. *The Quarterly Journal of Speech*, 71, 259–88.

Berger, P., Berger, B., and Kellner, H. 1973. *The Homeless Mind: Modernization and Consciousness*. New York: Vintage Books.

Bernstein, B. 1972. Social class, language, and socialization. In Giglioli, P.P. (ed.), *Language and Social Context*, pp. 173–78. Middlesex, England: Penguin Books.

Bock, P. 1969, 1974. *Modern Cultural Anthropology: An Introduction*. New York: Alfred A. Knopf.

Braithwaite, C.A. 1982. Cultural uses and interpretations of silence. M.A. thesis, University of Washington, Seattle.

Brown, R., and Gilman, A. 1960. The pronouns of power and solidarity. In Sebeok, T.A. (ed.), *Style in Language*, pp. 252–76. Cambridge: M.I.T. Press.

Burke, K. 1954, 1965. *Permanence and Change: An Anatomy of Purpose*. Indianapolis: Bobbs-Merrill.

———. 1968. *Counter-statement*. Berkeley: University of California Press.

———. 1950, 1969. *A Rhetoric of Motives*. Berkeley: University of California Press.

Canby, V. 1979. Screen: 'Kramer vs. Kramer.' *The New York Times*, December 19, 23, 1.

Carbaugh, D. 1987. Communication rules in Donahue discourse. *Research on Language and Social Interaction*, 21, 31–62.

———. 1988. *Talking American*. New Jersey: Ablex.

———. 1989. Fifty terms for talk: A cross-cultural study. *International and Intercultural Communication Annual*, 13, 93–120.

Corman, A. 1977. *Kramer vs. Kramer*. New York: Signet.

Donahue, P., & Company, 1979. *Donahue: My Own Story*. New York: Fawcett Crest.

Eastman, C. 1985. Establishing social identity through language use. *Journal of Language and Social Psychology*, 4, 1–20.

Estes, J. 1981. Playwright's wild air study. *Seattle Post-Intelligencer*, February 1.

Farb, Peter. 1972. *Word play: What happens when people talk*. New York: Alfred Knopf.

Fernandez, J. 1972. Persuasions and performances: Of the best in every body . . . and the metaphors of every man. *Daedalus*, 101, 39–60.

Finnegan, R. 1988. *Literacy and Orality: Studies in the Technology of Communication*. Oxford: Basil Blackwell.

Fortune. 1981. January 12, 103, 90–91.

Fox, R. 1977. The inherent rules of violence. In Collett, P. (ed.), *Social Rules and Social Behaviour*, pp. 132–49. Oxford: Basil Blackwell.

Frentz, T., and Farrell, T. 1976. Language-action: A paradigm for communication. *The Quarterly Journal of Speech*, 62, 333–49.

Friedman, M. 1962. *Capitalism and Freedom*. Chicago: University of Chicago Press.

Friedrich, P. 1977. Sanity and the myth of honor: The problem of Achilles. *Ethos*, 5, 281–305.

Gans, H. 1962. *The Urban Villages: Group and Class in the Life of Italian-Americans*. New York: Free Press.

Gardner, P. 1966. Symmetric respect and memorate knowledge: The structure and ecology of individualistic culture. *Southwestern Journal of Anthropology*, 22, 389–415.

Geduld, H.M. 1980. Film Review. *The Humanist*, March/April, 55.

Geertz, C. 1973. The *Interpretation of Cultures: Selected Essays*. New York: Basic Books.

Goffman, E. 1959. *The Presentation of Self in Everyday Life*. Garden City, N.Y.: Doubleday Anchor.

———. 1967. *Interaction Ritual: Essays on Face-to-Face Behavior*. Garden City, N.Y.: Anchor.

Golden, H., Jr. 1971a. Daley assails colleges for "agitation" and "hate." *Chicago Sun-Times*. July 23, 5.

———. 1971b. Simpson reads one in reply to Daley. *Chicago Sun-Times*, July 23, 5.

Gossen, G. 1974. *Chamulas in the World of the Sun: Time and Space in a Maya Oral Tradition*. Cambridge: Harvard University Press.

Gregg, R., and Hauser, G. 1973. Richard Nixon's April 30, 1970, address on Cambodia: The "ceremony" of confrontation. *Speech Monographs*. 40, 167–81.

Gumperz, J. 1982a. *Discourse Strategies*. Cambridge, England: Cambridge University Press.

———. 1982b. *Language as Social Identity*. Cambridge, England: Cambridge University Press.

Gumperz, J.J., and Hymes, D. 1972. *Directions in Sociolinguistics: The Ethnography of Communication*. New York: Holt, Rinehart & Winston.

Hamblen, C. 1979. The married woman's name: A metaphor of oppression. *Et cetera, A Review of General Semantics*, 36, 248–56.

Hannerz, U. 1969. *Soulside: Inquiries into Ghetto Culture and Community*. New York: Columbia University Press.

Hart, R., Carlson, R., and Eadie, W. 1980. Attitudes toward communication and the assessment of rhetorical sensitivity. *Communication Monographs*. 47, 1–22.

Hatch, R. 1980. Films. *The Nation*, January 26, 230, 90–91.

Hudson, R.A. 1980. *Sociolinguistics*. New York: Cambridge University Press.

Hsu, F. 1963. *Clan, Caste, and Club*. New York: Van Nostrand.

Hymes, D. 1962. The ethnography of speaking. In Gladwin, T., and Sturtevant, W.C. (eds.), *Anthropology and Human Behavior*, 13–53. Washington, D.C.: Anthropological Society of Washington.

———. 1964. Introduction. Toward ethnographies of communication. In Gumperz, J.J., and Hymes, D. (eds.), The ethnography of communication, *American Anthropologist*, 66 (part 2), 1–34.

———. 1967. Models of the interaction of language and social setting. *Journal of Social Issues*, 23, 8–28.

———. 1972. Models of the interaction of language and social life. In Gumperz, J.J., and Hymes, D. (eds.), *Directions in Sociolinguistics: The Ethnography of Communication*, pp. 35–71.

———. 1974. *Foundations in Sociolinguistics: An Ethnographic Approach*. Philadelphia: University of Pennsylvania Press.

"Jennifer James Show." 1981. KVI Radio. Seattle, Washington. March.

Katriel, T., and Philipsen, G. 1981. "What we need is communication": "Communication" as a cultural category in some American speech. *Communication Monographs*, 48, 302–17.

Keesing, R. 1970. Toward a model of role analysis. In Naroll, R., and Cohen, R. (eds.), *A Handbook of Method in Cultural Anthropology*, 423–53. Garden City, N.Y.: Natural History Press.

Kemnitzer, D.C. 1977. Sexuality as a social form: Performance and anxiety in America. In Dolgin, J.L., Kemnitzer, D.S., and Schneider, D.M. (eds.), *Symbolic Anthropology: A Reader in the Study of Symbols and Meanings*, 292–309. New York: Columbia University Press.

Kennedy, E. 1978. *Himself! The Life and Times of Mayor Richard J. Daley*. New York: Viking Press.

Kitagawa, E., and Taeuber, K. 1963. *Local Community Fact Book, 1960*. Chicago: University of Chicago Press.

Kohl, H. 1972. Names, graffiti, and culture. In Kochman, T. (ed.), *Rappin' and Stylin' Out: Communication in Urban Black America*, 109–33. Urbana: University of Illinois Press.

Komarovsky, M. 1962. *Blue Collar Marriage*. New York: Vintage Books.

Labov, W. 1966. *The Social Stratification of English in New York City*. Washington, D.C.: Center for Applied Linguistics.

Lichtenstein, G. 1980. Kramer vs. Kramer vs. the way it is. *Atlantic Monthly*, 245, 96–98.

Losing His Cool. 1971. *New York Times*, July 25, 5.

Mayor Daley's Blood Pressure. 1971. *Chicago Sun-Times*, July 24, 15.

Miner, H. 1956. Body ritual among the Nacirema. *American Anthropologist*, 58, 503–7.

Miner, M. 1971. Daley "bottled-up"—Oldberg. *Chicago Sun-Times*, July 24, 1.

Moerman, M. 1988. *Talking Culture: Ethnography and Conversation Analysis*. Philadelphia: University of Pennsylvania Press.

Naroll, R. 1970. Data quality control in cross-cultural surveys. In Naroll, R., and Cohen, R. (eds.), *A Handbook of Method in Cultural Anthropology*, pp. 927–45. Garden City, N.Y.: Natural History Press.

Ong, W.J. 1969. World as view and world as event. *American Anthropologist*, 71, 634–47.

———. 1982. *Orality and Literacy: The Technologizing of the Word*. London: Methuen.

Orth, M. 1979. Benton vs. Benton. *New York*, December 24, 12, 55, 57.

Philips, S.U. 1970. Acquisition of rules for appropriate speech usage. *Georgetown University Monograph Series on Languages and Linguistics*, 21, 77–94.

Philipsen, G. 1975. Speaking "like a man" in Teamsterville: Culture patterns of role enactment in an urban neighborhood. *Quarterly Journal of Speech*, 61, 13–22.

———. 1976a. Places for speaking in Teamsterville. *Quarterly Journal of Speech*, 62, 15–25.

———. 1976b. Speaking as a cultural resource. Paper presented at the Annual Convention of the Speech Communication Association. Chicago.

———. 1986. The ethnography of communication: From an assumptive to an empirical approach. Paper presented to the American Anthropological Association. Philadelphia.

———. 1987. The prospect for cultural communication. In Kincaid, D.L. (ed.), *Communication theory from Eastern and Western Perspectives*, 245–54. New York: Academic Press.

———. 1989. Speech and the communal function in four cultures. *International and Intercultural Communication Annual*, 13, 79–92.

Philipsen, G., and Carbaugh, D. 1986. A bibliography of fieldwork in the ethnography of communication. *Language in Society*, 15, 387–98.

Pitt-Rivers, J. 1966. Honour and social structure. In Persistiany (ed.), *Honour and Shame: The Values of a Mediterranean Society*, pp. 19–78. Chicago: University of Chicago Press.

Rich, F. 1979. Grownups, a child, divorce, and tears. *Time*, 114, 74–77.

Ricouer, P. 1977. The model of text: Meaningful action considered as text. In Dallmayr, F.R., and McCarthy, T.A. (eds.), *Understanding and Social Inquiry*, 316–34. Notre Dame, Indiana: University of Notre Dame Press.

Rosaldo, M.Z. 1982. The things we do with words: Ilongot speech acts and Speech Act Theory in philosophy. *Language in Society*, 11, 203–37.

Rosch, E. 1987. Linguistic Relativity. *Et cetera*, 44, 254–79.

Rosen, W., and Rosen, B. 1963. Introduction. In Shakespeare, W., *Julius Caesar*. New York: Signet.

St. George, R. 1984. "Heated" speech and literacy in seventeenth-century New England. In Hall, D.D., and Allen, D.G. (eds.), *Seventeenth-Century New England*, 275–322. Boston: Colonial Society of Massachusetts.

Sapir, E. 1921. *Language, An Introduction to the Study of Speech*. New York: Harcourt, Brace and Co.

Schlesinger, A., Jr. 1980. Growing pains. *Saturday Review*, March 1, 7, 34.

Schneider, D.M. 1976. Notes toward a theory of culture. In Basso, K.H., and Selby, H.A. (eds.), *Meaning in Anthropology*, 197–220. Albuquerque: University of New Mexico Press.

Schreiber, E. 1971a. Nepotism charge raises Daley's ire. *Chicago Tribune*, July 22, 1.

———. 1971b. Why Daley's temper is short. *Chicago Tribune*, July 23, 1.

———. 1971c. Daley no "Couch Case": Medic. *Chicago Tribune*, July 24, 4.

Scruton, Roger. 1979. "The significance of common culture." *Philosophy*, 54, 51–70.

Searle, J. 1976. A classification of illocutionary acts. *Language in Society*, 5, 1–23.

Seitel, P. 1974. Haya metaphors for speech. *Language in Society*, 3, 51–67.

Sennett, R. 1970. *The Uses of Disorder: Personal Identity and City Life*. New York: Vintage Books.

———. 1976. *The Fall of Public Man*. New York: Alfred A. Knopf.

Silverstein, M. 1979. Language structure and linguistic ideology. In Clyne, P.R., Hanks, W.F., and Hofbauer, C.L. (eds.), *The Elements: A Parasession on*

Linguistic Units and Levels, 193–247. Chicago: Chicago Linguistic Society.

Simon, J. 1980. Benton vs. the truth. *National Review*, February 8, 32, 168–69.

Suttles, G.D. 1968. *The Social Order of the Slum: Ethnicity and Territory in the Inner City*. Chicago: University of Chicago Press.

de Tocqueville, A. 1954. *Democracy in America*, vol. 2. New York: Vintage Books.

Turner, J. 1988. *A Theory of Social Interaction*. Stanford: Stanford University Press.

Turner, V. 1980. Social dramas and stories about them. *Critical Inquiry*, 7, 141–68.

Varenne, H. 1977. *Americans Together: Structured Diversity in a Midwestern Town*. New York: Teachers College Press.

Verschueren, J. 1989. Language on language: Toward metapragmatic universals. *IPrA Papers in Pragmatics*, 3, 5–144.

Weaver, R. 1964. *Visions of Order: The Cultural Crisis of our Time*. Baton Rouge: Louisiana State University Press.

Webb, E.J., Campbell, D.T., Schwartz, R.D., and Sechrest, L. 1966. *Unobtrusive Measures: Nonreactive Research in Social Sciences*. Chicago: Rand McNally.

Welsh, A. 1975. Brutus is an honorable man. *Yale Review*, 64, 496–513.

Westerbrook, C.L., Jr. 1980. Tale of Hoffman: Kramer vs. Kramer. *Commonweal*, February 15, 107, 87–88.

White, J.B. 1981. Homer's argument with culture. *Critical Inquiry*, 7, 707–25.

Whyte, W.F. 1943. *Street Corner Society: The Social Structure of an Italian Slum*. Chicago: University of Chicago Press.

Wiemann, J.M., and Harrison, R.P. (eds.), 1983. *Nonverbal Communication*. Beverly Hills: Sage Publications.

Wiener, N. 1954, 1967. *The Human Use of Human Beings: Cybernetics and Society*. New York: Avon Books.

Wierzbicka, A. 1986. Does language reflect culture? Evidence from Australian English. *Language in Society*, 15, 349–74.

Wister, O. 1929. *The Virginian: A Horseman of the Plains*. New York: MacMillan.

Zimmerman, D., and Wieder, D.L. 1977. The diary: Diary-interview method. *Urban Life*, 5, 479–98.

Index

COMEBACK CATCHER

STONE ARCH BOOKS
a capstone imprint

JAKE MADDOX
GRAPHIC NOVELS

Jake Maddox Graphic Novels are published by
Stone Arch Books, a Capstone imprint
1710 Roe Crest Drive
North Mankato, Minnesota 56003

www.mycapstone.com

Library of Congress Cataloging-in-Publication Data is available on the Library of Congress website.

ISBN: 978-1-4965-3700-3 (library binding)
ISBN: 978-1-4965-3704-1 (paperback)
ISBN: 978-1-4965-3720-1 (ebook PDF)

Summary: Eddie Jackson doesn't play baseball — not anymore. He loves playing catcher, but he's a nervous wreck when he's batting. So he quit the team after last summer's embarrassing championship strikeout. But when his old coach needs a backup catcher, Eddie finds himself back on the field. Will Eddie be able to overcome his fear of the spotlight and finally step up to the plate?

Editor: Abby Huff
Designer: Brann Garvey
Production: Gene Bentdahl

Printed in the United States 4995

COMEBACK CATCHER

Text by Eric Braun

Art by Bere Muñiz

Cover Art by Fern Cano

STARTING LINEUP
#13
EDDIE
#10
BIG LENNY

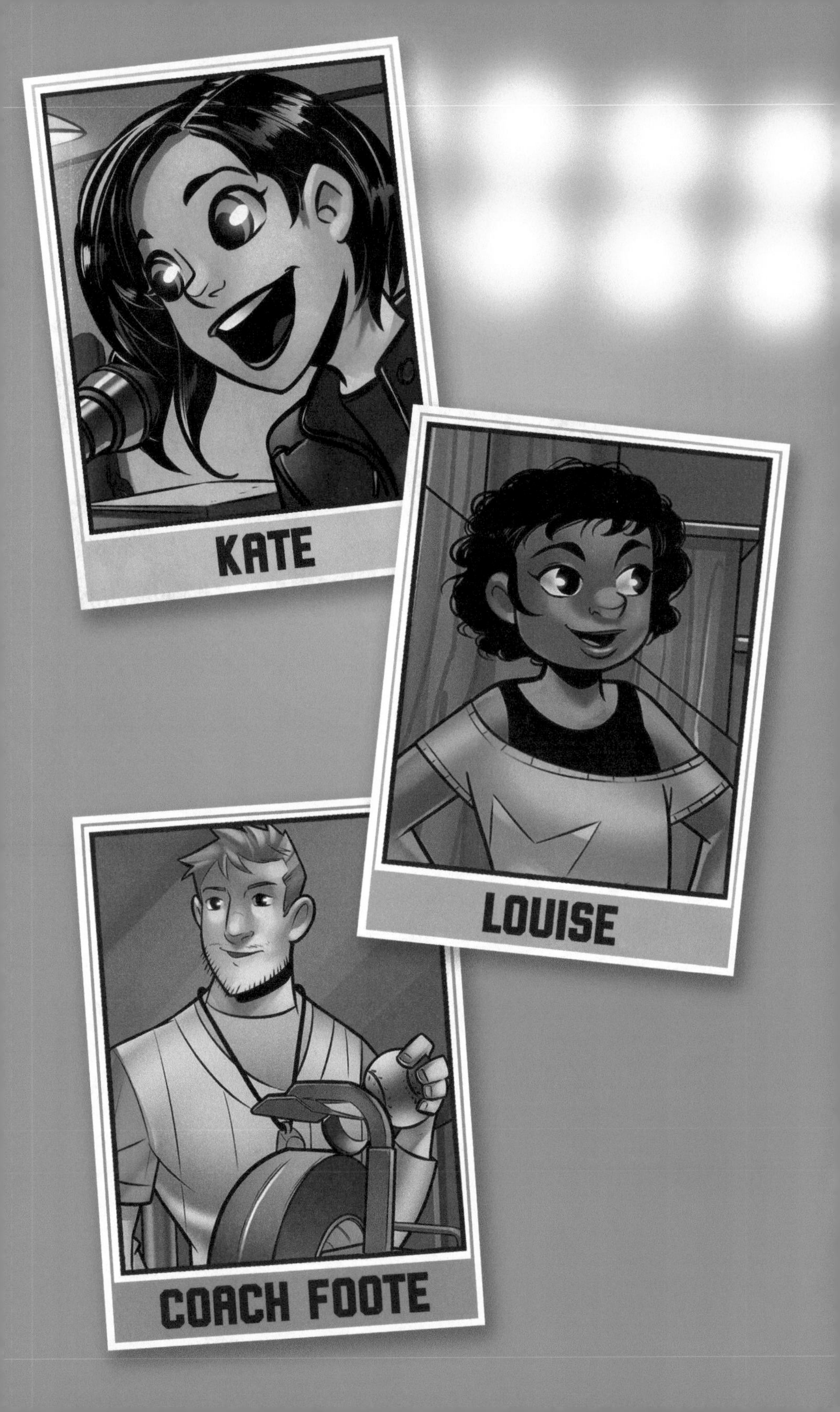
KATE
LOUISE
COACH FOOTE

CRACK!
I sure do miss that sound.
Not that *my* bat ever made it.
There you are! I thought I'd find you here.

Come on, Eddie. We're late for practice.
Practice?
Band practice.
Remember?
Right. Since I quit baseball last summer, band is the only kind of practice I have.
Hmm . . .

But I don't mind.
Our band totally rocks.
Ricky's stealing second base!
UNCLE CHARLIE
Our songs are all about baseball. We're big fans.
He steals third and home, just in case!
We even named the band Uncle Charlie — the nickname for a curveball.

Good practice, guys. But Lou, your last fill kind of clunked.
Try to keep it tight.
Sure, I'll work on it.
You were shredding tonight, Kate!
Thanks. I just hope we'll be ready for the Battle of the Bands.
I can't believe next Sunday is the big performance!
Don't worry. We'll be amazing.
Good night, rockers.
Don't forget — tomorrow's practice is at 3 p.m. sharp!
We'll be here, Kate!

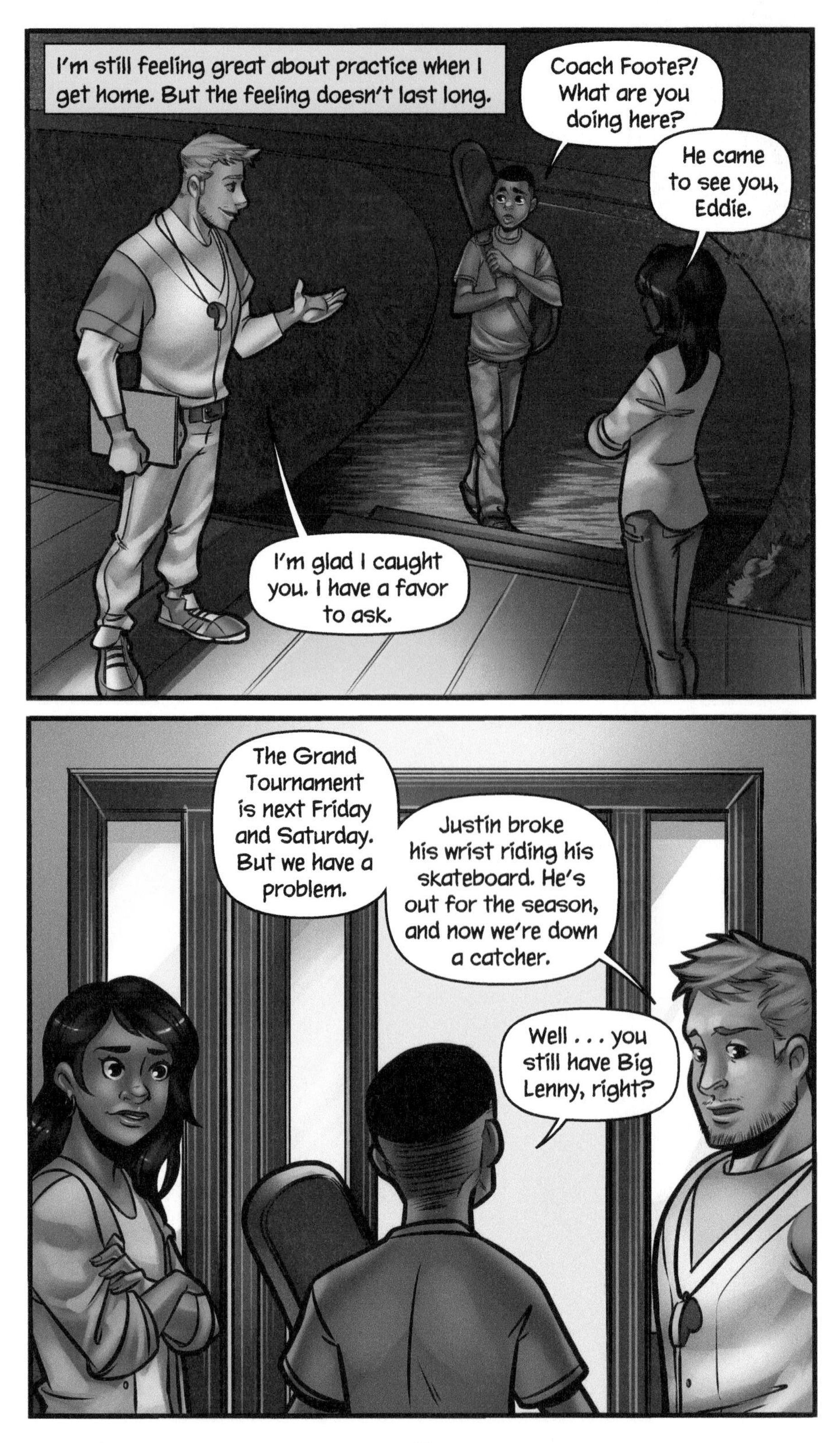
I'm still feeling great about practice when I get home. But the feeling doesn't last long.
Coach Foote?! What are you doing here?
He came to see you, Eddie.
I'm glad I caught you. I have a favor to ask.
The Grand Tournament is next Friday and Saturday. But we have a problem.
Justin broke his wrist riding his skateboard. He's out for the season, and now we're down a catcher.
Well . . . you still have Big Lenny, right?

The tournament is a lot of work. Lenny can't catch four games in two days in the heat of July. It's too much.
We need a good backup.
This doesn't have anything to do with me.
Eddie, don't be rude!
The team needs you, Eddie. You're one of the best catchers I've ever coached.
Sorry, Coach. I don't play baseball anymore.

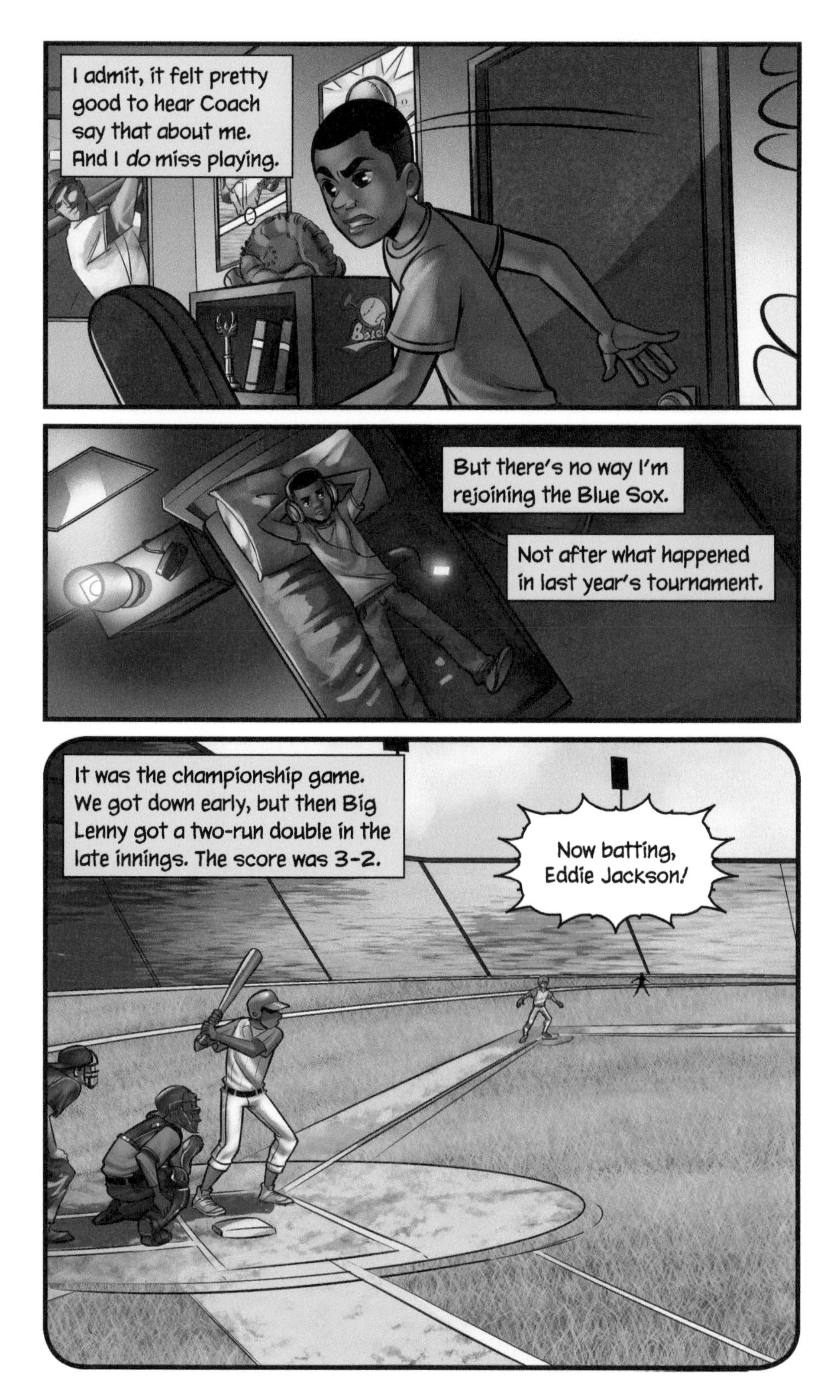
I admit, it felt pretty good to hear Coach say that about me. And I *do* miss playing.
But there's no way I'm rejoining the Blue Sox.
Not after what happened in last year's tournament.
It was the championship game. We got down early, but then Big Lenny got a two-run double in the late innings. The score was 3-2.
Now batting, Eddie Jackson!

We have a runner on third. Just get one hit, and we can tie it up. Strike out, and we lose.
No pressure!

Strike three! Lancers take home the win!
WHIFF
It was my fourth strikeout of the game — what fans call the Golden Sombrero.
I stranded three runners that day. If I'd gotten just one hit, we might've won.
But I didn't get a hit. I choked under the pressure. I let my team down . . . again.

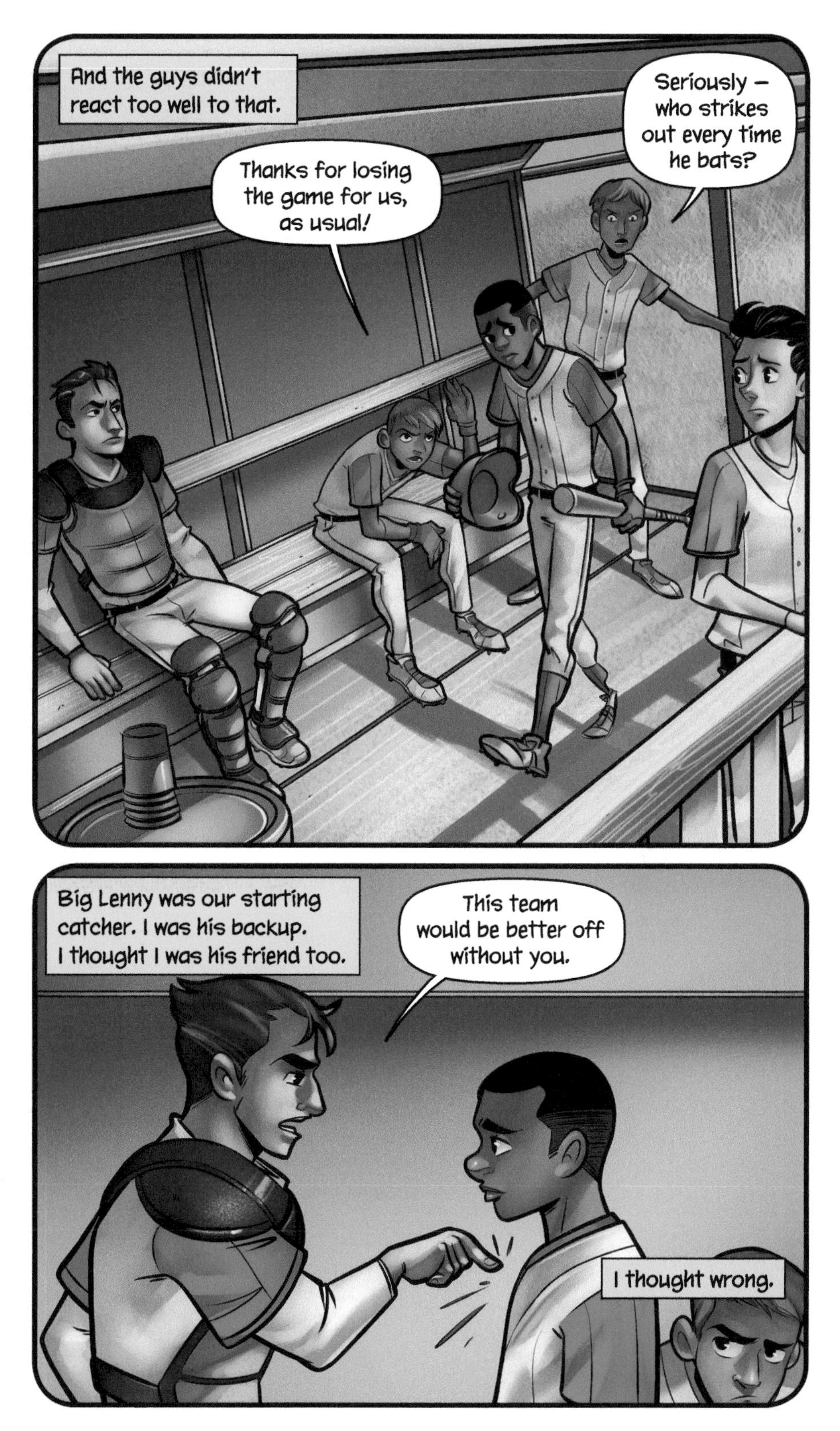
And the guys didn't react too well to that.
Thanks for losing the game for us, as usual!
Seriously — who strikes out every time he bats?
Big Lenny was our starting catcher. I was his backup. I thought I was his friend too.
This team would be better off without you.
I thought wrong.

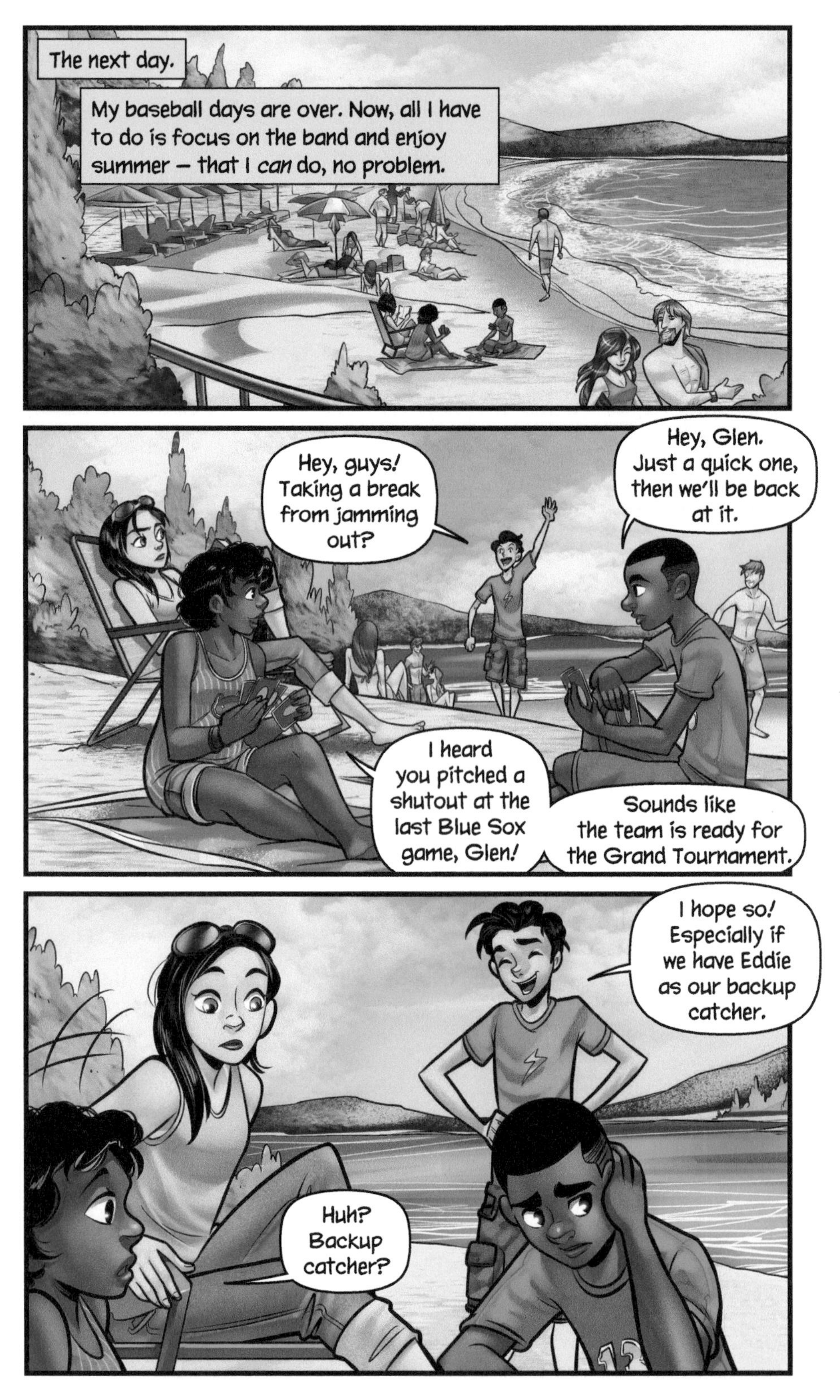
The next day.
My baseball days are over. Now, all I have to do is focus on the band and enjoy summer – that I *can* do, no problem.
Hey, guys! Taking a break from jamming out?
Hey, Glen. Just a quick one, then we'll be back at it.
I heard you pitched a shutout at the last Blue Sox game, Glen!
Sounds like the team is ready for the Grand Tournament.
I hope so! Especially if we have Eddie as our backup catcher.
Huh? Backup catcher?

Didn't you know? Coach wants Eddie on the team again.
Wait . . . isn't the tournament the same weekend as the Battle of the Bands?
Yeah, it is. But it doesn't matter. I'm done with baseball.
Being a great baseball player means playing good defense *and* offense. And I can't hit, so I shouldn't play.
Besides, after last year, it would be too embarrassing.
Hey, we would've lost by a lot more if you hadn't been catching. You call a great game, Eddie.
Plus, you threw out two base stealers that game. You were on fire!

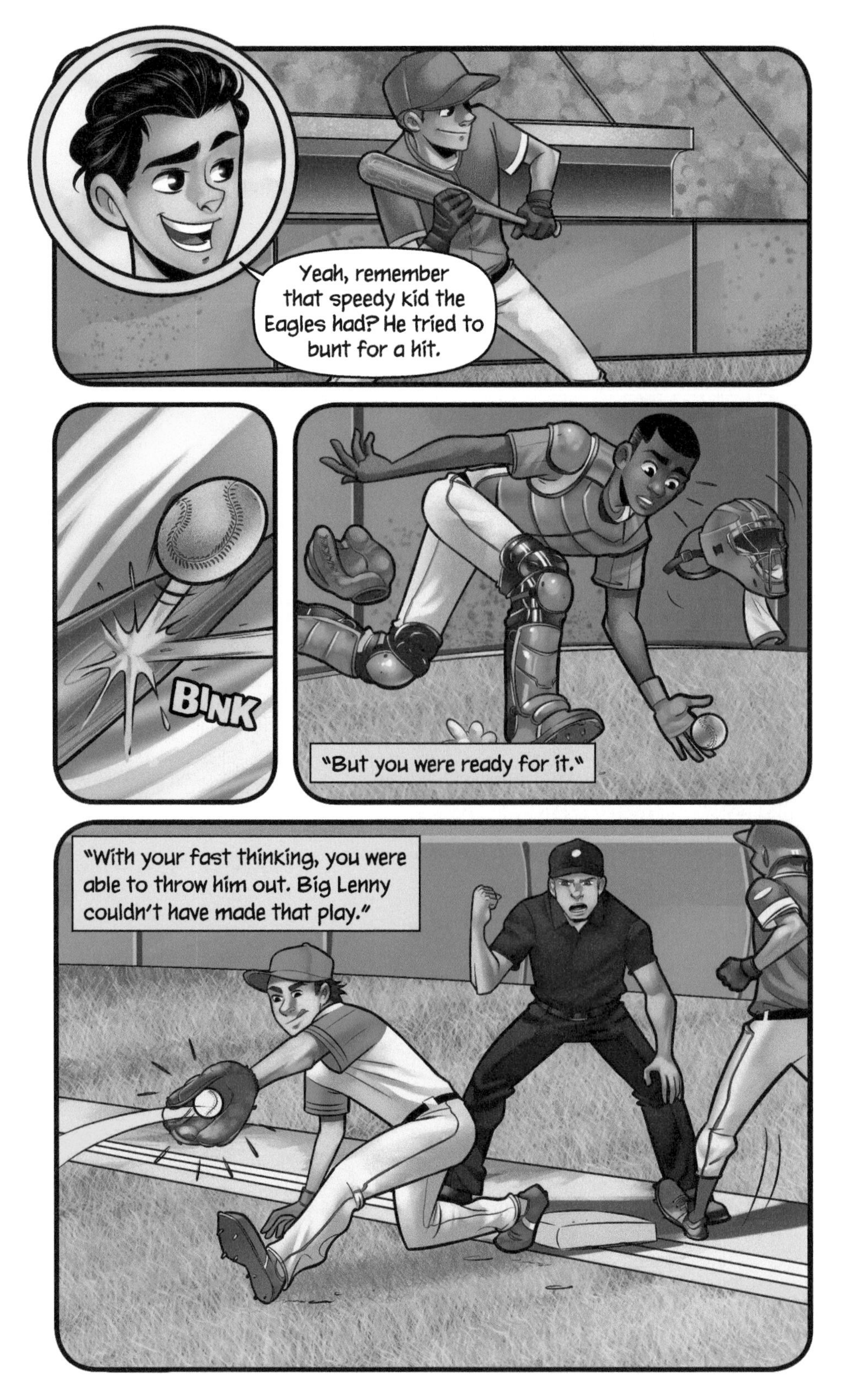
Yeah, remember that speedy kid the Eagles had? He tried to bunt for a hit.
BINK
"But you were ready for it."
"With your fast thinking, you were able to throw him out. Big Lenny couldn't have made that play."

Well, yeah. Being behind the plate is easy. No one pays attention to the catcher, so I can just focus on watching the other team's batters.
But when I'm batting, I feel like everyone is watching *me*, instead. That's what messes me up.
Really? I *like* the pressure of being in the spotlight. Like when we're on stage.
Ha, that's why you sing and play guitar, and I'm on bass.
Speaking of that, it's time for practice.
Blue Sox meet tomorrow at five, Eddie. See you there?
Don't hold your breath.
13

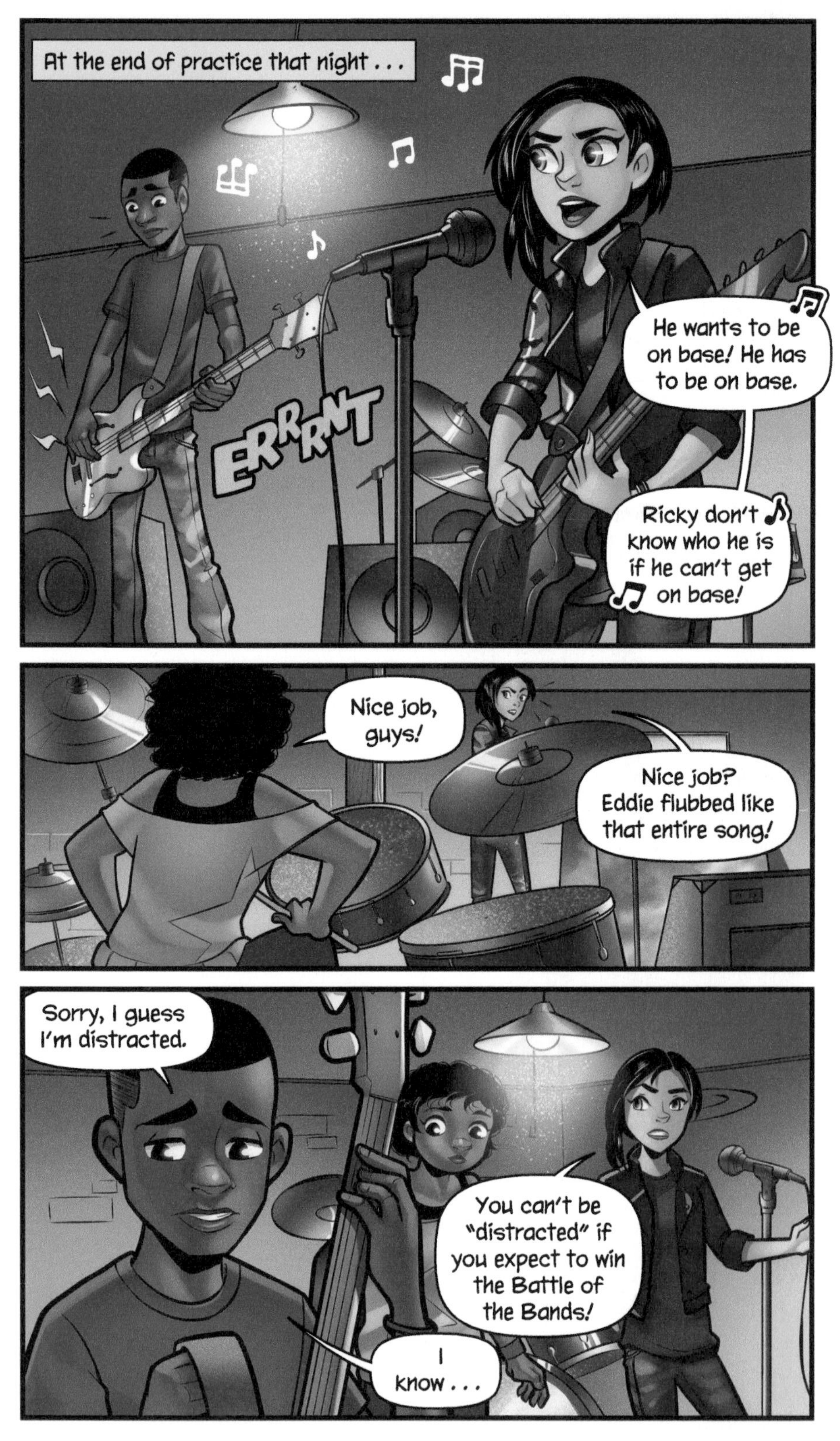
At the end of practice that night . . .
He wants to be on base! He has to be on base.
Ricky don't know who he is if he can't get on base!
ERRRNT
Nice job, guys!
Nice job? Eddie flubbed like that entire song!
Sorry, I guess I'm distracted.
You can't be "distracted" if you expect to win the Battle of the Bands!
I know . . .

Are you still thinking about the Blue Sox? I thought we settled it. You have to play!
Hey, give me that.
I never said I was going to play.
I mean . . . I really want to, but what if I bring the team down again? My nerves always get the best of me when I'm up to bat.
I can help you decide. The tournament ends Saturday. The Battle of the Bands is Sunday.
If you join the Blue Sox, we won't be able to practice before our performance.
You'll be messing up our chances to win.

Well, I think he should do it.
You do?
Definitely! You've been bummed out ever since the season started. Who cares if you strike out? You love baseball.

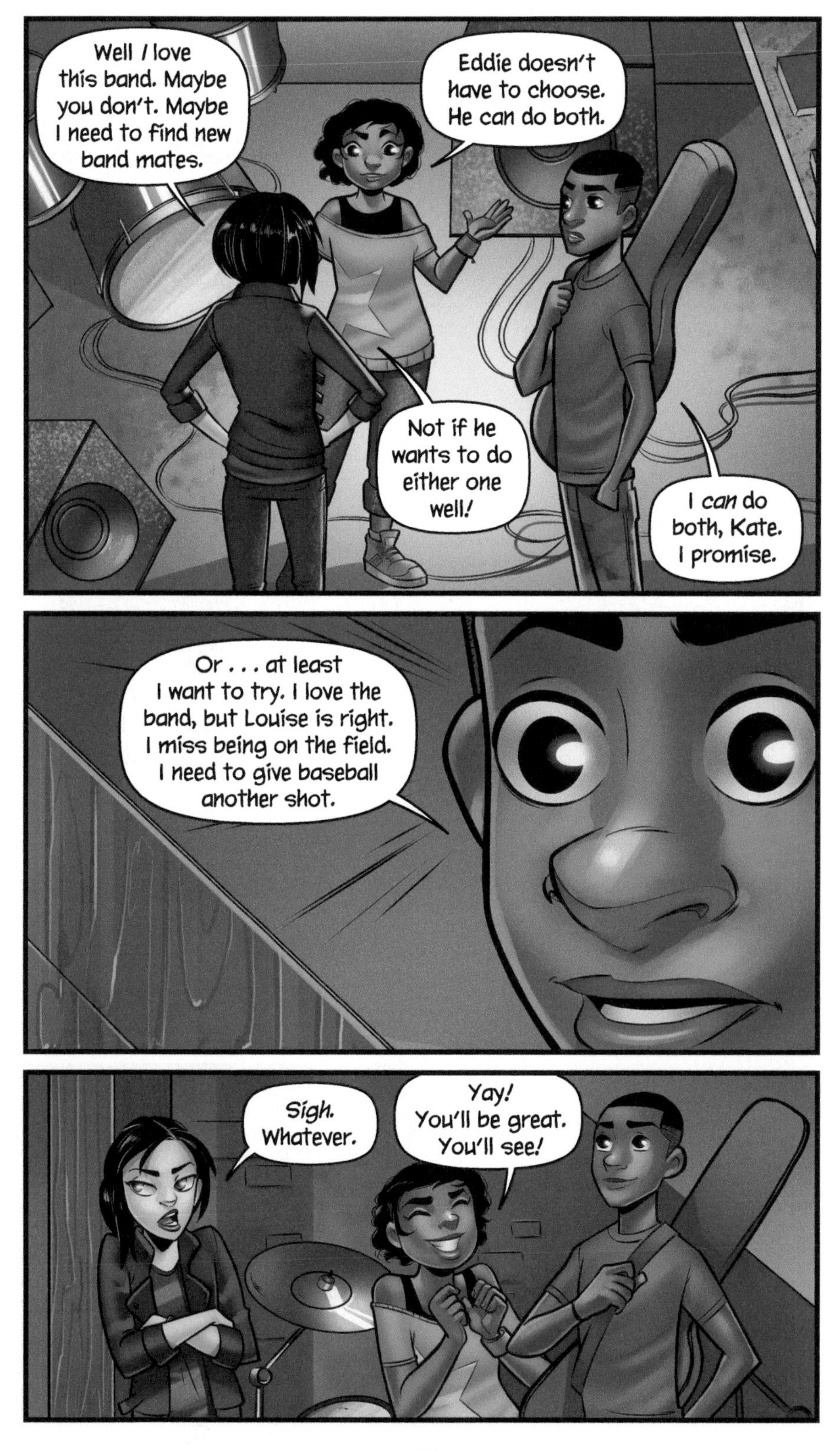
Well *I* love this band. Maybe you don't. Maybe I need to find new band mates.
Eddie doesn't have to choose. He can do both.
Not if he wants to do either one well!
I *can* do both, Kate. I promise.
Or . . . at least I want to try. I love the band, but Louise is right. I miss being on the field. I need to give baseball another shot.
Sigh. Whatever.
Yay! You'll be great. You'll see!

The next day.
Louise's support gave me some confidence back — at least a little.
I'm ready to play ball.
Eddie, welcome back!
Thanks, Coach.

Guys, you all remember Eddie?
Eddie "the K"? Sure, we remember.

He's the guy who can't hit to save his life.
Yeah, he's the no-hit catcher who lost us the tournament.

All right, let's start. Infielders, you're on field one. Outfielders, you're hitting in the cage.
Pitchers and catchers, you'll be in the bullpen with me.

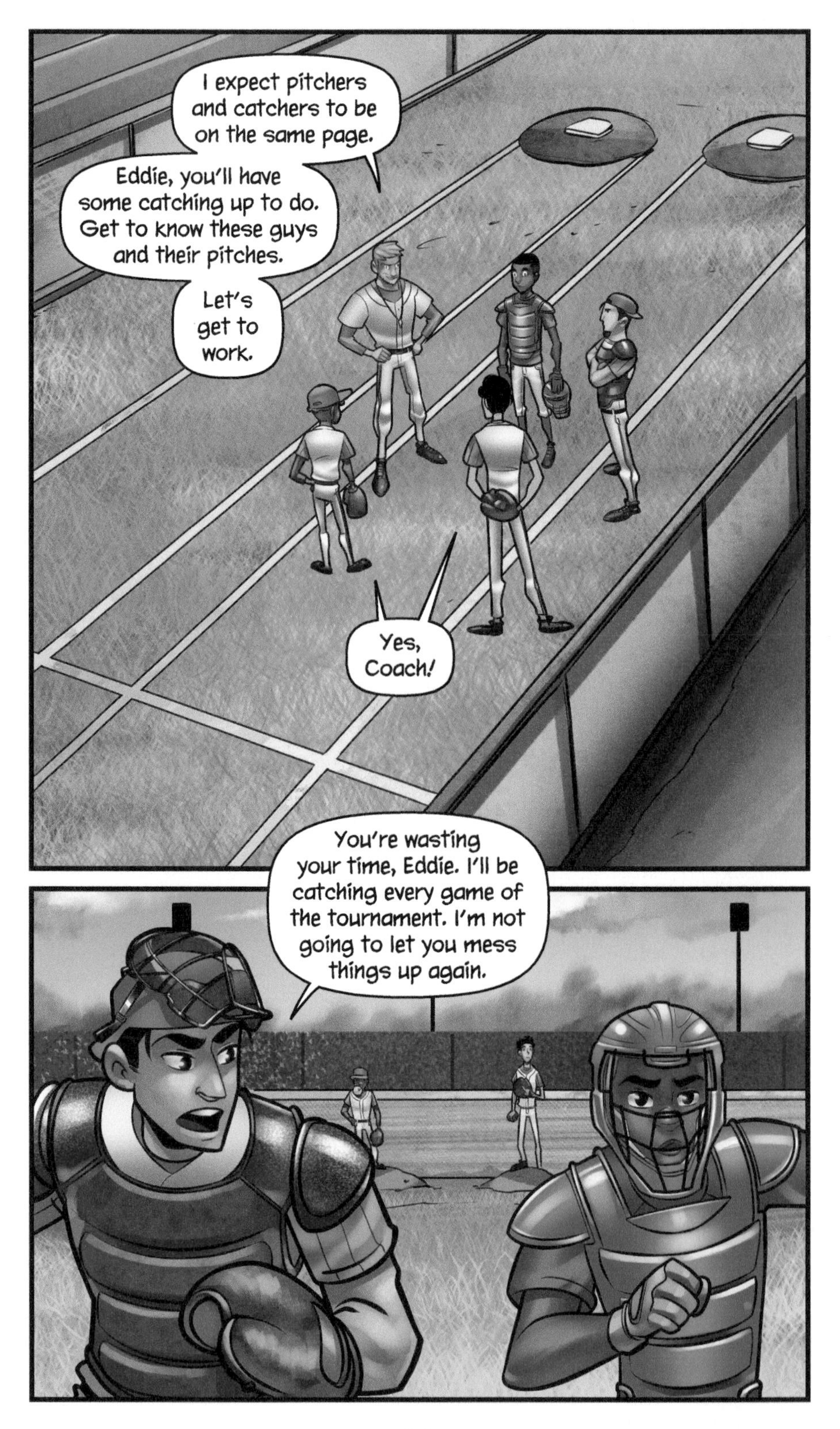
I expect pitchers and catchers to be on the same page.
Eddie, you'll have some catching up to do. Get to know these guys and their pitches.
Let's get to work.
Yes, Coach!
You're wasting your time, Eddie. I'll be catching every game of the tournament. I'm not going to let you mess things up again.

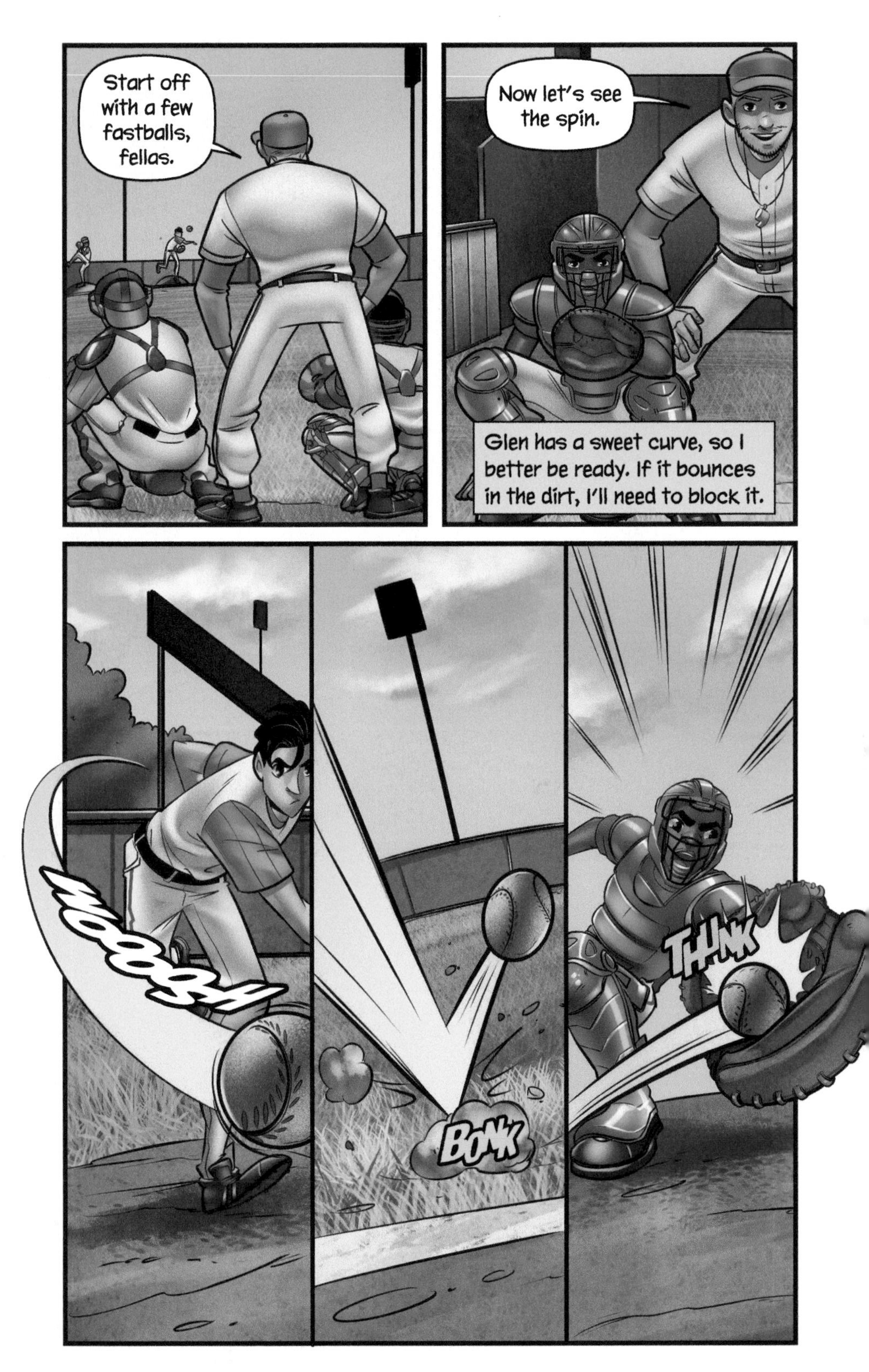
Start off with a few fastballs, fellas.
Now let's see the spin.
Glen has a sweet curve, so I better be ready. If it bounces in the dirt, I'll need to block it.
WOOOSH
BONK
THUNK

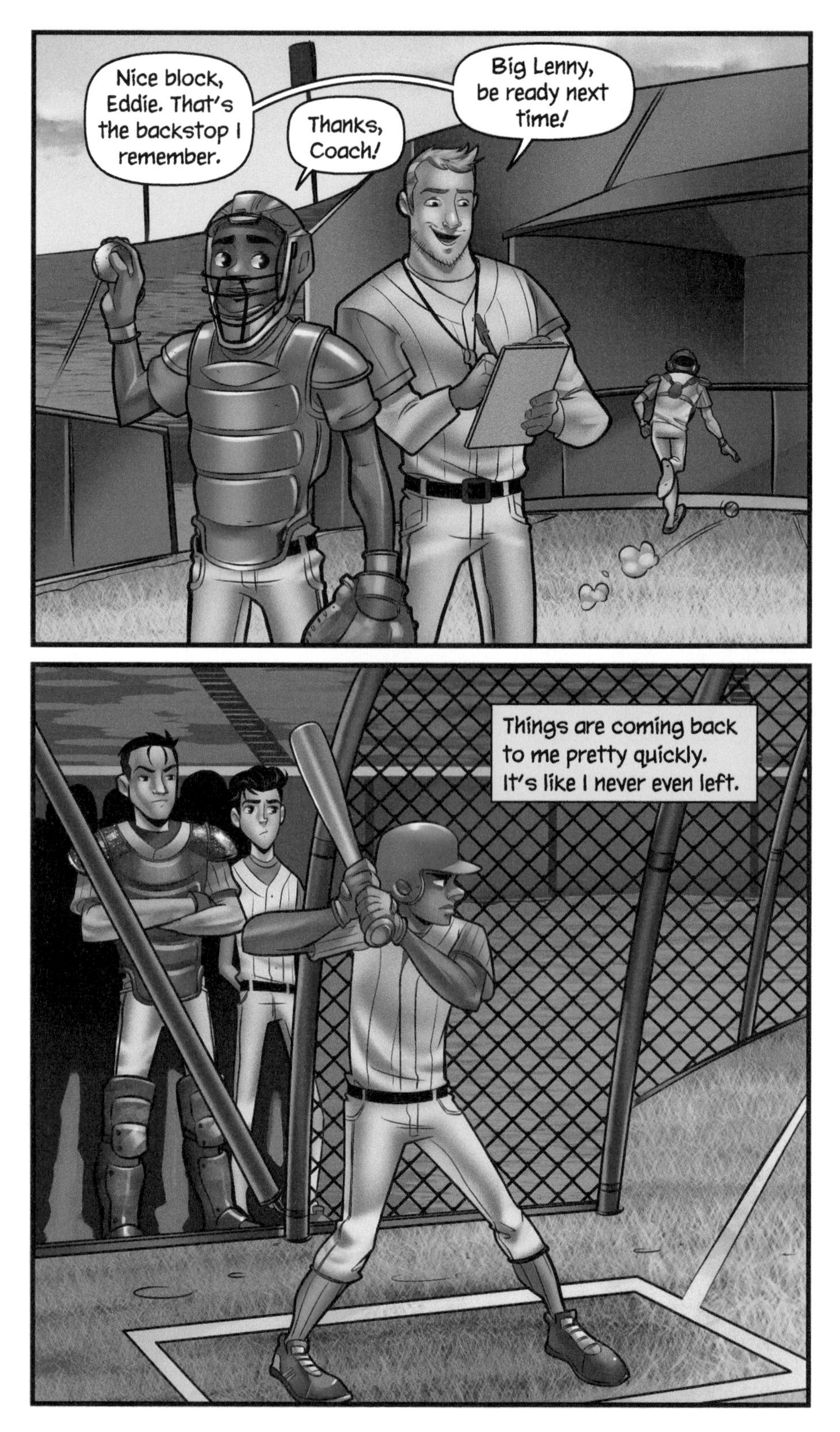
Nice block, Eddie. That's the backstop I remember.
Thanks, Coach!
Big Lenny, be ready next time!
Things are coming back to me pretty quickly. It's like I never even left.

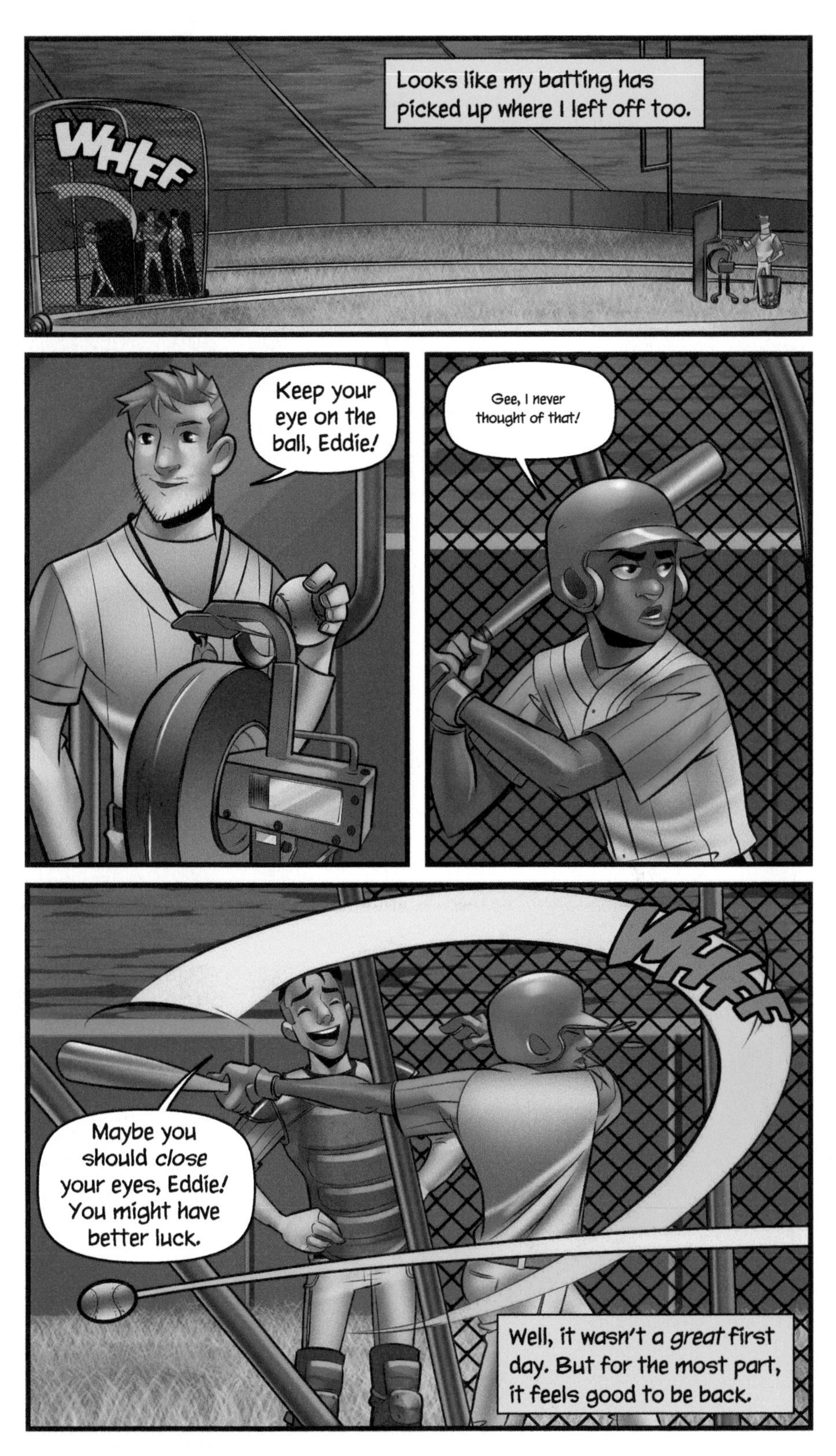
WHIFF
Looks like my batting has picked up where I left off too.
Keep your eye on the ball, Eddie!
Gee, I never thought of that!
WHIFF
Maybe you should *close* your eyes, Eddie! You might have better luck.
Well, it wasn't a *great* first day. But for the most part, it feels good to be back.

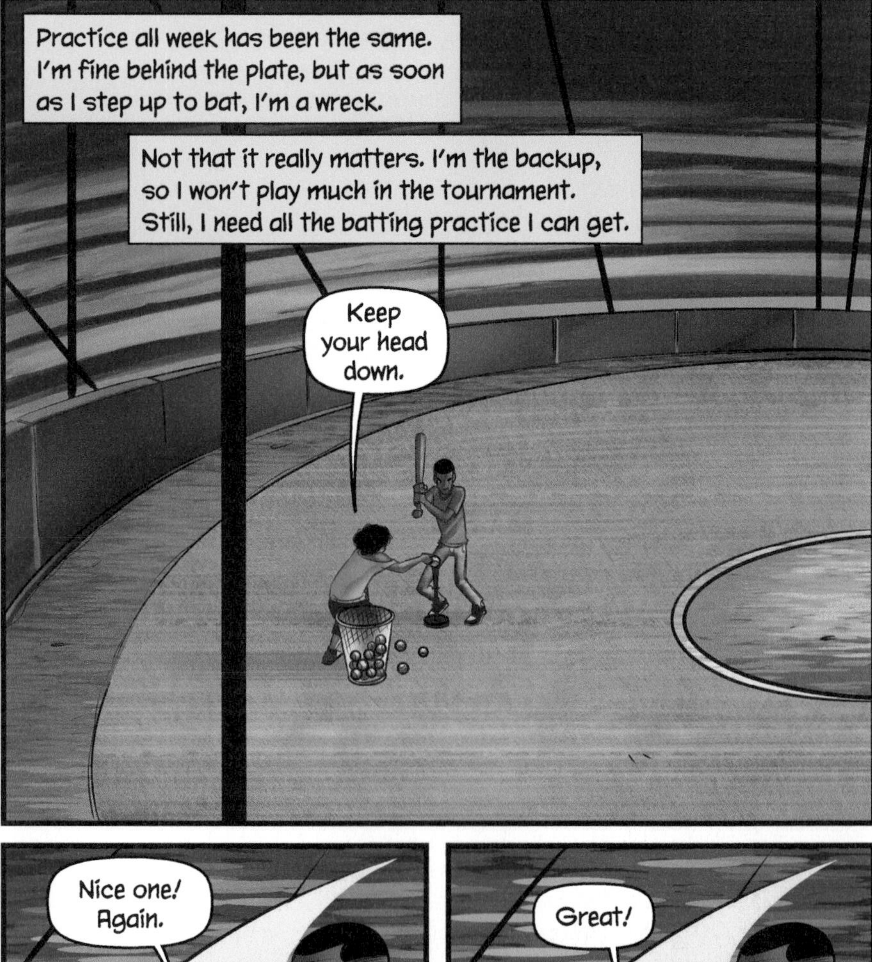
Practice all week has been the same. I'm fine behind the plate, but as soon as I step up to bat, I'm a wreck.
Not that it really matters. I'm the backup, so I won't play much in the tournament. Still, I need all the batting practice I can get.
Keep your head down.

Nice one! Again.
THWACK

Great!
THWACK
Sure it was great. It's not hard to hit off a tee — especially when there's no pressure.

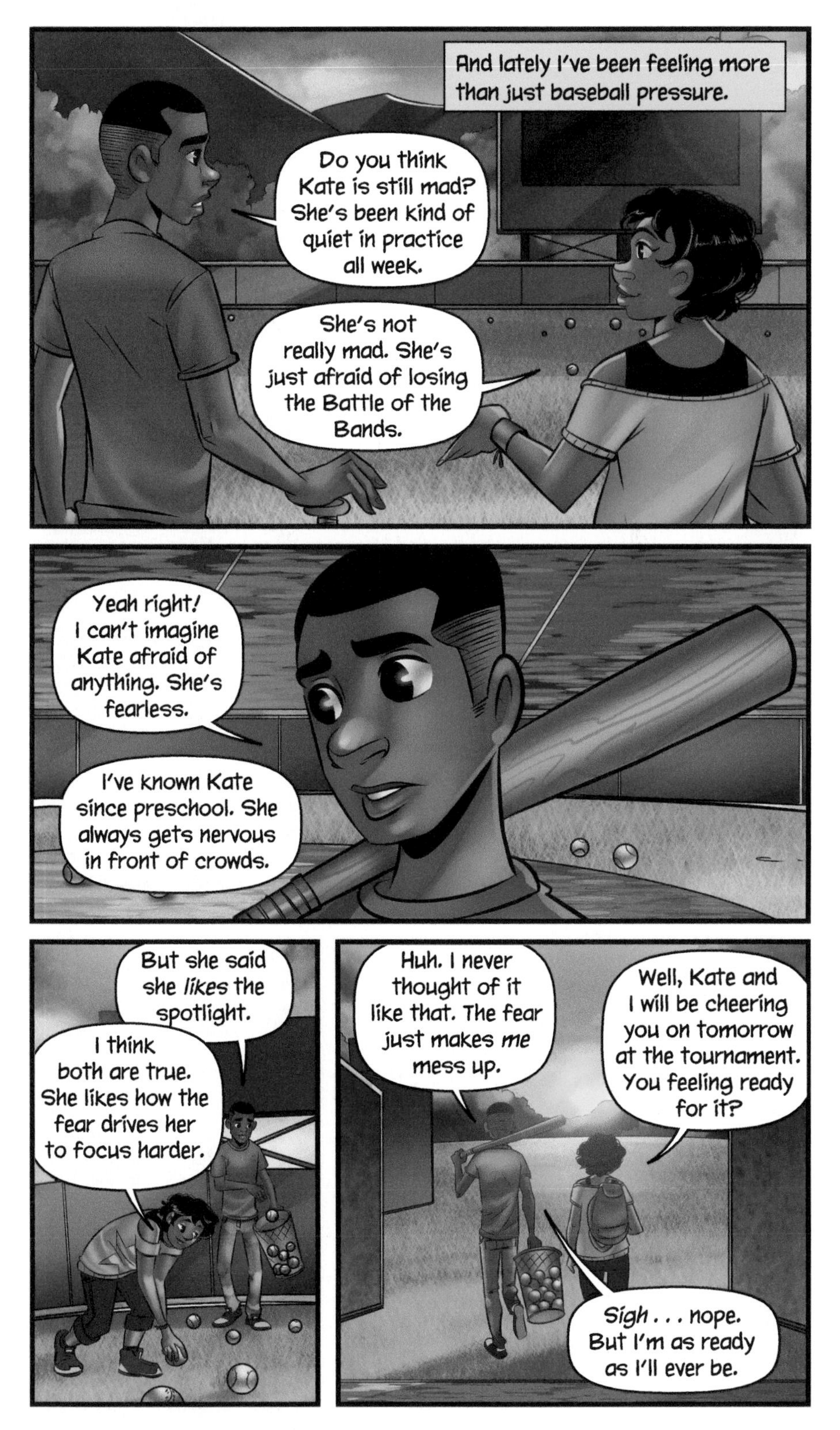
And lately I've been feeling more than just baseball pressure.
Do you think Kate is still mad? She's been kind of quiet in practice all week.
She's not really mad. She's just afraid of losing the Battle of the Bands.
Yeah right! I can't imagine Kate afraid of anything. She's fearless.
I've known Kate since preschool. She always gets nervous in front of crowds.
But she said she *likes* the spotlight.
I think both are true. She likes how the fear drives her to focus harder.
Huh. I never thought of it like that. The fear just makes *me* mess up.
Well, Kate and I will be cheering you on tomorrow at the tournament. You feeling ready for it?
Sigh . . . nope. But I'm as ready as I'll ever be.

Day one of the tournament. And my first real baseball game since last summer.
All right, fellas, this is it. All our hard work comes down to these two days.
We lose, we go home. We win, we move on to the next game. We win four times, we're the champs!
Lenny, you're catching and batting third.
I'm on the bench — as expected.

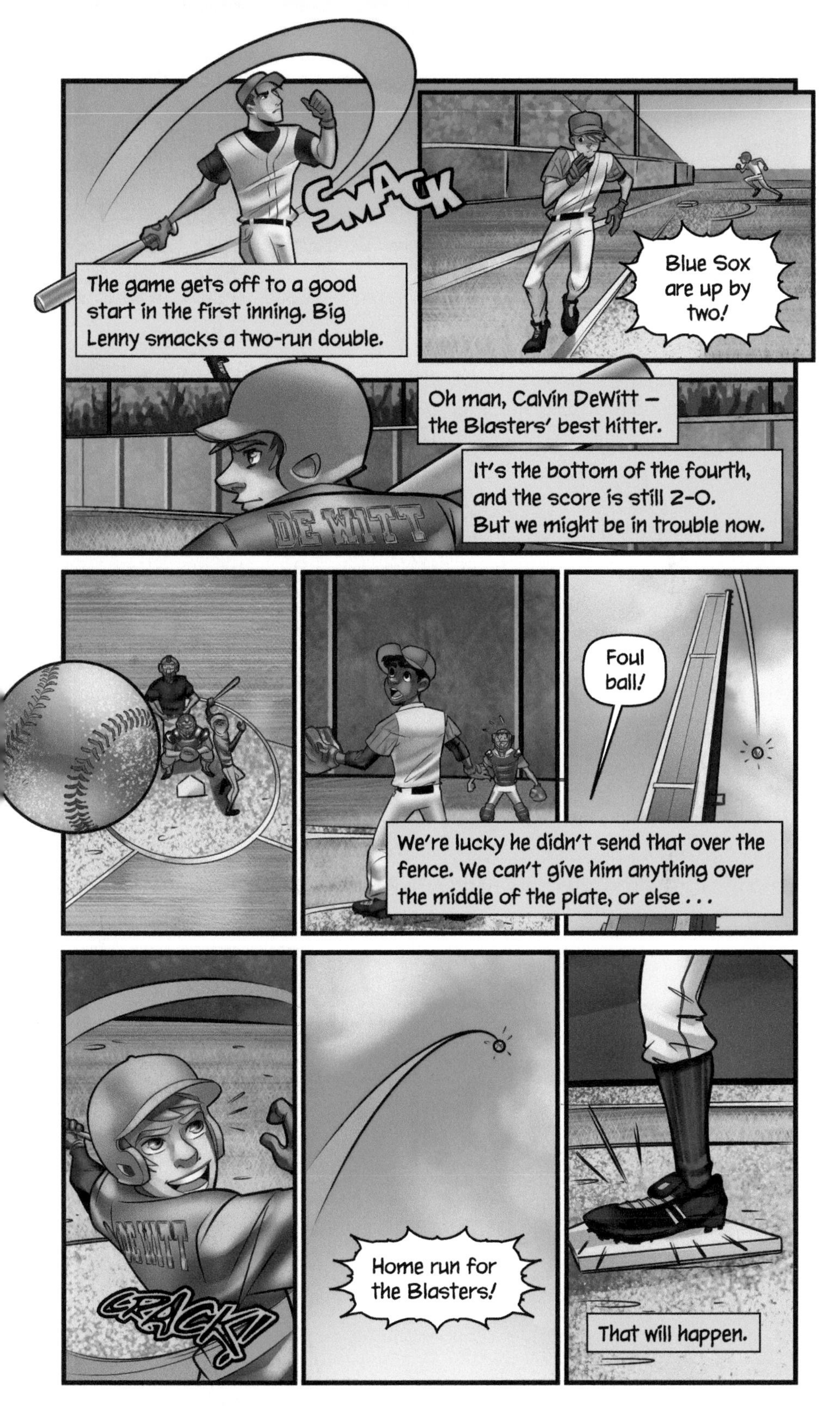
SMACK
The game gets off to a good start in the first inning. Big Lenny smacks a two-run double.
Blue Sox are up by two!
Oh man, Calvin DeWitt — the Blasters' best hitter.
DE WITT
It's the bottom of the fourth, and the score is still 2-0. But we might be in trouble now.
Foul ball!
We're lucky he didn't send that over the fence. We can't give him anything over the middle of the plate, or else . . .
DEWITT
CRACK!
Home run for the Blasters!
That will happen.

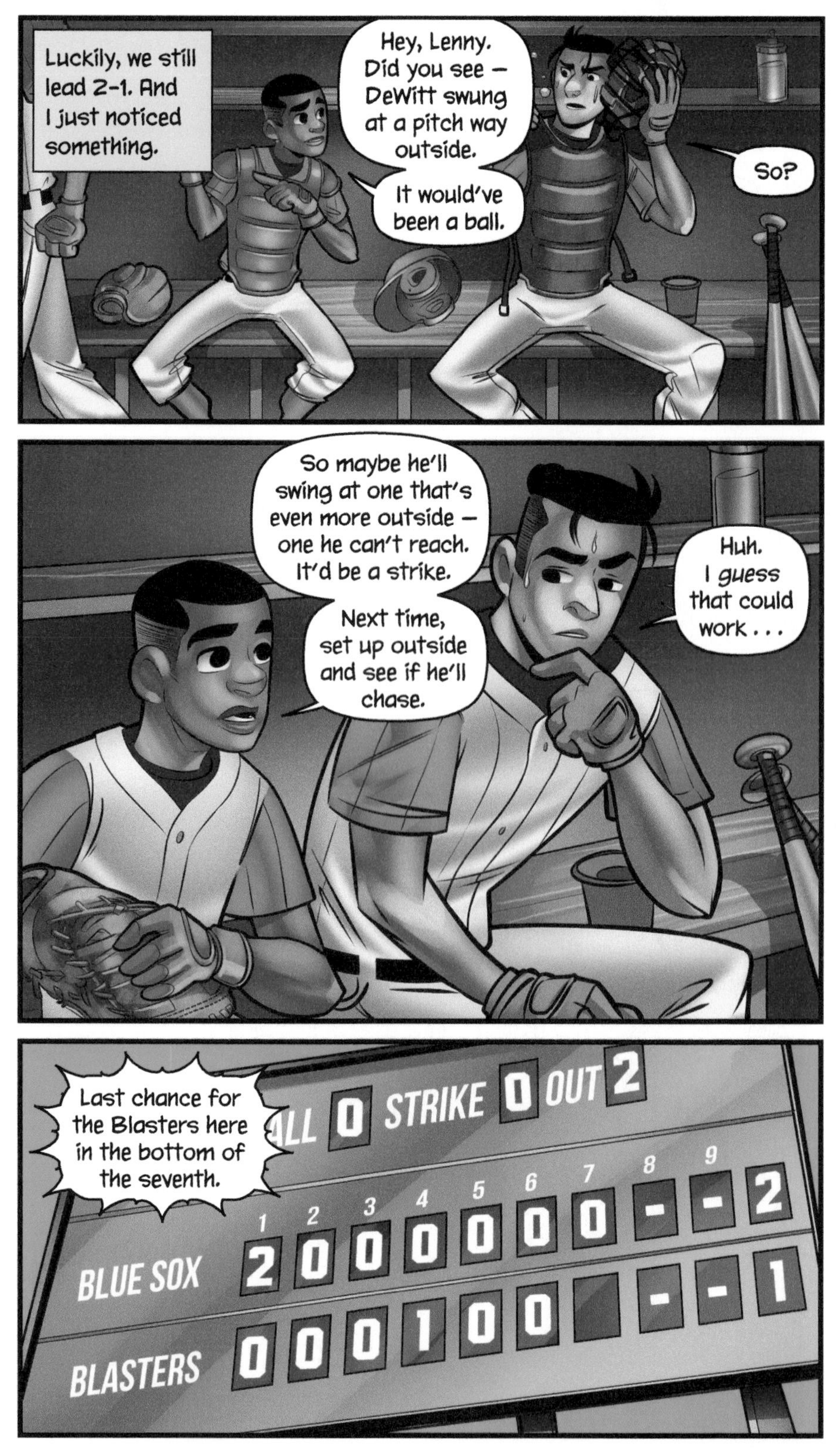

Luckily, we still lead 2-1. And I just noticed something.
Hey, Lenny. Did you see — DeWitt swung at a pitch way outside.
It would've been a ball.
So?
So maybe he'll swing at one that's even more outside — one he can't reach. It'd be a strike.
Next time, set up outside and see if he'll chase.
Huh. I *guess* that could work . . .
Last chance for the Blasters here in the bottom of the seventh.
ALL 0 STRIKE 0 OUT 2
1 2 3 4 5 6 7 8 9
BLUE SOX 2 0 0 0 0 0 0 - - 2
BLASTERS 0 0 0 1 0 0 - - 1

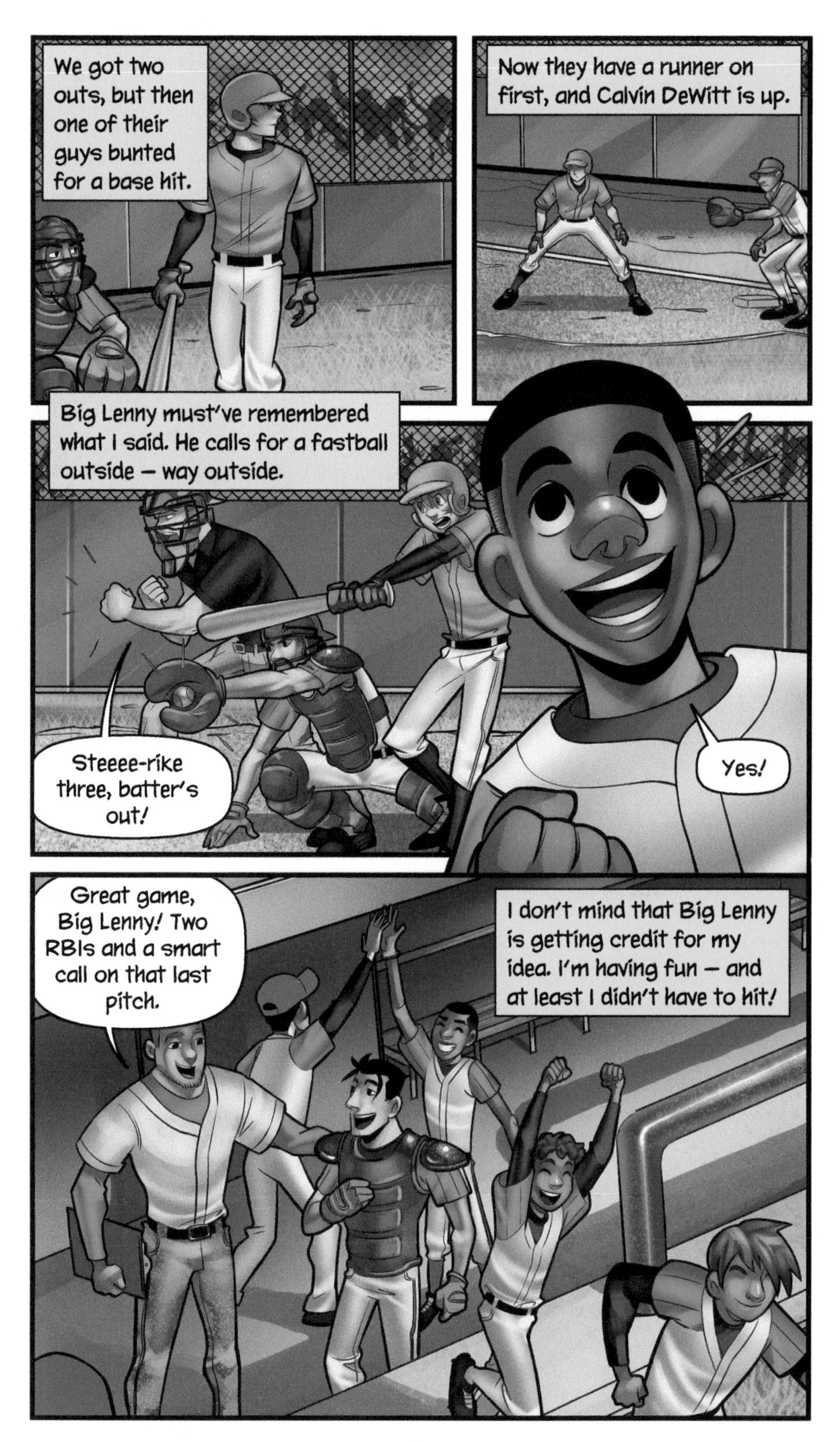
We got two outs, but then one of their guys bunted for a base hit.
Now they have a runner on first, and Calvin DeWitt is up.
Big Lenny must've remembered what I said. He calls for a fastball outside — way outside.
Steeee-rike three, batter's out!
Yes!
Great game, Big Lenny! Two RBIs and a smart call on that last pitch.
I don't mind that Big Lenny is getting credit for my idea. I'm having fun — and at least I didn't have to hit!

Big Lenny had a really good first game.
So Coach had him start the second game of the day too.
CRACK!
Home run!
That decision paid off right away.
But things changed in a hurry. And not in a good way.
The Bulls are running home for the tie!
Play at the plate! The throw from the outfield is in time . . .

He's out!
What a play by the catcher!
Big Lenny held onto the ball . . .
. . . even though he broke his finger.

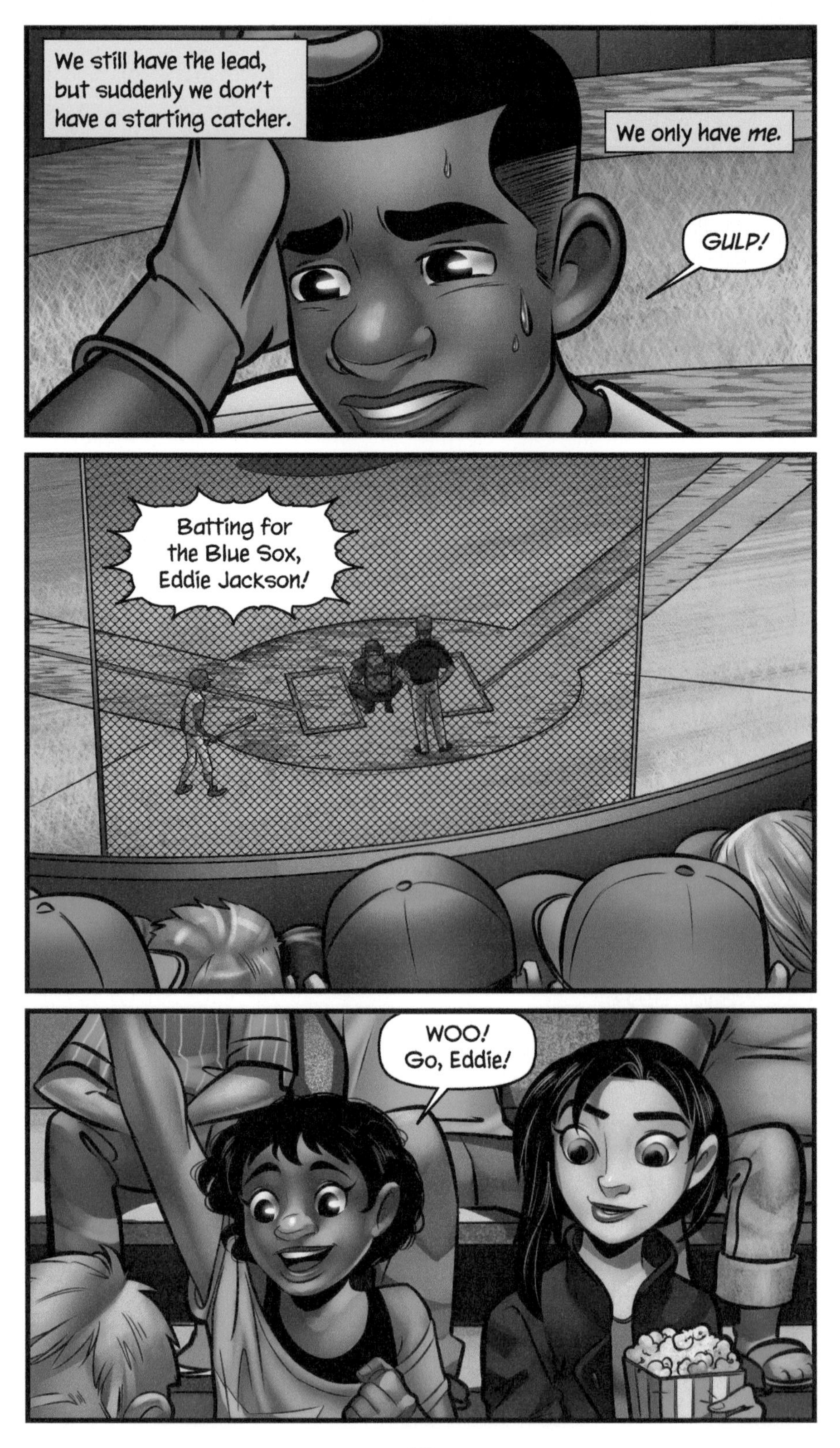
We still have the lead, but suddenly we don't have a starting catcher.
We only have *me.*
GULP!
Batting for the Blue Sox, Eddie Jackson!
WOO! Go, Eddie!

My first at-bat.
Oh man. This isn't going to be pretty.
Strike one!
Strike two!
Steeee-rike three! You're out!
Well that didn't go very well.

But I have a good
game behind the plate.

He's out! Game over!
Blue Sox take the win.
TAG
Great throw! We survive to play on day two.
Nice job, fellas! But be sure to get some rest tonight. It only gets tougher tomorrow.
Yeah, that's so — *gulp* — awesome.

Band practice that night.
Sorry I'm late. Coach was going over pointers for tomorrow. I came over as fast as I could.
No problem. By the way, great job stepping up during the game today!
We should get down to practice. "Ricky on Base" is up first.
I'm just glad I didn't ruin everything for the team with my horrible batting.
I forgot how terrifying it is being at the plate!
One, two, one-two-three-four!
CLICK
CLICK

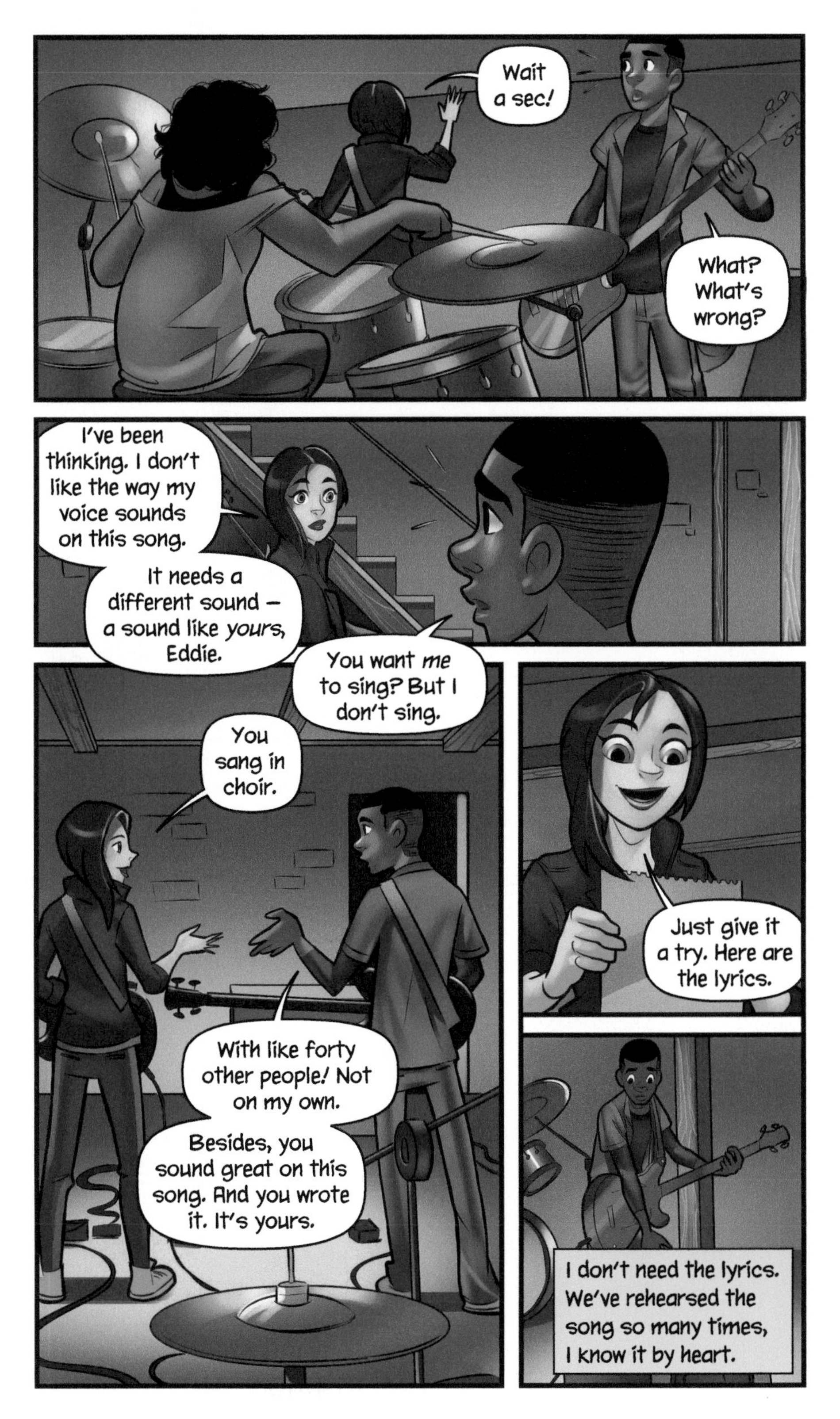
Wait a sec!
What? What's wrong?
I've been thinking. I don't like the way my voice sounds on this song.
It needs a different sound — a sound like *yours*, Eddie.
You want *me* to sing? But I don't sing.
You sang in choir.
With like forty other people! Not on my own.
Besides, you sound great on this song. And you wrote it. It's yours.
Just give it a try. Here are the lyrics.
I don't need the lyrics. We've rehearsed the song so many times, I know it by heart.

But that doesn't mean I can sing them.
Ricky takes a dangerous lead. Revs his —
Hold it!
What now?
Eddie, you have to move up. You're the singer. You need to be front and center.
. . . up front?
You have to get used to being the star. Don't think about us. Just settle into the song.
Ricky takes a dangerous lead.
Revs his engine, picks up speed.
Ricky's stealing second base.

To tell the truth, I love "Ricky on Base." I think it's Kate's best song.
Steals third and home, just in case!
It's about the MLB stolen base king, Ricky Henderson. He loved baseball so much, he never wanted to quit.
He just wanted to be on base.
Heeey, Ricky!
The more I got into the song, the more everything else kind of faded away.
Not bad, Mr. Jackson. Not bad at all.
Ha, yeah. Thanks!
UNCLE CHARLIE
Kate's right, I *wasn't* bad — once I just settled into the song.

Day two of the tournament.
Semi-final game vs. the Raiders.
WHIFF
Daijon is pitching. His slider is really sharp, and I've called for it a lot.
Strike three. You're out!
After all, it's working.
Hitting has been more of the same.
Come on, Eddie! Base hit gives us the lead!

CRACK!
But I'm getting more comfortable.
Foul!
Strike three. Batter's out!
WHIFF
Just a little.

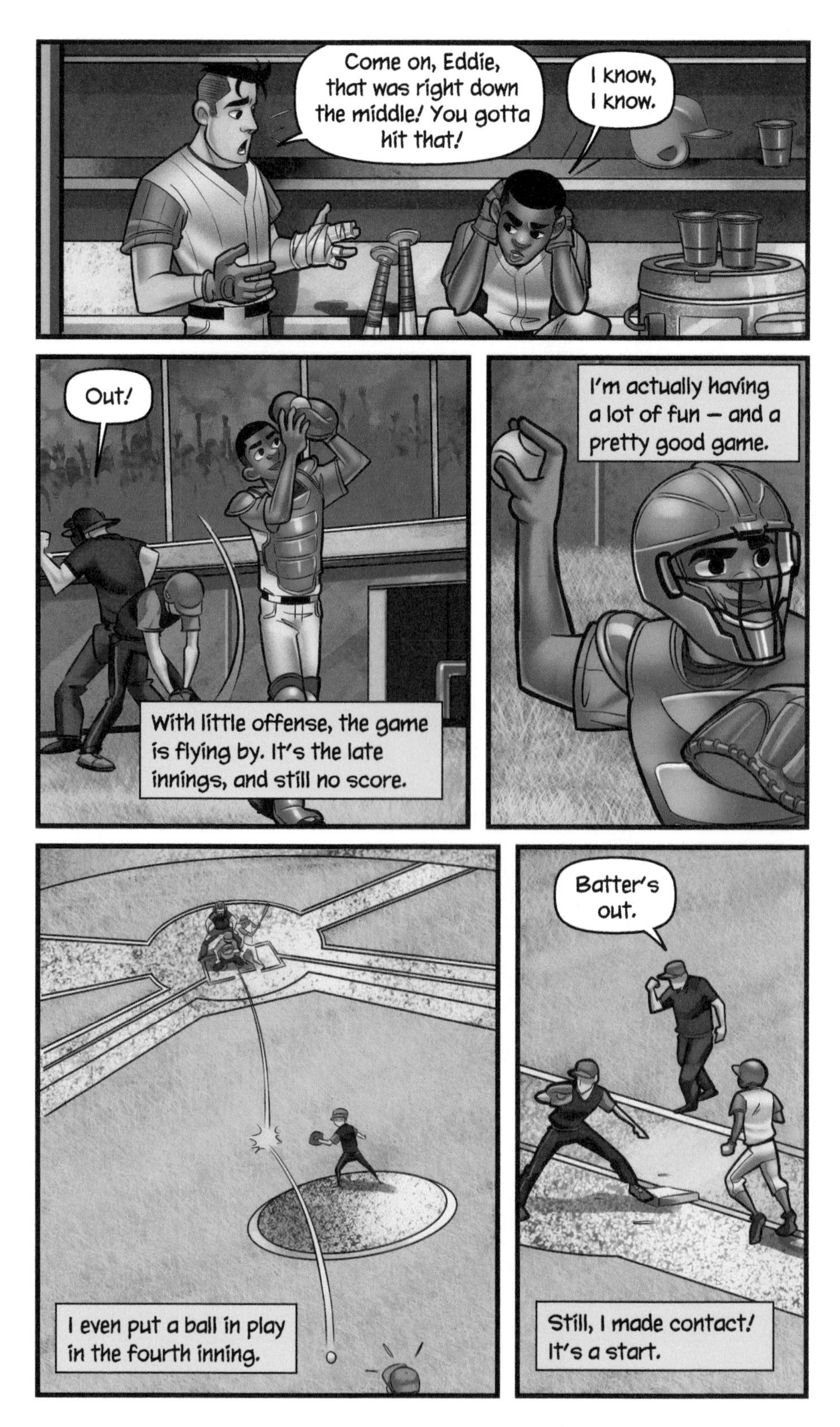
Come on, Eddie, that was right down the middle! You gotta hit that!
I know, I know.
Out!
With little offense, the game is flying by. It's the late innings, and still no score.
I'm actually having a lot of fun — and a pretty good game.
I even put a ball in play in the fourth inning.
Batter's out.
Still, I made contact! It's a start.

In the fifth inning, Daijon got a big hit with a runner on third.
It was only one run, but that's all we needed.
Daijon pitched a shutout. We got our third win.
BLUE SOX 0 0 0 0 1 0 0 - - 1
RAIDERS 0 0 0 0 0 0 0 - - 0

Just one more win to go.
Heck of a game, fellas. Daijon, a shutout! You and Eddie make a good team.
Get something to drink, have a snack, and stretch. Meet on field one for the final game in fifteen minutes.
Big Lenny doesn't look too happy. I know he wishes he could be playing.
Great game, Eddie! Your calls are killer today.
Thanks! I just hope I can keep it up for one more game.
Hey, is that who I think it is?
DeAndre Simmons, the kid who struck me out four times in one game last year? Yep.
Looks like he's pitching this game.

Well, I'm doomed.
Hey, don't let that guy intimidate you. Just settle in. Focus.
Yeah, you got this.
Ugh. I'm starting to wish I chose band practice over the Blue Sox.
Oh, we're having band practice tonight.
You didn't think you were getting out of that, did you?
Hey Eddie, warm me up. I think Uncle Charlie is biting today!

WHIFF
Glen's right. Uncle Charlie is biting, and the Lancers are swinging and missing.
Unfortunately, DeAndre is throwing pure gas.
Come on, guys. Can't *anyone* get a hit off this guy?
Good swing, Eddie! You'll get it next time.
WHIFF

After six innings, it's still 0-0.
Things aren't looking good.
DeAndre is up third next inning.
He totally hammered Uncle Charlie last time. What are we going to do?
Let's give him plenty of fastballs inside. He'll either strike out or walk.

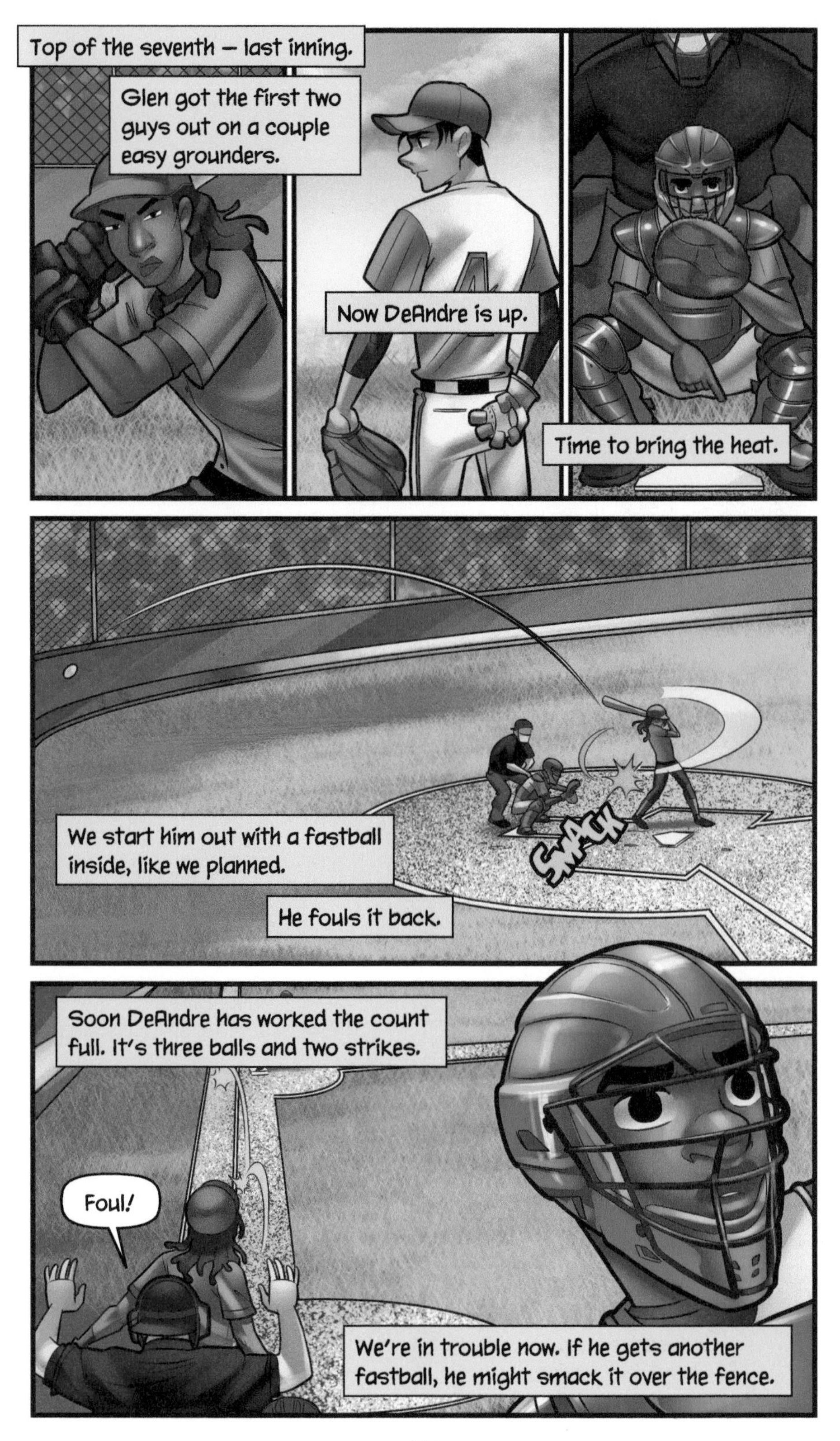
Top of the seventh — last inning.
Glen got the first two guys out on a couple easy grounders.
Now DeAndre is up.
Time to bring the heat.
We start him out with a fastball inside, like we planned.
SMACK
He fouls it back.
Soon DeAndre has worked the count full. It's three balls and two strikes.
Foul!
We're in trouble now. If he gets another fastball, he might smack it over the fence.

Meeting on the mound.
That was close.
No kidding! We need to get him out. I think it's time for Uncle Charlie.
You sure?
Trust me. Just bury it.
This has to work.
You're out!
TUNK

Great call, Eddie!
See? Told ya.
Bottom of the seventh. The game is still tied 0-0.
All right, fellas, how about a little rally here? All we need is one run!
You're up first, Eddie.
Eddie, wait.
Uh . . . hey, Lenny. What's up?

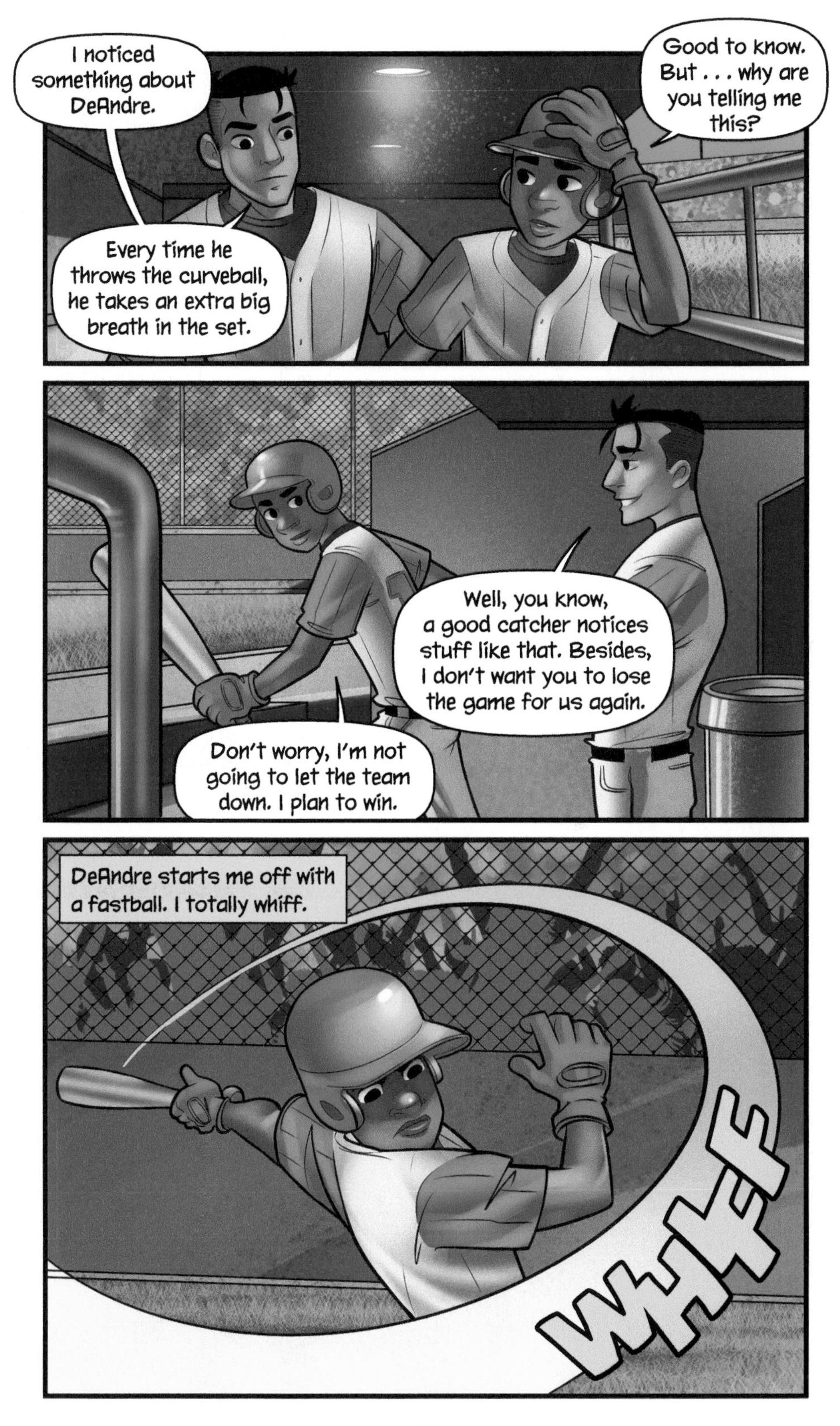
I noticed something about DeAndre.
Good to know. But . . . why are you telling me this?
Every time he throws the curveball, he takes an extra big breath in the set.
Well, you know, a good catcher notices stuff like that. Besides, I don't want you to lose the game for us again.
Don't worry, I'm not going to let the team down. I plan to win.
DeAndre starts me off with a fastball. I totally whiff.
WHIFF

Come on, Eddie!
You Can do it!
You got this!
Right. Just settle into the moment, Eddie.

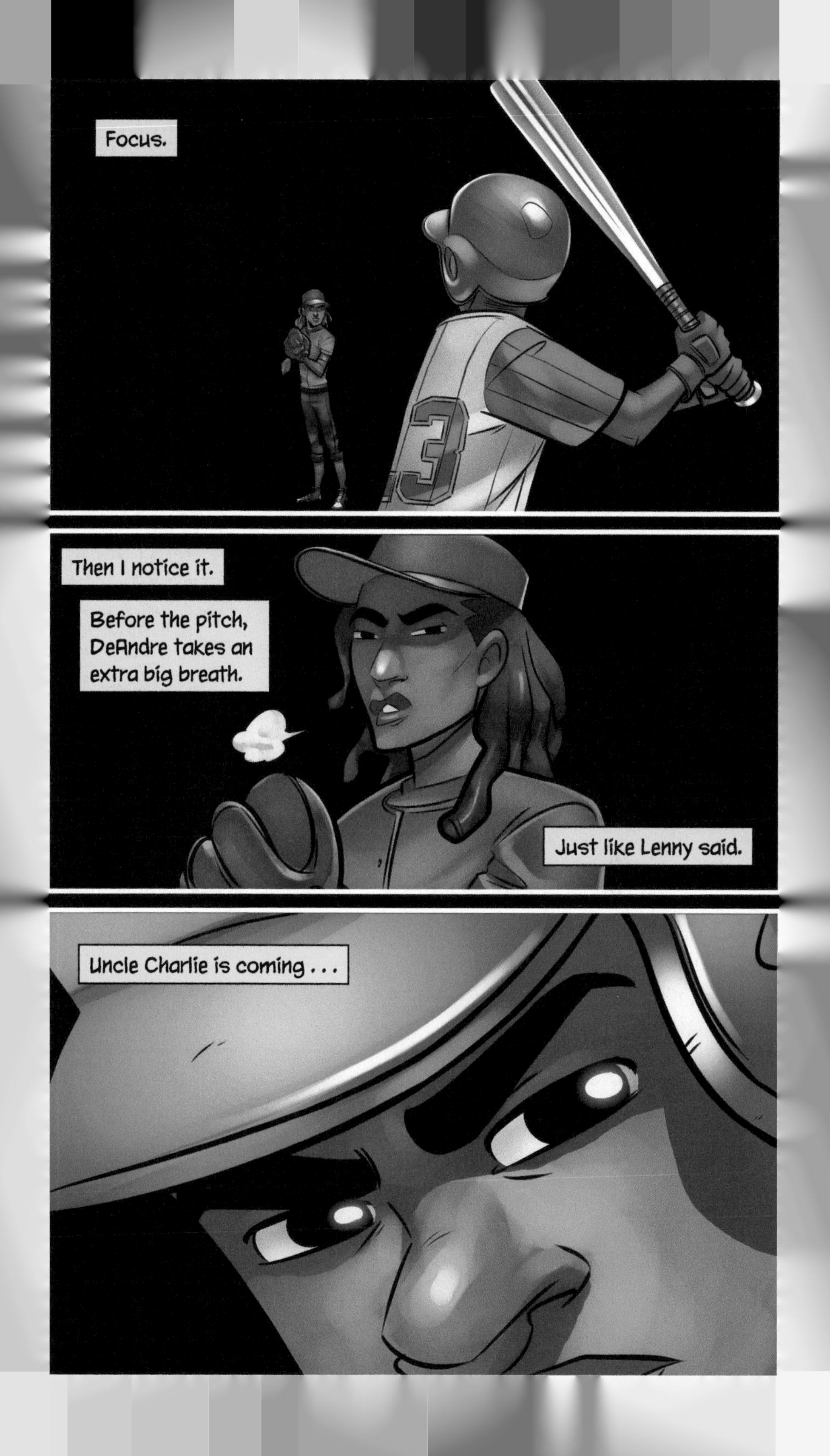
Focus.
Then I notice it.
Before the pitch, DeAndre takes an extra big breath.
Just like Lenny said.
Uncle Charlie is coming . . .

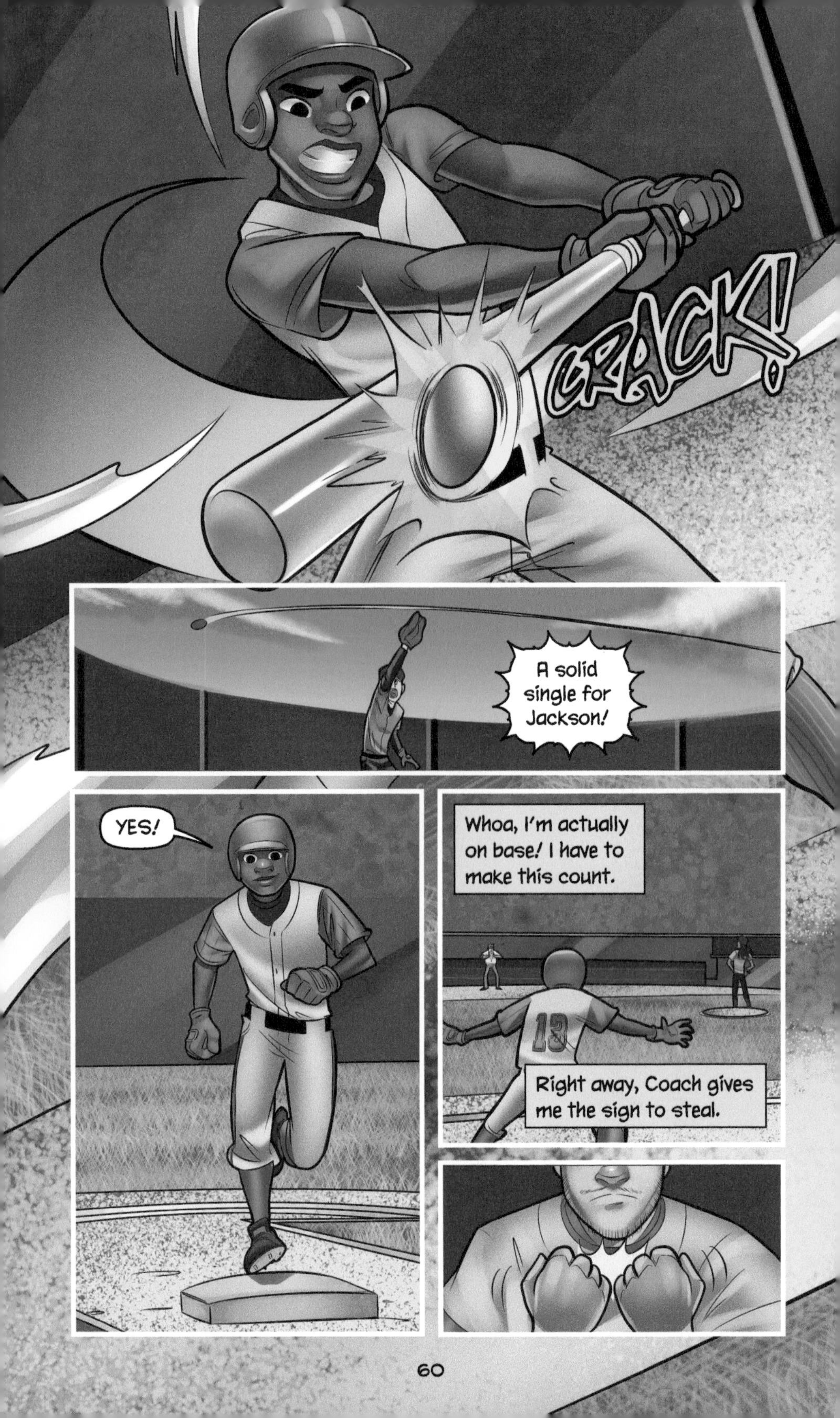
CRACK!
A solid single for Jackson!
YES!
Whoa, I'm actually on base! I have to make this count.
13
Right away, Coach gives me the sign to steal.

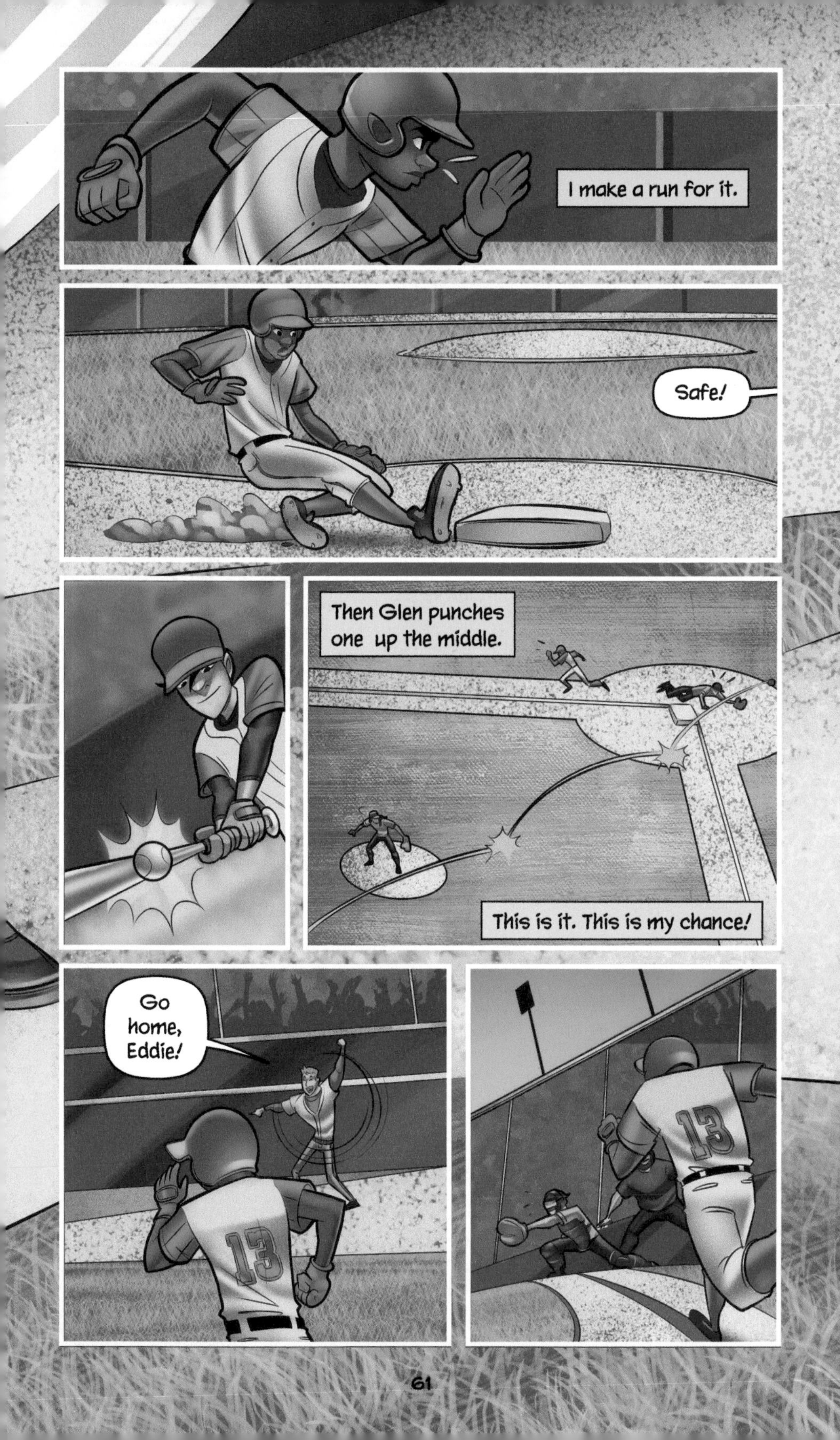
I make a run for it.
Safe!
Then Glen punches one up the middle.
This is it. This is my chance!
Go home, Eddie!
13
13

Safe!
Blue Sox win, 1-0! We have our new tournament champions!
Nice wheels, Eddie!

Good game.
Good game.
Hey, you were decent out there, Eddie. Good, even.
But not as good as me, obviously.
Obviously.
You know . . . even though the tournament is over, there's still more baseball to be played this summer.
The team could use another good catcher.
That'd be cool. Count me in!

Eddie! I'm so proud of you!
Us too! You looked so calm out there – not nervous at all.
Oh, I was *super* nervous. But I used that energy to help me focus, instead of freaking out.
Sounds like you're finally getting used to the spotlight.
Who knows, maybe soon you'll be leaving the band and breaking into a solo career.
Ha, yeah I don't think that'll happen *anytime* soon.
Let's all celebrate the big win by going out for tater-tot nachos and malts!
How about it?
That sounds great, Mom, but we have to practice.
The Battle of the Bands is tomorrow.
We have to get ready.

We can skip practice tonight. I think somebody's earned a celebration.
YAY!
Of course, that means we practice bright and early in the morning.
Of course.

VISUAL QUESTIONS

1. Eddie likes baseball, but he quit the team. In your own words, write a paragraph about why he decided not to play on the Blue Sox.

2. The art in graphic novels can tell you a lot about what a character is feeling. Describe how you think Eddie is feeling here. What in the text and art makes you think that? Look back at page 13 if you need help.

3. What can you see in the background of this panel? Why is Eddie thinking about band practice as he gets ready to bat against DeAndre? Talk about your answer.

4. Compare and contrast how Eddie performs when he's playing catcher and when he's up to bat. What would you prefer, catching or batting?

5. What three actions are being shown here? How do they connect to each other? Write a narrative paragraph that describes what happens during these three panels.

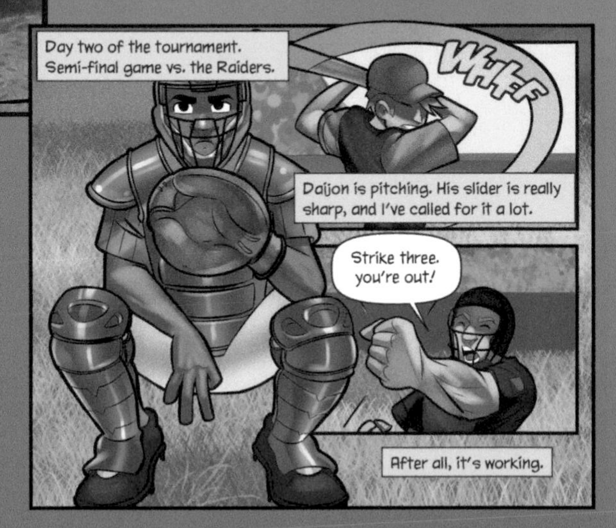

BALLPARK LINGO

Baseball has been played in the United States since the 1800s. Since then, lots of slang and colorful terms have entered the sport. It can be confusing if you're new to the field. Read on, and in no time you'll be talking like a true pro baseball player!

Ace — the best pitcher on a team

Bag — a base

Battery — the pitcher and the catcher

Beanball — a pitch purposefully thrown to hit the batter, often aimed at the head; this pitch can result in a warning, ejection, or suspension

Can of corn — a fly ball that takes very little effort to catch; also an easy play made on the field

Cannon — a strong arm

Cookie — a pitch that is easy to hit

Dish — home plate

Gas — a pitch thrown with a lot of speed and power; "throwing gas" or "bringing the heat" can also mean to throw a fastball

Fireballer — a pitcher known for throwing fastballs; also called a flamethrower or power pitcher

Golden sombrero — when a batter strikes out four times in one game; if a player strikes out five times, it's called a platinum sombrero

Goose egg — a zero on the scoreboard

Grand slam — hitting a homerun when there is a runner on every base, resulting in four runs; also called a grand salami or a grand ol' ding dong

Hill — the pitcher's mound

K — the abbreviation for a strikeout

Knuckleball — a slow pitch where the ball is thrown with little or no spin; the ball travels through the air unpredictably, making it difficult to hit

Lumber — a baseball bat

Rhubarb — a fight or scuffle on the field

Slugger — a powerful hitter

Southpaw — a left-handed pitcher

Strand — to leave players on base at the end of an inning; stranding runners means the team has missed a good scoring opportunity

Tater — a home run; other terms for a home run include homer, big fly, dinger, bomb, and blast

Uncle Charlie — a curveball

Wheels — a player's legs; a player who can quickly run the bases is described as "having wheels"

GLOSSARY

backup (BAK-uhp)—a person or thing who can take the place of another

bullpen (BUL-pen)—an area where pitchers can warm up before or during a baseball game

confidence (KON-fi-duhns)—the belief that you can succeed or do something well

credit (KRED-it)—recognition or praise for doing something

distracted (dis-TRAK-tid)—unable to pay attention

focus (FOH-kuhss)—to keep all of your attention on something or someone

pressure (PRESH-ur)—the stress or burden you feel when you need to do something important

react (ree-AKT)—to act or behave because of something that has happened

settle (SET-uhl)—to become comfortable and calm

spotlight (SPOT-lahyt)—a strong beam of light, often used on a theater stage; if someone is in the spotlight, they're the center of attention

tournament (TUR-nuh-muhnt)—a series of games between several teams that ends with one winner

whiff (WIF)—to swing and miss a pitch

READ THEM ALL!

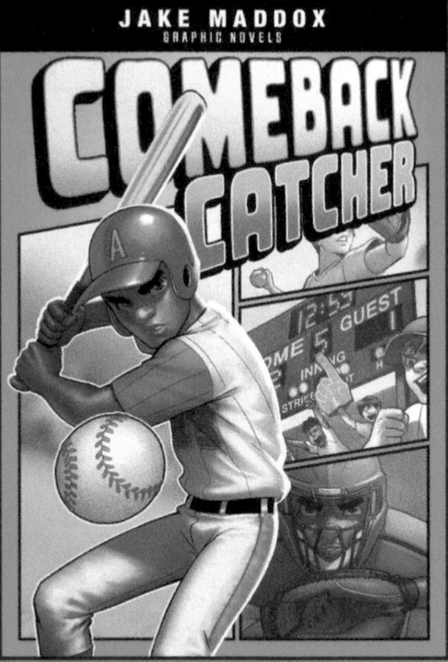
JAKE MADDOX
GRAPHIC NOVELS
COMEBACK CATCHER
GUEST

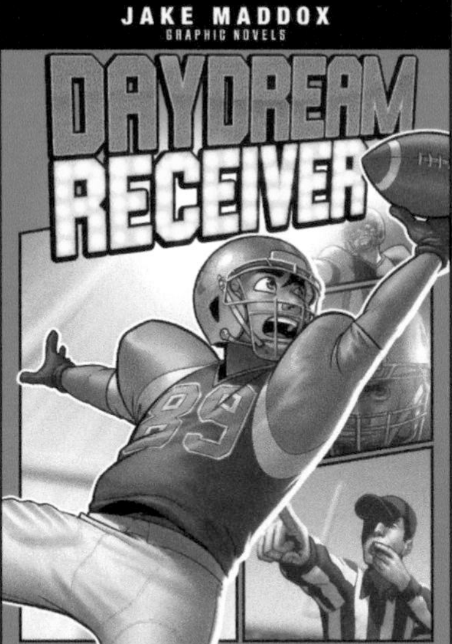
JAKE MADDOX
GRAPHIC NOVELS
DAYDREAM RECEIVER

JAKE MADDOX
GRAPHIC NOVELS
DOUBLE SCRIBBLE
JAKE MADDOX
GRAPHIC NOVELS
SOCCER SWITCH

ABOUT THE AUTHOR

Eric Braun has written more than one hundred books for kids and teens, including many about sports. He coaches youth baseball and soccer, has two sports-loving sons, and has suffered many disappointments as a lifelong fan of the Minnesota Twins.

Berenice Muñiz is a graphic designer and illustrator from Monterrey, Mexico. In the past, she has done work for publicity agencies, art exhibitions, and she's even created her own webcomic. These days, Berenice is devoted to illustrating comics as part of the Graphikslava crew. In her spare time, “Bere” loves to draw, read manga, watch animated movies, play video games, and fight zombies.